Code Leader

Code Leader

Code Leader

Using People, Tools, and Processes to Build Successful Software

Patrick Cauldwell

WILEY

Wiley Publishing, Inc.

Code Leader: Using People, Tools, and Processes to Build Successful Software

Published by
Wiley Publishing, Inc.
10475 Crosspoint Boulevard
Indianapolis, IN 46256
www.wiley.com

Copyright © 2008 by Wiley Publishing, Inc., Indianapolis, Indiana

Published simultaneously in Canada

ISBN: 978-0-470-25924-5

Manufactured in the United States of America

10 9 8 7 6 5 4 3 2 1

Library of Congress Cataloging-in-Publication Data is available from the publisher.

*To my wife Vikki, who has supported me through many wacky endeavors, taken up the slack when I've overcommitted myself, and generally been the best wife and mother **ever**.*

About the Author

Patrick Cauldwell somehow found his way to a career in software despite earning a bachelor's degree in East Asian Studies. From a work-study job in the student computer lab at college through early jobs in quality assurance and localization, and finally into full-time software engineering, Patrick has always been interested in what makes computers tick. He's worked in a wide range of software operations, from very large projects at Intel to a very small start-up to a consulting job in the midst of the .COM boom.

Patrick pursues his passion for talking and writing about software development as often as possible. He teaches computer science classes at the Oregon Institute of Technology, speaks at numerous developer conferences across the country, and once talked about the challenges of building a highly scalable eCommerce web site as part of a 12-city developer road show.

After working for several product companies, Patrick recently returned to consulting full time.

Foreword

I have worked with Patrick Cauldwell, in one form or another, at two different companies for more than half of my 15-year career in software. He has been almost a constant in my professional life, and I am a better programmer for working with him. Why am I telling you this, dear reader, and why should you care? Because you should always strive to surround yourself with people who are smarter than you, and when you can't, you should at least read their books.

Patrick is a pragmatist with a purist's knowledge. He has a deep understanding of what "smells" right, and he knows when and how to find the right balance to get the job done. This philosophy of balanced "pure pragmatism" pervades this book and makes it useful.

He moves back and forth between code and prose as if they were the same thing — useful, because for many of us, they are. Rather than including large formal code listings and leaving the reader huge chunks of code to grok, he weaves code in and out of his prose with the result being a practical, eminently readable book about the art and science, but most importantly, the process of modern software engineering.

There are dozens of books that include lists of tools and techniques, but few attempt to put these tools into the larger context of actually shipping successful software. I've found, while reading this book, that it's full of concepts that are intuitively obvious, but often forgotten within the scope of a large project. It's so nice to not just be preached the what and the how, but also the why. These are the practical concepts that we *aren't* taught in school, but only learn after hard-won battles in the real world.

Scott Hanselman
Author of ComputerZen Blog, www.computerzen.com
Senior Program Manager, Developer Division, Microsoft Corporation

Credits

Acquisitions Director
Jim Minatel

Development Editor
Maryann Steinhart

Technical Editor
Douglas Parsons

Production Editor
Dassi Zeidel

Copy Editor
Foxxe Editorial Services

Editorial Manager
Mary Beth Wakefield

Production Manager
Tim Tate

Vice President and Executive Group Publisher
Richard Swadley

Vice President and Executive Publisher
Joseph B. Wikert

Project Coordinator, Cover
Lynsey Stanford

Proofreader
Kathy Pope, Word One

Indexer
Robert Swanson

Acknowledgments

Big thanks to Scott Hanselman, who has long been a good friend and who has always encouraged me to tackle new challenges. Thanks also to Chris Brooks and Tom Cook, who gave me the chance to put many of the ideas in this book into practice. I would also like to thank Jim Minatel, Maryann Steinhart, and the rest of the folks at Wiley for making this book possible.

Contents

Contents

Contents

Introduction

Writing software is a complicated business. Once upon a time, software was written by an exclusive hacker priesthood that emerged from big businesses like the telephone company or big industrial concerns. Most of them were electronics engineers who needed to write software to control hardware devices that they built. Those early "programmers" mostly did just that. They wrote code to solve tangible problems, such as opening and closing phone switches and making sure that conveyor systems in automobile factories worked the way they were supposed to. A very few of them wrote operating system software or device drivers or networking protocols. In my first software job, I worked with a very complex (for 1992) network backup program that backed up client PCs to a tape drive attached to a Novell server. The system had to manage network traffic, multiple clients waiting for the same tape drive on the server, full and incremental backup sets, and so on. That piece of software was written almost entirely by two developers.

Those days are over. The vast majority of software today is written by professional software developers to solve business problems. There is often no hardware device involved except for the PC itself. Online commerce, business-to-business computing, financial and accounting software, and banking or healthcare software are what many if not most of us work on today. There are no device drivers involved, no hardware switches, no robots — these are business problems that can be solved by software.

Along with changes in the nature of the problems to be solved with software has come a huge increase in the complexity of the software systems that we must design and build. The advent of the Web has meant that much of the software written today is designed to be distributed across more than one computer, and potentially used by many hundreds of thousands of customers. It is no longer enough to write software that solves a problem; it must also be fast, scalable, reliable, and easy to use. Ever since the infamous .COM bubble burst, software must also be affordable, both to build and to support. Total cost of ownership is becoming an increasingly important issue for software firms, sometimes more so than building new features.

Luckily, the tools used to write software have improved at least as rapidly as the complexity of the software has increased. Most software today, particularly business software, is written in high-level languages that remove much of the drudgery once associated with day-to-day programming tasks. That frees developers to concern themselves with solving business problems rather than with pure "coding" tasks.

The combination of these various trends has meant that professional developers can't just be coders any more if they want to advance in their careers. Gone are the days when a project could be saved at the last minute by the heroic efforts of a super-genius coder. Although I'm sure that still happens here and there, it certainly isn't the norm. Most modern software projects are just too complicated to make that work. Even a medium-sized software project these days is too much for one person to fully comprehend in all of its detail. That means that we must work on teams on almost all software projects. Granted, that might be a team of two or three in some cases, but more often it's a team of 10 or more developers. That means that to get ahead in the software industry these days you have to know just as much about how to help teams work together as you do about writing code, even if you are not in a project management or personnel management role. A team lead, technical lead, or architect must be able to keep a team of developers on track and working well together, just as much as he or she needs to be able to turn requirements into code.

That isn't to say that they should become project managers — that's a completely different subject, and this book is not about project management, although all of the topics covered in it apply equally well to any project management methodology. It falls to the team lead to be familiar with strategies that make it easier for teams of developers to work together in ways that enhance rather than detract from their productivity.

Those strategies range from high-level development philosophies, such as Test-Driven Development (TDD) or Continuous Integration (CI), to more concrete development process issues, from source code control and static analysis to techniques involving code construction, such as programming by contract and how to deal with errors and tracing. Taken collectively, all these strategies and techniques are designed to make it easier for teams of developers to work together in ways that allow them to coordinate their work for highest productivity, and to produce software that is easy to build, support, and maintain. In today's software job market, those are ultimately the skills that separate the career professional from the hacker, and the great developer from the average one.

Being able to write good code is still a prerequisite, of course, but there are several other exceptional books that cover that subject in depth. *Code Complete* by Steve McConnell and *The Pragmatic Programmer: From Journeyman to Master* by Andrew Hunt and David Thomas are excellent examples. If you want to make the transition from solid coder to team lead, however, you need to know more than how to write a tight `for` loop.

Who This Book Is For

This book is for the career developer who wants to take his or her skill set and/or project to the next level. If you are a professional software developer with 3–4 years of experience looking to bring a higher level of discipline to your project, or to learn the skills that will help you transition from software engineer to technical lead, then this book is for you. The topics covered in this book will help you focus on delivering software at a higher quality and lower cost. The book is about practical techniques and practices that will help you and your team realize those goals.

This book is for the developer who understands that the business of software is, first and foremost, business. Writing code is fun, but writing high-quality code on time and at the lowest possible cost is what makes a software project successful. A team lead or architect who wants to succeed must keep that in mind.

Given that target audience, this book assumes a certain level of skill at reading code in one or more languages, and basic familiarity with building and testing software projects. It also assumes that you have at least a basic understanding of the software development life cycle, and how requirements from customers become testable software projects.

Who This Book Is Not For

This is not a book for the entry-level developer fresh out of college, or for those just getting started as professional coders. It isn't a book about writing code; it's a book about how we write code together while keeping quality up and costs down. It is not for those who want to learn to write more efficient or literate code. There are plenty of other books available on those subjects, as mentioned previously.

This is also not a book about project management or development methodology. All of the strategies and techniques presented here are just as applicable to waterfall projects as they are to those employing Agile methodologies. While certain strategies such as Test-Driven Development and Continuous Integration have risen to popularity hand in hand with Agile development methodologies, there is no coupling between them. There are plenty of projects run using SCRUM that do not use TDD, and there are just as many waterfall projects that do. To learn more about development methodologies, I suggest *Rapid Application Development* by Steve McConnell, or anything from the XP series beginning with Kent Beck's *eXtreme Programming eXplained*. While XP itself may not be as popular today as once it was, that first book is a fantastic introduction to the Agile philosophy.

Why I'm Writing This Book

I've been writing code professionally for the last 16 years. In that time, I have worked for companies ranging from less than 20 people to 65,000. I have worked on projects with one or two other developers, and on at least one that had nearly 200 developers working on it. I have seen both sides of the .COM bubble. While working for a consulting company during the .COM boom, I saw the nature of software change radically (and rapidly) from desktop applications to web sites to highly distributed applications. I saw some projects succeed, and more than a few fail spectacularly. Many of those projects failed because the developers working on them didn't have the skills they needed to work effectively together. An improperly used source control system can cause just as many schedule delays as changing requirements. Developers who cannot work effectively with their quality-assurance teams are not likely to deliver high-quality software.

In my own career transition from individual contributor to team lead to architect, I've learned that putting policies in place to help developers work together is at least as important as finding people who are good at writing code. The most brilliant architecture will fail if it is implemented in a way that is too buggy or too expensive to support.

In writing this book I hope to get more developers excited about process, about working well with others, and about building software that is easy and less expensive to create and to support. I think those things are at least as exciting as building a faster hashtable or a better reader-writer lock, if not more so.

Philosophy versus Practicality

There are a lot of philosophical arguments in software development. Exceptions versus result codes, strongly typed versus dynamic languages, and where to put your curly braces are just a few examples. I certainly have opinions about each and every one of those debates, but I have done what I could to steer clear of them here. Most of the chapters in this book deal with practical steps that you as a developer can take to improve your skills and improve the state of your project. I make no claims that these practices represent *the* way to write software. They represent strategies that have worked well for me and other developers who I have worked with closely.

Philosophy certainly has its place in software development. Much of the current thinking in project management has been influenced by the Agile philosophy, for example. The next wave may be influenced by the Lean methodologies developed by Toyota for building automobiles. Because it represents a philosophy, the Lean process model can be applied to building software just as easily as to building cars. On the other hand, because they exist at the philosophical level, such methodologies can be difficult to conceptualize. I have tried to favor the practical over the philosophical, the concrete over the theoretical. This should be the kind of book that you can pick up, read one chapter, and go away with some practical changes you can make to your software project that will make it better.

That said, the first part of this book is entitled ''Philosophy'' because the strategies described in it represent ways of approaching a problem rather than a specific solution. There are just as many practical ways to do Test-Driven Development as there are ways to manage a software project. You will have to pick the way that fits your chosen programming language, environment, and team structure. I have tried to describe some tangible ways of realizing TDD, but it remains an abstract ideal rather than a one-size-fits-all technical solution. The same applies to Continuous Integration. There are numerous ways of thinking about and achieving a Continuous Integration solution, and I have presented only a few. Continuous Integration represents a way of thinking about your development process rather than a concrete or specific technique.

The second and third parts of this book represent more concrete process and construction techniques that can improve your code and your project. They focus on the pragmatic rather than the philosophical.

Every Little Bit Helps

You do not have to sit down and read this book from cover to cover. While there are interrelationships between the chapters, each chapter can also stand on its own. If you know that you have a particular problem, such as error handling, with your current project, read that chapter and try to implement some of the suggestions in it. Don't feel that you have to overhaul your entire software project at once. My hope is that the various techniques described in this book can all incrementally improve a project one at a time.

If you are starting a brand-new project and have an opportunity to define its structure, then by all means read the whole book and see how it influences the way you design your project. If you have to work within an existing project structure, you might have more success applying a few improvements at a time.

In terms of personal career growth, the same applies. Every new technique you learn makes you a better developer, so take them one at a time as your schedule and projects allow.

Examples

Most of the examples in this book are written in C# because that is the language that I currently do most of my work in. However, the techniques described in this book apply just as well to any other modern programming language with a little translation. Even if you are unfamiliar with the inner workings or details of C# as a language, the examples are very small and simple to understand. Again, this is not a book about how to write code, and the examples in it are all intended to illustrate a specific point, not to become a part of your software project in any literal sense.

How This Book Is Structured

This book is organized into three sections, Philosophy, Process, and Code Construction. The following is a short summary of what you will find in each section and chapter.

❑ Part I (Philosophy) contains chapters that focus on abstract ideas about how to approach a software project. Each chapter contains practical examples of how to realize those ideas.

    ❑ Chapter 1 (Buy, not Build) describes how to go about deciding which parts of your software project you need to write yourself and which parts you may be able to purchase or otherwise leverage from somewhere else. In order to keep costs down and focus on your real competitive advantage, it is necessary to write only those parts of your application that you really need to.

    ❑ Chapter 2 (Test-Driven Development) examines the Test-Driven Development (or Test-Driven Design) philosophy and some practical ways of applying it to your development life cycle to produce higher-quality code in less time.

    ❑ Chapter 3 (Continuous Integration) explores the Continuous Integration philosophy and how you can apply it to your project. CI involves automating your build and unit testing processes to give developers a shorter feedback cycle about changes that they make to the project. A shorter feedback cycle makes it easier for developers to work together as a team and at a higher level of productivity.

❑ The chapters in Part II (Process) explore processes and tools that you can use as a team to improve the quality of your source code and make it easier to understand and to maintain.

    ❑ Chapter 4 (Done Is Done) contains suggestions for defining what it means for a developer to "finish" a development task. Creating a "done is done" policy for your team can make it easier for developers to work together, and easier for developers and testers to work together. If everyone on your team follows the same set of steps to complete each task, then development will be more predictable and of a higher quality.

    ❑ Chapter 5 (Testing) presents some concrete suggestions for how to create tests, how to run them, and how to organize them to make them easier to run, easier to measure, and more useful to developers and to testers. Included are sections on what code coverage means and how to measure it effectively, how to organize your tests by type, and how to automate your testing processes to get the most benefit from them.

    ❑ Chapter 6 (Source Control) explains techniques for using your source control system more effectively so that it is easier for developers to work together on the same project, and easier to correlate changes in source control with physical software binaries and with defect or issue reports in your tracking system.

    ❑ Chapter 7 (Static Analysis) examines what static analysis is, what information it can provide, and how it can improve the quality and maintainability of your projects.

❑ Part III (Code Construction) includes chapters on specific coding techniques that can improve the quality and maintainability of your software projects.

    ❑ Chapter 8 (Contract, Contract, Contract!) tackles programming by contract and how that can make your code easier for developers to understand and to use. Programming by contract can also make your application easier (and therefore less expensive) to maintain and support.

❑ Chapter 9 (Limiting Dependencies) focuses on techniques for limiting how dependent each part of your application is upon the others. Limiting dependencies can lead to software that is easier to make changes to and cheaper to maintain, as well as easier to deploy and test.

❑ Chapter 10 (The Model-View-Presenter Model) offers a brief description of the MVP model and explains how following the MVP model will make your application easier to test.

❑ Chapter 11 (Tracing) describes ways to make the most of tracing in your application. Defining and following a solid tracing policy makes your application easier to debug and easier for your support personnel and/or your customers to support.

❑ Chapter 12 (Error Handling) presents some techniques for handling errors in your code that if followed consistently, make your application easier to debug and to support.

❑ Part IV (Putting It All Together) is simply a chapter that describes a day in the life of a developer who is following the guiding principles and using the techniques described in the rest of the book.

❑ Chapter 13 (Calculator Project: A Case Study) shows many of this book's principles and techniques in actual use.

Errata

Every effort is made to ensure that there are no errors in the text or in the code. However, no one is perfect, and mistakes do occur. If you find an error in one of our books, like a spelling mistake or faulty piece of code, we would be very grateful for your feedback. By sending in errata, you may save another reader hours of frustration, and at the same time, you will be helping us provide even higher-quality information.

To find the errata page for this book, go to www.wrox.com and locate the title using the Search box or one of the title lists. Then, on the book details page, click the Book Errata link. On this page you can view all errata that has been submitted for this book and posted by Wrox editors. A complete book list, including links to each book's errata, is also available at www.wrox.com/misc-pages/booklist.shtml.

If you don't spot "your" error on the Book Errata page, go to www.wrox.com/contact/techsupport .shtml and complete the form there to send us the error you have found. We'll check the information and, if appropriate, post a message to the book's errata page and fix the problem in subsequent editions of the book.

p2p.wrox.com

For author and peer discussion, join the P2P forums at p2p.wrox.com. The forums are a Web-based system for you to post messages relating to Wrox books and related technologies, and interact with other readers and technology users. The forums offer a subscription feature, which provides email notifications when posts are made on topics of your choosing. Wrox authors, editors, other industry experts, and your fellow readers are present on these forums.

At http://p2p.wrox.com you will find a number of different forums that will help you not only as you read this book, but also as you develop your own applications. To join the forums, just follow these steps:

1. Go to p2p.wrox.com, and click the Register link.

2. Read the terms of use, and click Agree.

3. Complete the required information to join as well as any optional information you wish to provide, and click Submit.

4. You will receive an email with information describing how to verify your account and complete the registration process.

You can read messages in the forums without joining P2P, but in order to post your own messages, you must join.

Once you join, you can post new messages and respond to messages that other users post. You can read messages at any time on the Web. If you would like to have new messages from a particular forum emailed to you, click the Subscribe to this Forum icon by the forum name in the forum listing.

For more information about how to use the Wrox P2P, be sure to read the P2P FAQs for answers to questions about how the forum software works as well as many common questions specific to P2P and Wrox books. To read the FAQs, click the FAQ link on any P2P page.

Code Leader

Part I
Philosophy

1

Buy, Not Build

The very basis of our jobs as developers is to write code. If you can't write code, there is no work for you to do as a software engineer. We spend long years learning to write better, tighter, faster, more elegant code. There comes a time, however, when what we really need to do is *not* write code. It turns out to be one of the hardest parts of the job: learning when to say no and letting someone else do the work. Why should you say no? Isn't writing code what we do? Yes, it is what we do. Yet the reality of the business of software engineering is that business owners or project sponsors or whoever holds the purse strings don't hire us to write code. Sounds odd, doesn't it? But it's true. They don't hire us to write code. They hire us to solve problems using software. Sometimes (in fact, most of the time) that means we get to write code. But more often than we like to think, what we really should do is let someone else do the fun part.

As software systems have become increasingly complex, it has become impossible for any one developer to know everything there is to know about building a single system. We'd like to believe that isn't the case, but unless you are working on a very small project devoted to a very narrow domain, it's true. Someone who is an expert in crafting HTML to look exactly right in every browser and still knows how to write kernel-mode hardware drivers might exist somewhere in the world, but he certainly isn't in the majority. There is simply too much to know, which naturally leads to specialization. So we end up with some developers who know the ins and outs of HTML, and others who write device drivers.

Even in the case of a moderately sized commercial project, no average team of developers will be able to write all the software that it needs to accomplish its goals — nor should it. We get paid to solve problems that businesspeople have, not to write code because it's fun. Okay, the fact that for most of us writing code also happens to be fun comes as a nice bonus, but our business is really *business*.

So what's the point of all that? It is that before we write a single line of code for any project, we should be asking ourselves one simple question: *Is this code providing business value to my customers?*

At the core of that question lies an understanding of what business value means to your organization. For example, if your company sells online banking software, then the core business value that you are delivering to your customers is *banking*. When it comes time to build your banking web site, and you need to ask the user what day he wants his bills paid, you might want to add a calendar control to your web page. That certainly makes sense, and it will make the user's experience of your software better. It's tempting (because we all like to write code) to immediately start writing a calendar control. After all, you can write one in no time, and you always wanted to. Besides, nobody else's calendar control is as good as the one that you can write. Upon reflection, however, you realize that there is nothing about being able to write a calendar control that provides value directly to online banking customers. "Of course there is," you say. "The users want a calendar control." True, they do. But the business of a company that builds banking software is not to build calendar controls.

Cost versus Benefit

As I said, this is one of the hardest parts of this job to really get your head around. We've all encountered and suffered from the "not invented here" syndrome. Every developer thinks that he writes better code than any other developer who ever lived. (That's healthy and exactly the way it should be. It leads to continuous improvement.) Besides, some stuff is more fun than other stuff. It would be fun to spend time writing the perfect calendar control. But what business value does it provide? If you work for a company that builds control libraries and competes daily with a dozen other control vendors, then by all means you should be working on the perfect calendar control. That's your business. But if you write banking software or health care software or warehouse management software, then you need to let those control vendors worry about the calendar controls.

Luckily, there are developers who specialize in writing user interface (UI) controls so that the rest of us don't have to. The same principal applies to a very wide range of services and components. It's not just things like controls or serial drivers.

As the complexity of software has increased, so has the level of support provided by operating systems and base class libraries. Only 10 years ago if you wanted to write a windowing application, you had to start by writing a message pump, followed closely by windowing procedures for each and every window in the application. Most of us would never think of writing code at that low a level now because there wouldn't be any point to it. It's been done; problem solved. If you're writing in C#, there are now not one but two window management systems (Windows Forms and Windows Presentation Foundation) that handle all the work in a much more complete way than you would ever have enough time to do yourself. And that's okay. As software becomes bigger and more complex, the level of problems we write code to solve has moved up to match it. If you wrote a bubble sort or a hashtable yourself anytime in the last five years, then you have wasted both your own time and your employer's money (unless you happen to be one of the relatively small number of developers building base class libraries).

The key is evaluating the benefits versus cost at the level of individual software components. Say that you write banking software for a living, and you need a hashtable. There happens to be a hashtable built into the class library that comes with your development environment, but it doesn't perform quite as fast as it could. Should you write a 20% faster hashtable yourself? No. The time it takes you to write a better hashtable costs your employers money, and it has gained them nothing. Another aspect of the increasing complexity of software is that performance issues have changed in scope. Coupled with the fact that Moore's Law (the number of transistors that can be placed in an integrated circuit doubles every two years) still seems to be working, increasing complexity means that the extra 20% you get out of that perfect hashtable is likely to mean absolutely nothing in the greater scope of your project.

There are a few narrow exceptions to this general principal. There are always cases where some piece of software that is critical to your application has already been written but lacks a key bit of functionality — functionality that might constitute a competitive advantage for your company. Let's say that your application needs a calendar control, and you have one that does just about everything that you need. However, you have just been told that there is a deal in the works with a customer in the Middle East that could mean big money for your company. The calendar control that you have been using doesn't support alternative calendars such as those used in much of the Middle East. Now you might just find it a competitive advantage to write your own calendar control. Sure, it's not core to your business, but if it means getting a deal that you might not get otherwise, then it adds business value.

Unfortunately, it is situations such as this, coupled with the inherent desire to write more code, that makes it difficult to decide when to buy and when to build. It is often not a simple question to answer. It almost always comes down to money. I think that this is one of the core issues that separate "computer science" from "software engineering." Software engineers always have to keep in mind that they cost money. Academic "computer scientists" have a much different value proposition to consider. Coming up with activities that are grantworthy is vastly different (although no less difficult) from trying to decide which software to write and which to buy to save your company time and money. Writing software that could have been purchased at less cost is a good way to get your project canceled. No project owner is likely to question the need to write software that adds business value to your project if the value is real and demonstrable.

The part of the equation that can be particularly galling to software engineers is that the 80% solution often ends up being just fine. It's hard to let go of that last 20% and accept the idea that the overall project will come out just fine even if every piece isn't 100% the way you want it to be. The last 20% is almost never worth the money that it costs your project's sponsors. This means that if a component that you can buy off the shelf solves most of your problem, it's almost certainly more cost-effective than trying to write it yourself.

Creating a Competitive Advantage

So what should you be writing? The parts that constitute a competitive advantage for your organization. Software is a competitive business, and the part of any project that you have to do yourself is the part that will beat the competition. If you are writing banking software, that's probably the part that talks to the bank's mainframes, and not calendar controls. If you are writing inventory management software, it's probably the algorithms that decide when to order new parts, not the drivers for a bar code scanner. The important part is to focus on the key piece of your project, which provides the most business value to your customers. That is, after all, our real job. Writing code is fun, but what we really do is solve problems for business owners.

It can be very difficult to decide which parts you really should write yourself and which you can leave to someone else. Sometimes the choice is clear. Most of us wouldn't consider writing an SQL query engine just so that our project could use a database. We would use MySQL or purchase a commercial database product. That one seems pretty clear. An SQL engine intuitively feels too big to take on, and it would require such specialized skills to implement that it is easy to see why it makes sense to buy one. Low-level components also tend to be easy to write off. Even if the product must communicate over the WAN, most of us wouldn't start by writing a TCP/IP stack. It's been done. Our value proposition as software engineers lies in solving problems and writing code in a way that *hasn't* been done.

Base Class Libraries

One of the most productive activities you can spend time on is learning your base class library (BCL). Every language and development platform comes with some kind of base class library. Whether that means the .NET BCL, the standard Java libraries, the basic Ruby class library, or the stdlib for C++, you will receive a sizable return on investment if you spend some time getting to know all of its ins and outs. The more you know about your BCL (or basic application programming interfaces (APIs) or built-in methods or whatever they happen to be called), the less likely you are to find yourself writing code that has already been written. It will take some time. Over the years, the code most of us write has moved toward ever-higher levels of abstraction. The base libraries have grown larger and larger over time, and continue to do more for us. That enables us to focus more on business problems and less on plumbing. We don't have to write windowing procedures or bubble sorts, so we can concentrate on complex algorithms and better user experiences.

This is another area where the 80% solution is usually good enough. For example, the .NET BCL comes with a ReaderWriterLock implementation that does exactly what you would expect it to do. It allows multiple readers to access the same resource without blocking, and it causes writes to be done one at a time. Additionally, a write operation blocks all readers until the write is finished. I have heard it said that the .NET Framework 1.1 implementation is susceptible to a condition whereby it basically blocks everyone, even if there is no write operation pending. I've never seen it happen in my code, but the developer who told me about it had looked into the code and proclaimed that it was a theoretical possibility. The solution he proposed was to write his own ReaderWriterLock that would theoretically be faster and not prone to this problem. I would never use this as a reason *not* to use the ReaderWriterLock in the BCL. The fact is that the one in the BCL is done. Every line of code I don't have to write (and more importantly maintain) saves my team time and money. I would absolutely go forward with the BCL version unless I found out that my code was actually experiencing the theorized problem, and that it really had an impact on my users.

That second part is just as important. If I looked at my application while it was running and saw that once a week I got a deadlock on a ReaderWriterLock that caused one web server to recycle itself, I would probably go right on using the BCL class. The fact that a handful of users would have to relogin to my site once a week wouldn't make it worth spending the time and effort to rewrite the ReaderWriterLock, or worse, to try to come up with an alternative solution that worked around it. Consider your actual Service Level Agreement with your customers before deciding to write a single line of code you don't have to.

Of course, your application might not be able to tolerate that kind of failure, in which case you would have to make that hard choice about rewriting or working around the problem class. Making those decisions is what project sponsors pay us for. Before you decide, though, take a hard look at what is good enough versus what you would like to have in a perfect world. The reality is that almost always, you can live with the less-than-perfect solution and still deliver valuable functionality to your customers.

To know which components you really do have to write from scratch, you should be intimately familiar with your platform's libraries. That doesn't necessarily mean that you have to know every method of every class. It means that you should have a broad understanding of which functionality your application might need is provided by the framework, and which is not. That way when it comes up in a project meeting that the project really needs functionality XYZ, you can make a high-level estimate based on whether the class library already has that functionality or you will have to write your own. It may turn out that the BCL already has only 60% of what you need, in which case you may be able to reuse parts of its implementation. Or you might have to start from scratch. Either way you will be making an informed choice.

Open Source Software

Whether to incorporate Open Source software (OSS) into any given project is a huge and potentially controversial issue. Legal, moral, or other questions aside, let's pursue it from the buy-versus-build perspective.

Like any other third-party component, Open Source or other freely available software may save you a lot of time and money by replacing code you would otherwise have to build and maintain yourself. Truly Open Source, or even "source available" software is additionally attractive because if any issues come up, you can probably fix them yourself.

On the other hand, there are good reasons for not choosing an Open Source component. Before you decide to adopt any Open Source component, take a good look at the code. There are some very well-designed and built Open Source software projects, and there are some less-well-designed and built ones. If incorporating an OSS component into your project (legal issues aside) means that you are adopting a body of code that you didn't write, it may turn out to be more trouble than it is worth. If the code looks overly complicated or poorly designed, or is difficult to build or test, you may want to think about writing that part yourself rather than relying on the OSS project. You could easily end up spending more time and effort dealing with buggy or unreliable code that is difficult to debug than if you had started from scratch.

A common argument in favor of OSS projects is that there is a whole community of people who can help you solve any problems you have with the project. For a large and active project, that is certainly true. However, just because a project has been released to the OSS world doesn't mean that there is anyone around who is working on it or who knows how it works. Before adopting any OSS component, see how active the community is, how often new releases are made, and how active the source base is. That will give you some hints as to how much help you can expect if you have problems.

There are some very useful, and even a few brilliant, Open Source projects that you may be able to take advantage of to save you time and money on your project. Just keep in mind that "freely available" isn't the same thing as "free." "No charge" does not equal "no cost."

Taking Advantage of Your Platform

As software in general has become more complex, so too has the operating system software that powers computers. More and more services are provided by the operating system "out of the box," and those services are there for you to take advantage of. Operating systems provide simple services such as encryption, as well as potentially complex services such as LDAP directories, authorization systems, and even database systems. Every function, subsystem, or application provided by an operating system platform represents work that you don't have to do, and code you don't have to write or maintain. That can save time and money when building an application.

Design

Just as it behooves every developer to know all the features provided by his or her base class libraries, it behooves every architect to learn about all the services provided by each operating system. Before designing any new system, it's important to isolate those features that you can rely on an OS to provide and those that you will have to construct yourself, or buy from a third party.

As with any other buy-versus-build decision, the key to this process is understanding a sufficient percentage of your requirements early in the design process so that you can decide if the services provided by the platform are "good enough."

I recently hosted a discussion session that centered on Microsoft's Authorization Manager, which ships as a part of its Windows 2003 Server operating system. Windows Authorization Manager provides a role-based authorization system that can be integrated into other applications. You can add users, organize those users into groups, and then assign those users and groups to roles. Those roles, in turn, are assigned rights to operations or sets of operations. When your application runs, you can ask Authorization Manager if user X can execute operation Y, and get back a yes or no answer. Authorization Manager represents exactly the kind of software it would be nice not to have to write. It is very useful as part of another application that requires security, but it is functionality that is "generic" enough not to provide what for most applications would represent a "competitive advantage." One of the participants in the discussion asked, "Why would I use the one provided by Microsoft when I could just write it myself?" The implication was that if he wrote it himself, he would have full control and could achieve that perfect 100% solution instead of compromising by using the Microsoft implementation. My response was exactly the opposite: "Why would I write it myself when Microsoft's already done it for me?"

Do I really need more than what is provided? In all likelihood, no. Even if there were "nice to have" features that were missing, I might choose to work around those deficiencies. Why? Because there is nothing about a simple role-based authorization system that gives my product an advantage over the competition. It then becomes more advantageous for me to save the time and money it would take for me to write the 100% solution. Delivering software faster and cheaper represents more of a competitive advantage in many cases than adding additional features.

Risk

There is always a risk, however. If you bank on functionality provided by the operating system (or any third-party software, for that matter), you could find yourself backed into a corner. Months into your development process, it might turn out that some functionality that is critical will be impossible to implement using the third-party software. If that happens, the only alternative is to write it yourself after all, only now you have to do it with time and resources you didn't budget for at the beginning of the project.

The best way to mitigate this risk is by building a "baseline architecture." If you can build out as much of your design as possible in "width" rather than "depth" (meaning that you touch as much of the macro-level functionality of the system as you can without going into detail), you will have a much better estimate of whether any third-party systems will meet your needs. It is particularly important to include third-party or operating system functionality into that baseline architecture because that is where the greatest risk often lies. As long as you can implement enough critical functionality in your baseline, you can be reasonably sure you won't end up backed into a corner later on.

Building a baseline architecture is discussed in greater detail in later chapters.

Services

Operating systems provide a wide range of services. Some of those services are in the form of simple method calls, such as encryption or text formatting. Others — such as messaging or networking services — are more complex. Once upon a time, applications had to include their own routines for 3D graphics, but now those are provided by subsystems like OpenGL and DirectX. Some operating systems even provide whole applications such as an LDAP directory (Microsoft's Active Directory Lightweight Directory Services is one example) or a database (such as the Berkeley DB that ships with many *nix systems).

The one thing that all of those services have in common is that they represent functionality that can be exploited by developers writing non-operating-system software. Every time you can take advantage of such a service, you are not writing code that you will have to maintain someday. That shaves valuable time off of your development schedule, and can save a great deal of money in maintenance. Supporting code already written can be much more expensive than developing it in the first place, so code not written is that much cheaper.

In terms of risk management, the larger the scale of functionality you rely on the OS providing, the riskier it is. If all you need is an encryption routine, the risk is very low. It either works or it does not. If you are relying on an OS-provided LDAP directory, on the other hand, you had better do some baselining to make sure that it really does what you need it to do before committing to it. That is a much more risky proposition, and it must be approached with considerably more caution.

As with any other buy-versus-build decision, take a look at the features provided by your operating system and decide which parts of your software are core to your business and which parts you can rely on someone else to write and maintain. Write only the code that provides your software with its competitive advantage, and leave the busy work to other people whenever you can.

Third-Party Components

In addition to features provided by base class libraries and operating systems, there's a third category of code you don't have to write. That is third-party components provided by ISVs (independent software vendors) — which basically means everyone except us and the operating system vendors. There are a number of types of third-party components, ranging from small things like networking libraries and sets of UI components, all the way up to very expensive and complex applications such as messaging systems like IBM's MQ series.

The reason to choose any of those third-party solutions is that they represent work you don't have to do. That has to be balanced against the risk associated with not being in control, although there are often ways to mitigate that risk. Many component vendors will provide you with source code at an additional cost, which is a great way to lessen risk. If you have the source code, it is easier to diagnose and possibly fix any problems that may come up, or to add new features that are specific to your application. Other vendors, particularly smaller ones, are happy to make changes to accommodate your needs in exchange for a commitment to purchase X units, and so on.

Evaluating third-party components can be tricky. Every vendor will tell you that its product will solve all of your problems, so the only way to know for sure is to try it out. Purchasing a third-party component based solely on the demos given by technical salespeople is just asking for trouble. Get a trial copy, a sample license, or whatever will allow you to get that software in your hands for real testing. Try it out in what you think is a real scenario for your business to see if it really does what it is supposed to do.

Take the time to evaluate not just the product itself, but also the documentation, samples, and developer support. The most feature-rich of third-party components is useless if you can't figure out how to program against it or can't get support from the company you purchased it from.

One of the most common places to use third-party components is in the user interface. User interface code and components such as calendars, date pickers, and grids are excellent candidates for the use of third-party software. UI components are necessary for most applications but are hard and extremely time-consuming to develop. A good UI control should be easy to use, feature rich, and support complex user interaction, all of which means lots of code to write, and a great deal of testing. It would be nice, then, to just buy someone else's controls.

There are dozens of vendors for every platform providing rich suites of UI widgets. Unfortunately, the user interface is often where applications have the most detailed and stringent requirements. Most companies have a very specific vision of how users will interact with their applications, and very detailed requirements regarding look and feel. The details of how an application looks and interacts with the user can end up being a competitive advantage and differentiates applications from one another in terms of user perception. For that very reason, UI components are among the hardest to shop for. It can be very difficult to find components that provide all the functionality you want and are still configurable enough to match your application's look and feel. Luckily, control vendors are often willing to work with you to meet your needs, including writing custom code or a customized version of their components. Those are details that need to be worked out ahead of time.

It is also very important to spend some time working with the different suites available to evaluate their ease of use, documentation, customizability, and feature set. Don't assume that you can learn everything about a set of components by getting the demo or looking at sample applications. Try them out to see for yourself before committing to any specific suite. If source code is available, try to get a sample so that you can evaluate how easy it would really be to make changes or debug problems if you had to. You can save large amounts of time and money by relying on off-the-shelf user interface components, but you do have to choose carefully from among the available options.

Summary

Writing code is fun, and it is what we do, but ultimately it is not what we get paid for. Providing business value to your project's sponsors can often best be achieved by purchasing someone else's code. It can be difficult to balance the savings incurred by not writing code against the risks posed by adopting and relying on code you don't own, however. Focus on writing the parts of your application that provide the most value to your project sponsors, and buy everything else if you can. Building a baseline architecture that incorporates the functionality of all the third-party software is one of the best ways to mitigate the risk of adopting third-party code and helps ensure that you find any potential problems early on.

2

Test-Driven Development

Your first response to Test-Driven Development, or TDD, may be that it feels like a good way to encourage developers to write their unit tests. After you have spent some time with TDD, however, that becomes its least interesting aspect. Let's take a quick look at what TDD is and where it came from, then move on to the fascinating parts.

Test-Driven Development arose out of early literature around XP and other agile methods and was put forth, first and foremost, as a way to support refactoring. The idea was that writing your tests first forced you into thinking about tests, which in turn encouraged you to write more. The more tests you had, the easier it was to practice *refactoring*, or the art of making small incremental changes to your code to improve its structure. Proper refactoring involves making very small organizational changes to your code, then making sure that your tests still pass. Without proper test coverage, refactoring is much more difficult.

> See Martin Fowler's excellent book *Refactoring: Improving the Design of Existing Code (Addison-Wesley, 1999)* for more information on this practice.

The process of TDD is often described, in abbreviated form, as "Red, Green, Refactor," meaning that first you write tests so that the tests fail (causing a "red light" in most testing GUIs), then you write code to make the tests pass (causing the "light" to turn green), and then you are free to refactor or improve the structure of your code, safe in the knowledge that the tests still pass. Once the refactoring is complete, the cycle begins again:

- ❑ Write tests that fail.
- ❑ Write code to make the tests pass.
- ❑ Refactor your code to improve its structure.
- ❑ Repeat.

The hardest part about making this cycle work is self-discipline. As developers, the thing we like to do most is write code — code that solves problems. Writing tests for many developers seems like drudgery or busy work. Some feel it's a waste of time or that someone else should be writing their tests. It is always tempting to "just write a little code" before you start writing the tests for it. You see a problem, and you want to code your way out of it. It can be very difficult to stick to writing tests first, then writing code to make them pass. However, there are a number of compelling reasons for writing the tests first:

1. If you wait, you won't really write the tests. This is just human nature. In almost every software development shop, the most important metric is success, which means that as soon as your code works, you've accomplished your primary goal, and the organization will reward moving on to write more code above going back to write unit tests.

2. Writing the tests first forces you, as the developer, to think about your interfaces. It is very easy to write an interface in a vacuum and then discover that it doesn't work when someone tries to consume your interface. If you write the tests first, you are both consumer and producer, and that leads to much better design. Tests help to define your contract.

3. Tests can provide documentation that is often more accessible to other developers than written documentation would be. Unit tests reflect the way the developer who wrote those tests thought about how the code was designed to be used. Tests define our expectations. If the same developer writes both the unit tests and the code to make those tests pass, then the tests reflect the *intent* of that developer. Writing the tests first expresses that intent more clearly than writing tests later to fit the code you have already written.

TDD can also be very useful when doing pair programming. The most effective way to use TDD to pair is for one person to write the test that expresses his or her intent and for the other person to write the code that makes that test pass. This can be done at a very physical level, passing the keyboard back and forth. First one developer writes the test and then passes the keyboard to the second developer, who then must make the test pass. The pair then jointly decides if any refactoring needs to be done, and the cycle begins again. This time the developers switch roles, trading test writing for implementation tasks. This method is not only fun, but also leads to a very high level of productivity and very consistent interface design, because two pairs of eyes have been on the code, and two developers are forced to agree on the intent of their interface.

Test-Driven Development applies to your whole software development lifecycle, not just to the beginning of the process. Tests define the requirements of your system as understood at the time the tests were written. In fact, in some agile projects, tests might be the only concrete representation of the project's requirements, if the developers have direct access to their customer and the customer doesn't provide written requirements beyond story cards.

One of the most important ways to use TDD may come after the release of your project. Every time a defect in your code is reported, the first thing you should do is write a test that exposes the defect. If you get a bug report and immediately create a test that causes the bug to happen, then you can be secure in the knowledge that when your tests pass, the defect is resolved. This provides a great way to ensure success in fixing the bug, and the test remains as part of the total unit test corpus, providing regression testing so that you know the bug won't reoccur due to future changes. Those new tests may represent aspects of the system that were never properly tested before (this is why code coverage metrics are important; more on that later), or it might mean that the developer who wrote the initial code had an incorrect or incomplete understanding of the requirements.

Yes, It Means Writing More Code

While it is certainly helpful to buy code you don't need to write and to take full advantage of the code provided by your platform, writing fewer lines of code should never be considered a design goal.

It is more important in the long run (and will end up saving you time and money) to write more code rather than less to achieve your architectural or design goals.

Writing unit tests is a seminal example. I have often heard developers complain that if they really follow TDD, they will end up writing more code than if they just wrote code first and had Quality Assurance or Test personnel test their code at a functional level.

However, that assumes that writing less code is in itself a design goal. It should not be. Your team may set as a design goal that refactoring should be easy or that code coverage should be as high as possible to avoid defects before shipping. Those are practical goals that will make your team more productive and save your organization money. Achieving those goals may require that you write more code (in the form of thorough and complete tests) than you would otherwise. That doesn't mean that you have written "extra" or "too much" code. It means that you have written the amount of code necessary to achieve your goals, or those of your organization. Just as to outside observers it may seem like pair programming should result in half as much code as two developers working alone (yet we know that isn't true), writing "extra" test code may, in fact, keep you from writing "too much" code in the form of code that never gets called, or that doesn't directly contribute to fulfilling your software's requirements, as embodied in its tests.

The goal of any software team should be to write no more code than is necessary to achieve their goals, not to write as little code as possible.

So there's much more to TDD than just increasing your test coverage (the percentage of your code exercised by your tests) or supporting refactoring. One of the most important things we can use tests for is communicating with other developers (and sometimes ourselves) about our code.

Tests Define Your Contract

When you write tests first, then write code to make them pass, it forces you to focus on the contract that your code is making with the rest of the system. Every piece of code has a contract, whether implicit or explicit. Every piece of code does something (or at least it should), and what the code does and how it is called by other code constitutes its contract. We'll talk more about contracts in Chapter 8, "Contract, Contract, Contract!," but for now we'll look at how writing tests helps define your contracts and why that's important.

As an example, imagine a simple calculator interface that adds, subtracts, multiplies, and divides integers. It's easy to imagine how such an interface would be implemented, but there are several ways it could be used. Thirty years ago, most serious calculators used Reverse Polish Notation (RPN). RPN is convenient from the implementer's perspective, because it uses a stack to store operands and operators, and it's very useful for implementing complex calculations. It would be easy to write an RPN-style calculator interface, such as the following:

```
public interface IRPNCalculator
{
    int Op1 { get;set;}
    int Op2 { get;set;}
    int Add();
    int Subtract();
    int Multiply();
    int Divide();
}
```

If you were to write the tests for this interface before implementing it, you might end up with a test like this:

```
[Test]
public void Add()
{
    IRPNCalculator calc = new Calculator();
    calc.Op1 = 2; //set the first operand
    calc.Op2 = 2; //set the second operand
    int result = calc.Add();   //call the Add method,
                               //which acts on the operands
    Assert.AreEqual(4, result); //assert (using our Unit
                                //testing framework)
                                //that the result should be 4
}
```

Testing Frameworks

The examples in this book that involve unit tests are written using the popular NUnit testing framework. It is freely available at www.nunit.org. Most unit test frameworks available for .NET or other coding environments work very similarly. Tests are defined in NUnit using a .NET custom attribute called [Test]. This marks the code as something that the testing framework should know about. In other environments such as Java or Smalltalk, naming conventions or other devices may be used instead of attributes.

The end result is the same. The testing framework identifies some methods as unit tests, and then provides some means of running those tests and reporting the results. NUnit ships with both a GUI- and a command line–based test runner. In addition, a number of third-party products provide test runners that work with NUnit tests, such as TestDriven.NET, JetBrains' ReSharper, and others. These test runners provide the typical red light/green light user interface that is familiar to anyone using a testing framework. If any of the tests fail, the light turns red. When all the tests pass, it turns green. It provides an intuitive and immediate way for developers to find out if their tests are passing.

The testing framework also provides a common method for reporting the success or failure of your tests. This is typically done via Assertions about what results you expect. For example, if you expect your Add method to return a 4, you would use the Assert.AreEqual(4, addResult) method (in NUnit) to assert that the result you got back from the Add method equals 4. If the value of addResult is not equal to 4, the test will fail.

This starts to expose some issues, however. If you have ever used a physical RPN calculator, you know that they are designed for long-running, relatively complex calculations. For example, even a comparatively simple calculation such as (2 + 2) * 8 on an RPN calculator would be entered as:

```
2 (enter key) 2 + 8 *
```

If you tried this simple calculation on the interface defined in the previous code, you might end up with code that looked like this:

```
[Test]
public void AddComplex()
{
    IRPNCalculator calc = new Calculator();
    calc.Op1 = 2;
    calc.Op2 = 2;
    calc.Op1 = calc.Add();
    calc.Op2 = 8;
    int result = calc.Multiply();
}
```

This is not a straightforward, easy-to-understand way to use this interface. You would have to carefully document this kind of behavior. This interface does what it is supposed to do but not in a way that is intuitive for the consumer. You wouldn't necessarily find this out unless you had written the tests first. It is very easy to design an interface like this, implement it fully, and then find out that it's difficult, or sometimes even impossible, to use in the way you had envisioned. If you had written the tests before even defining the interface, you might come out with something more like this:

```
[Test]
public void AddBetter()
{
    IRPNCalculator calc = new Calculator();

    calc.Push(2);
    calc.Push(2);
    calc.Add();
    calc.Push(8);
    calc.Multiply();
    int result = calc.Result();
}
```

This test feels like much more intuitive code for someone who has used a physical RPN calculator, and it will be easier to grasp intuitively with less documentation and less cost to support later. This test suggests an interface more like:

```
public interface IRPNCalculator
{
    void Push(int operand);
    int Result();
    void Add();
    void Subtract();
    void Multiply();
    void Divide();
}
```

15

By writing the test first, the developer is also forced to consume the interface under test and is much more likely to come up with something usable and easy to understand with less documentation required. In the example preceding this paragraph, if another developer who had to consume your IRPNCalculator interface looked at the tests, it should be obvious how the interface is to be used without having to resort to external written documentation.

In this way, the tests that you write define and exemplify the contract that your code implements. You end up with better code coverage, easier to refactor code, and a firm contract that is understood first by the developer writing the code and also by those who will consume that code.

Tests Communicate Your Intent

In a perfect world, your code would stand on its own and communicate your intent without resorting to written documentation. Martin Fowler asserts in his book *Refactoring* that if you feel you need to add comments to your code to properly express your intent, then you need to refactor. It should be obvious to anyone who views your code what it was you intended it to do and how it is intended to be used. This might be a little idealistic and really represents more of a theoretical goal than an actual state of affairs. It is also harder to achieve in designs that are less strictly object oriented. In today's Service Oriented Architecture (SOA) or other message-passing-style architectures, the semantics of the code can be harder to determine solely by reading the code.

In cases where the design may be less intrinsically clear, tests can help to communicate your intent better than external written documentation or code comments. For example, take the following version of your calculator interface:

```
public enum Operator
{
    Add,
    Subtract,
    Multiply,
    Divide
}

public interface IRPNCalculator2
{
    void Push(int operand);
    void Push(Operator theOperator);
    int Result();
}
```

This interface may in many ways be easier to use than the versions previously discussed, but it might be harder to understand at first glance. The equivalent test might look like this:

```
[Test]
public void AddADifferentWay()
{
    IRPNCalculator2 calc = new Calculator2();
    calc.Push(2);
    calc.Push(2);
    calc.Push(Operator.Add);
```

```
        calc.Push(8);
        calc.Push(Operator.Multiply);
        int result = calc.Result();
        Assert.AreEqual(32, result);
}
```

This test very clearly communicates to a reader how this IRPNCalculator2 interface is to be used and how it corresponds to the pattern used by a physical RPN calculator.

It is easy to write an interface that does everything it is supposed to do, but in a way that makes the semantics of the interface unclear. The first calculator interface shown in this chapter is a perfect example:

```
public interface IRPNCalculator
{
    int Op1 { get;set;}
    int Op2 { get;set;}
    int Add();
    int Subtract();
    int Multiply();
    int Divide();
}
```

This interface works functionally, but its semantics aren't immediately clear. The intent of the interface's designer doesn't come through. If you consider the simple calculation $(2 + 2) * 8$, it is not apparent how you would use the previously listed interface to do the calculation.

Semantically, the interface assumes that all calculations are binary, having two operands. For these simple integer methods, that may be true. However, for a complex calculation, the consumer of the interface has to keep track of the running total by reassigning the result of each operation to one of the operand properties.

```
[Test]
public void AddComplex()
{
    IRPNCalculator calc = new Calculator();
    calc.Op1 = 2;
    calc.Op2 = 2;
    calc.Op1 = calc.Add();
    calc.Op2 = 8;
    int result = calc.Multiply();
}
```

Not only is this cumbersome, but it is also difficult to understand from a semantic perspective. While I would never suggest that you write an interface like the one immediately preceding this paragraph, it still demonstrates how writing tests can communicate your intent. It should be clear from looking at the test code previously listed how the interface designer intended the interface to be used, even if that intent produced something rather awkward.

Another key area in which writing tests can help to express developer intent is error handling. Error handling can be difficult and time-consuming to document, if that documentation takes the form of prose or technical documentation. You can quickly communicate your intent as to how errors should be handled through test writing.

Some languages have first-class constructs for declaring what errors a specific piece of code might generate. For example, in Java it is possible to declare which exceptions a given method might throw and compel the callers of that method to handle those exceptions. In C#, that's not possible to do declaratively, so the best you can do while coding the method is to add the list of possible exceptions to the written documentation for that method.

However, tests can be used to communicate much of the same information. If your tests define your requirements, negative test cases should define your expectations about how errors will be reported. To achieve the best possible code coverage with your tests, you have to test negative as well as positive results so that all possible error paths are executed. NUnit allows us to define "expected exceptions" for any test. That means you can declare that a given test must throw the specified exception. If it does not, the test fails.

If I have an interface method that takes an object, the code would look like this:

```
public interface SendMail
{
    void SendEMailMessage(Message message);
}
```

There is nothing about this interface that specifies what happens if I pass a null Message object to the SendEMailMessage method. However, I can specify my intent by creating the following test code:

```
[Test]
[ExpectedException(typeof(ArgumentNullException))]
public void NullMessageReturnsArgumentNullException()
{
    SendMail mail = new MailSender();
    mail.SendEMailMessage(null);
}
```

The ExpectedException attribute tells the test framework (again, NUnit in this example) that this method should result in an exception. Not just any exception, either, but an exception of type ArgumentNull Exception. If the SendEMailMessage method doesn't throw that exception when I pass a null Message object, the test will fail.

This very clearly expresses intent. It implies that the method will explicitly check the value of the incoming Message object against the value null, then throw a very specific exception type if it is null. If the method didn't check the incoming value, it might well throw a NullReferenceException when passed a null value. That implies that the incoming value isn't being validated, and hence the behavior is not part of the method's contract. By expecting an ArgumentNullException, the test expresses the fact that part of the SendEMailMessage's contract with the outside world is to check the incoming value of Message and act accordingly. That part of the contract (and hence the developer's intent) would not be clear without the test code.

Seen from another angle, you could say that the test expresses the *requirement* that the SendEMailMessage method throw an ArgumentNullException when passed a null Message object.

Summary

Test-Driven Development provides us with better code coverage, more ability to refactor efficiently, quicker feedback about the quality of our code, and a mechanism for formalizing regression testing.

More important, TDD provides every developer with the opportunity to write better-designed interfaces that more closely meet the requirements defined for them, and to more clearly express his or her intent for how the interface should be used and how errors should be handled.

It is this finer expression of contract and of intent that in the long run provides at least as much, if not more, benefit from TDD than simply quality assurance.

3

Continuous Integration

If you are working by yourself on all of your software projects, Continuous Integration may not be for you. Most of us don't have that luxury, however. Modern software development is almost always done by teams, and sometimes by very large teams. Even in small companies, a single project may involve 5–10 developers, and those developers need to be able to work together in as efficient a manner as possible.

In the past, when most software development followed the waterfall model, developers largely worked independently. Each developer worked on one task, a subsystem, or some other piece of the overall project. Individual developers kept from stepping on each other's toes by using source control systems that relied on pessimistic locking. At some point in the waterfall project schedule, time was set aside for an integration phase, in which each developer checked in all of his or her work, and the long process of integration began. That integration process was inherently unpredictable. If many developers are all working in isolation and then integrating their work, there is no way to predict ahead of time how long that process will take. Because integration traditionally happened at the end of a cycle, that unpredictability came at a critical juncture.

On even a medium-sized project, that integration phase might last a week or two, as everyone figured out how to make all their changes work together. Interfaces might have changed, new components might have to be integrated, or other incompatibilities might crop up. Only at the end of that integration phase could the code be tested, which meant testers were often idle.

More and more projects today are being run using Agile methodologies such as Scrum or XP. In these methodologies, a single iteration may only last a month, sometimes only a few weeks. If your entire cycle only lasts one month, there is no room in the schedule for a one-week integration phase. To make such a schedule work, incompatibilities must be detected as quickly as possible so that they can be addressed right away.

If a dedicated integration phase is to be avoided, integration must become a part of the developer's routine. Integration has to happen at every level of the project, as often as possible. The more often integration happens, the less time it will take as a percentage of the project, since each integration will be much easier.

These new scheduling realities have led to the philosophy of Continuous Integration.

Integrate Early and Often

The primary tenet of Continuous Integration (CI) is "integrate early and often." The more often you integrate, the less work it is for everyone. The best way to achieve this level of integration is to set up a CI server, which is a dedicated server machine responsible for "continuously" building and testing all the code in a given project. There are a number of software packages, some commercial and some freely available, that facilitate the creation of such a server. Once a CI server is up and running, it becomes the responsibility of every developer to keep it running smoothly and successfully.

The two biggest goals of any Continuous Integration effort should be:

1. To make sure that there is always a testable version of your software that reflects the latest code.
2. To alert developers to integration problems as quickly as possible.

Keeping Testers Working

One of the issues that came up during waterfall projects was that until the integration phase of the project was completed, the testers often had nothing to test. If one test pass through the software took less time than a development/integration cycle, testers might be idle, with little to do besides writing test plans. In a perfect world, we would like to keep testers busy all the time, with each feature being tested as soon as it is coded. This makes the most efficient use of testing resources and provides developers with as short a feedback cycle as possible. After a given piece of code is written, developers tend to move on to the next problem and to lose focus on what they just completed. The more time that elapses between when code is initially created and when defects are reported, the harder it is for the developer who wrote that code to go back and fix the defect. If testers can report defects as soon as features are completed, they will be easier and cheaper to address.

The only way for testers to be able to provide that level of feedback is for the software to be built and assembled into an executable state as quickly as possible after new features are written. To this end, part of the job of the CI server is to produce executable code from the latest source as often as possible. How "continuous" that really is will depend on the specifics of your project, including how long it takes to compile and test, and how often new code is checked into the system.

With new executables produced every time a feature is added, testers are kept working, and features get validated more quickly. If everything is working smoothly, by the end of an iteration all of the features delivered for the iteration should be tested with very little delay.

Keeping Developers Working

If any of the developers on a project deliver breaking changes, it can cause delays for everyone. If someone checks in a change that causes the build to break, such as an interface change, then anyone depending on that interface has to wait until the problem is resolved. That means productivity lost and time spent on something other than adding business value to your software. The faster that the team is informed of the breaking change, the faster they will be able to get it fixed and the less time will be lost. The Continuous Integration server is there to help shorten that cycle of notification. If the CI server builds every time a change is checked in, and the build breaks, then it should be easy to correlate the change to the problem. Part of the job of the CI server becomes reporting failures and providing enough information to match up the specific change that occurred with the problem that resulted. That makes it easier to locate the breaking change, and easier to fix it.

However, "breaking the build" still has a cost associated with it. If the build breaks, no one can count on the integrity of the source code, and no executables will be produced for testing until it is fixed. If everyone is following the right process, the build should never break. That turns out to be a tall order for a number of reasons. There is a whole set of dependencies that have to be in place to make a CI build work correctly. Those include the source control system you are using, the completeness of your unit tests, the nature of your build script, and so forth.

If your team's CI process is working correctly, then every time a developer checks in a change, he or she will have already completed the process of integration.

Before making any code changes, the developer checks out all of the latest source code, and makes sure that everything builds and that all the tests pass. If everyone is following the process, then the latest source code in the integration branch should build and pass the tests (more on integration branches in Chapter 6, "Source Control"). Only when all the tests pass should any additional changes be made to add a new feature or fix a defect. When the coding is all done, again it should build and all the tests should pass. Before checking anything back into source control, the developer once again updates to the latest version of the source, and again makes sure that all the code builds and passes tests. Then, and only then, can the developer check in the new code changes. That puts the burden of integration on the developer making the changes, not on the rest of the team. This process is illustrated in Figure 3-1.

This does require a certain level of sophistication in both process and tools. For example, for this to really work, your source control system must make sure that you can't check in changes without first updating. That way the integration work has to be done, or at least the latest code has to have been checked out, before anything new can be checked in. That puts the burden for making sure that the integration work has been done on the person introducing changes. Either he or she makes sure that everything is integrated, or the build breaks, and it is obvious who is responsible.

Barriers to Continuous Integration

So why doesn't every team already practice Continuous Integration? Because it's hard. Establishing a solid CI practice takes a lot of work and a great deal of technical know-how. There are a number of tools and processes that have to be mastered. Setting up a CI server requires that your build, unit test, and executable packaging processes all be automated. That means mastering a build scripting language, a unit testing platform, and potentially a setup/install platform as well. Once all that is done, you have to be familiar enough with how your source control system works, and how developers will work with it, to integrate the build process with the CI server. You may need debug and release builds, and you may have to orchestrate the building of multiple projects if your dependencies are complex.

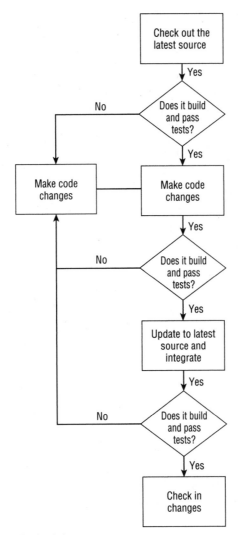

Figure 3-1

Not only does CI require that someone on your team understand how to set up all of these disparate systems, but it also requires an understanding of, and commitment to, the process by every member of your team. One of the hardest parts of establishing a good CI process is just getting everyone to buy into the idea that it is important and worth spending time on. Most developers who have been in the industry for a while are used to doing things differently. Only a few years ago, most developers were used to working on waterfall projects, with source control systems that used pessimistic locking, where each developer "checked out" and "locked" the files they were working on so that no one else could make changes to them. That promoted a working style that featured checking out files, making large numbers of changes over a period of days or weeks, and then checking in those changes all at once at the end of the cycle. It can be very difficult to convince developers who are comfortable with that style that Continuous Integration is a good idea.

One of the principles that every developer must be committed to if CI is to work is frequent check-ins, or "commits" as they are known in CVS/Subversion lingo. Every developer must check in everything they have done at least once a day. Never let the sun go down on uncommitted code. Once everyone is used to the idea, start encouraging even more frequent commits. The more often people are committing to the integration tree, the easier it is for everyone to do their integration work, since they will only have to deal with a small number of changes at a time. The longer any member of the team goes without committing their work, the more their code may drift away from the rest of the integration tree. That makes it harder to do the integration later on when they do commit.

CI can seem like more work in the short term, since each developer has to be responsible for integration. To make that integration work, developers must be comfortable making changes in "other people's" code. If people in your organization have a high degree of "code ownership" or emotional investment in their code, transitioning to CI can be uncomfortable.

Granted, following a good CI process certainly does involve more steps and a more detailed understanding of process than the old pessimistic locking model. It (usually) requires a higher degree of facility with source control systems. It also requires that every developer be comfortable making the changes required to integrate with the rest of the system before checking in their changes. That means they may need to have a better understanding of how the whole system works. Of course, that understanding has a large number of other benefits for the team.

If everyone is willing and able to follow the process, they will quickly discover how much easier the integration process becomes for everyone, and how much less time they spend waiting around for someone else to deal with integration issues.

Build Servers

The first step toward Continuous Integration is getting a build server set up. There must be an automated way to build and test your code, and a machine dedicated to making that happen. Furthermore, that build server needs to be set up as closely as possible to resemble your production system, to lend the maximum validity to your automated tests.

There are a lot of compelling reasons for using a dedicated build server. Builds need to happen on a predictable schedule, and they need to run as fast as possible to provide the best level of feedback. Unit tests need to run in the same environment every time for the most reliable results. Executable code delivered to testers needs to be built in the same environment every time to provide the best test results. All of these issues argue for not only a dedicated build server, but also a good one. Many organizations will trivialize the role of their build servers and use virtualized servers, or low-quality, older hardware, to host their build servers. This is a mistake. The faster and more reliably the build happens, the less time people will spend waiting for it or fixing it, and developer time is always more expensive than hardware. A build that takes 10 minutes on a local developer's machine may take 20–30 minutes if run on a virtual server or downlevel hardware. In his seminal paper on Continuous Integration, Martin Fowler suggests that a build that can be kept to less than 10 minutes will yield the best results for the team.

By running on dedicated hardware, your build will be creating executable code in the same environment every time it is built. If done correctly, the build will then represent a consistent product based on the latest source files. Every developer has seen a case where code built on one developer's machine functions differently from code built on another developer's machine. They might have different compiler or library versions, or other dependencies that are out of sync. They might have different versions of the source code, despite their best efforts. If the build is done on a dedicated server, even if the build comes out wrong, it will be consistent. Of course, it is incumbent on whomever sets up the build server to make sure that it isn't wrong.

Automating a Build Process

Before a dedicated server can take over your build, it must be in a state that requires no human intervention. For very large and complex software projects, that may be a tall order. If you are lucky enough to be working on a project that consists of only one piece, with limited dependencies, it may already build without intervention, using only the integrated development environment (IDE) your developers use to write the software. For example, if you are using Visual Studio .NET and all of your application code belongs to the same solution, you might be able to rely on the IDE to build everything using the command line option. The latest versions of Visual Studio .NET make it even easier by using the new MSBuild format natively to describe projects in the IDE. MSBuild projects are designed to be run automatically, which makes automating newer Visual Studio builds much more straightforward. The same is true of some Java IDEs, which may use Ant or another automated build script format natively.

These automated build script formats are very similar to the traditional "make file" format common in the days of C and C++ compilers. Most of them use XML or something similar to make them easier to parse than the old make files, and easier to edit using tools or by hand if you are familiar with XML. Ant (an Apache project) is popular in the Java world. NAnt (the Open Source .NET port of Ant) and MSBuild are popular in the .NET world. Rake is a Ruby build tool, which uses script files written in that language. There are also commercial products available, such as FinalBuilder or VisualBuild.

The key to any automated build file is that it must orchestrate all of the steps necessary to produce your application without a human being needed to push buttons or copy files. That might seem like a trivial problem to solve, and for very simple scenarios, it might be that simple. However, in many modern software projects, the build needs to coordinate compiling, linking, building resources, creating a setup/install package, and deploying components to the right locations so that testing can take place automatically as well.

Even a very simple project can quickly produce a fairly complex build script. A simple class library project created by Visual Studio .NET 2005 requires a build script like the following (MSBuild):

```
<Project DefaultTargets="Build" xmlns="http://schemas.microsoft.com ↵
/developer/msbuild/2003">
  <PropertyGroup>
    <Configuration Condition=" '$(Configuration)' == " ">Debug</Configuration>
    <Platform Condition=" '$(Platform)' == " ">AnyCPU</Platform>
    <ProductVersion>8.0.50727</ProductVersion>
    <SchemaVersion>2.0</SchemaVersion>
    <ProjectGuid>{F293A58D-4C0E-4D54-BF99-83835318F408}</ProjectGuid>
    <OutputType>Library</OutputType>
    <AppDesignerFolder>Properties</AppDesignerFolder>
    <RootNamespace>MVPSample.Core</RootNamespace>
    <AssemblyName>MVPSample.Core</AssemblyName>
  </PropertyGroup>
  <PropertyGroup Condition=" '$(Configuration)|$(Platform)' == 'Debug|AnyCPU' ">
    <DebugSymbols>true</DebugSymbols>
    <DebugType>full</DebugType>
    <Optimize>false</Optimize>
```

```
      <OutputPath>bin\Debug\</OutputPath>
      <DefineConstants>DEBUG;TRACE</DefineConstants>
      <ErrorReport>prompt</ErrorReport>
      <WarningLevel>4</WarningLevel>
    </PropertyGroup>
    <PropertyGroup Condition=" '$(Configuration)|$(Platform)' == 'Release|AnyCPU' ">
      <DebugType>pdbonly</DebugType>
      <Optimize>true</Optimize>
      <OutputPath>bin\Release\</OutputPath>
      <DefineConstants>TRACE</DefineConstants>
      <ErrorReport>prompt</ErrorReport>
      <WarningLevel>4</WarningLevel>
    </PropertyGroup>
    <ItemGroup>
      <Reference Include="System" />
      <Reference Include="System.Data" />
      <Reference Include="System.Xml" />
    </ItemGroup>
    <ItemGroup>
      <Compile Include="Class1.cs" />
      <Compile Include="Properties\AssemblyInfo.cs" />
      <Compile Include="SurveyPresenter.cs" />
    </ItemGroup>
    <Import Project="$(MSBuildBinPath)\Microsoft.CSharp.targets" />
    <!-- To modify your build process, add your task inside one of the ↵
targets below and uncomment it.
         Other similar extension points exist, see Microsoft.Common.targets.
    <Target Name="BeforeBuild">
    </Target>
    <Target Name="AfterBuild">
    </Target>
    -->
</Project>
```

All this build file describes is the debug and release configurations of a library consisting of three source files.

An Ant file for building a Java package might look like this (from the Ant documentation). An NAnt script for building the same project might look similar, as NAnt is the .NET version of Ant.

```
<project>

    <target name="clean">
        <delete dir="build"/>
    </target>

    <target name="compile">
        <mkdir dir="build/classes"/>
        <javac srcdir="src" destdir="build/classes"/>
    </target>

    <target name="jar">
        <mkdir dir="build/jar"/>
        <jar destfile="build/jar/HelloWorld.jar" basedir="build/classes">
```

```
                <manifest>
                    <attribute name="Main-Class" value="oata.HelloWorld"/>
                </manifest>
            </jar>
        </target>

        <target name="run">
            <java jar="build/jar/HelloWorld.jar" fork="true"/>
        </target>

    </project>
```

A Rake script written in Ruby might look like this (from the Rake docs):

```
task :default => [:test]

task :test do
  ruby "test/unittest.rb"
end
```

One big advantage to Rake is that the build scripts are defined in the same language that the compile is targeting, assuming that you are using Rake to build Ruby code, that is. Many of the other build platforms involve working in a second language such as XML, which means one more thing for developers to have to learn.

Many things that your build process might need to do go beyond the scope of the tool you are using. For example, NAnt doesn't necessarily ship with support for your version control system, and MSBuild may not natively support your unit testing framework. Luckily, they all support some form of plug-in architecture. Developers building other tools that are commonly used in builds may have the forethought to produce NAnt/MSBuild/Ant plug-ins that ship with their tools. Code coverage tools such as NCover, static analysis tools, and testing frameworks such as MbUnit all come with plug-ins for use with various build systems. If the tools themselves don't provide plug-ins, the Open Source community probably has. It may take some time to gather all the components you need to get your build automated, but it is always possible.

You may still find yourself writing custom build plug-ins if you have very specific requirements. For example, if you use a custom system for creating version numbers for your software components, you may need to write a custom plug-in that generates those numbers and inserts them into your code in the right location(s).

As builds become more complex and build scripts become longer, it is tempting to assign someone to be the "build guy." Creating complex build scripts in a "foreign" language can take a fair amount of expertise in both the scripting language and the build process. This tends to be a job that the lowest person on the totem pole gets stuck with. Resist that temptation. In the long run, you will be better off if a senior developer or possibly even the architect writes the initial version of the build script. It takes a fair amount of vision to build a flexible build script that will serve the needs of the team as the project grows. That task should not be left to the least experienced member of the team, or you will more than likely end up with a build that is brittle and difficult to maintain.

Furthermore, everyone on the team should be expected to have some facility with the build system. If there is only one person on the team who understands how the build works, your project is exposed to the classic "beer truck problem." If that one developer leaves or gets hit by a beer truck, it will take time and effort better spent someplace else to train another person to take it over. If the "build guy" stays home sick and the build breaks, someone really needs to know how to fix it. That is not to suggest that everyone on the team needs to be an expert, but everyone should at least have an idea of how the build script works and how to make changes or fix problems with the build. If Continuous Integration is to succeed, there can be no "single point of failure" in your CI process, such as the build guy staying home sick. If the build isn't working, your CI process isn't working.

Expanding the Build Process

Getting your software to build automatically is the first step. In order to get your CI process off the ground, your tests must be automated as well. To validate each integration, you need the software to not only build, but to also pass all of the unit tests as well.

Usually unit tests aren't difficult to add to your process. Most of the popular unit testing frameworks are designed to be run from a command shell, which means that they can also be integrated into an automated build process. Most of the testing frameworks also have plug-ins for integrating directly with automated build tools. It is important to be able to create reports based on your unit testing results, and most of the test tools can create XML results files that can be styled into HTML for reporting or read by other tools. The following example is an XML report generated by an MbUnit test run:

```xml
<?xml version="1.0" encoding="utf-8"?>
<report-result xmlns:xsi="http://www.w3.org/2001/XMLSchema-instance" xmlns:xsd=
"http://www.w3.org/2001/XMLSchema" date="2007-10-11T22:04:52.953125-07:00">
  <counter duration="0.03125" run-count="1" success-count="1" failure-count=
"0" ignore-count="0" skip-count="0" assert-count="1" />
  <assemblies>
    <assembly name="TDDSample" location="TDDSample.DLL" full-name=
"TDDSample, Version=1.0.0.0, Culture=neutral, PublicKeyToken=null">
      <counter duration="0.03125" run-count="1" success-count="1"
failure-count="0" ignore-count="0" skip-count="0" assert-count="1" />
      <version major="1" minor="0" build="0" revision="0" />
      <namespaces>
        <namespace name="TDDSample">
          <counter duration="0.03125" run-count="1" success-count="1"
failure-count="0" ignore-count="0" skip-count="0" assert-count="1" />
          <namespaces />
          <fixtures>
            <fixture name="SimplestTestFixture" type=
"TDDSample.SimplestTestFixture">
              <counter duration="0.03125" run-count="1" success-count="1"
failure-count="0" ignore-count="0" skip-count="0" assert-count="1" />
              <description />
              <runs>
                <run name="SimplestTestFixture.SimplestTest" result=
"success" assert-count="1" duration="0.03125" memory="40960">
                  <invokers />
                  <warnings />
                  <asserts />
                  <Description />
                  <console-out />
                  <console-error />
```

```
            </run>
          </runs>
        </fixture>
      </fixtures>
    </namespace>
  </namespaces>
  </assembly>
 </assemblies>
</report-result>
```

Such an XML report can be formatted as HTML or rich text for reporting, or it can be read programmatically in order to pass or fail your build.

Once you can run your unit tests automatically, you are ready to get our CI process off the ground. You should be able to automatically build and run at least your unit tests, and you should be able to fail your build if any of the unit tests fail. Failing the build is important. As your process matures, you will find more and more reasons to fail your build. If the build fails, it means that you are not meeting your own expectations, and that is something you need to know right away. When the build fails, it communicates just as much or more than when it succeeds.

Another thing you may want to add to your build is code coverage analysis. Coverage tools such as NCover can be integrated into your build process and used as criteria to fail the build. You can set a threshold for acceptable code coverage levels, and if the code coverage drops below that threshold, your build will fail. If you are working with legacy code that has very few unit tests, or if you are just starting to integrate code coverage analysis into your build, it is a good idea to start out with a relatively low level of coverage. Start by measuring your existing code coverage level, and then set the acceptable level in your build process accordingly. If you find that you only have 52% coverage, set your acceptable level at 50–51%. That way, if your code coverage level falls, your build will fail. That will alert you to the fact that people are checking in more code that doesn't have test coverage, which is unacceptable. This will work out better than trying to set the bar too high right off the bat, say 85–90%, and then having the build fail for long periods while you try to achieve that level of coverage. Your build failing should be a symbol of current expectations not being met, not a gauge of future expectations. Even if your level is set low, it forces developers to check in tests to go with their code or risk breaking the build. Over time, that should raise the percentage of code coverage, since more new code will have better test coverage. That should allow you to slowly raise the bar on your build process to keep from backsliding.

Other things you may want to add to your build include static analysis tools such as NDepend or FxCop. These are both .NET tools, but similar tools exist for other platforms. NDepend is a static analysis tool that measures metrics such as cyclomatic complexity, coupling between your libraries, and other aspects of dependency that you may wish to know about for every build. NDepend can be set up to fail your build based on rules that you establish. The tool itself comes with a set of built-in rules, and you can add your own using its internal rule definition language. Built-in rules include things like cyclomatic complexity. You can, for example, fail the build if any method has a CC rating of more than 25. NDepend comes with suggested thresholds for most of its metrics so that you can establish a baseline set of criteria for success or failure of your build. The rules can also trigger warnings rather than failures, so you might decide that for some rules you want to be notified on a violation rather than have the build fail.

FxCop is another static analysis tool provided freely by Microsoft for use with .NET libraries. FxCop comes with a number of very useful rules and provides a set of interfaces for writing custom rules on your own. FxCop's primary focus is on the usability of library code, and thus most of its built-in rules are centered on that goal. FxCop will tell you if you misspell words in your public method or property names, if you are passing unused parameters, if your methods aren't properly validating the parameters passed into them, and so on. These are all very useful rules that will help you catch problems that customers may have with your interfaces before you ship your code. On the other hand, if you are not building library code that will be used directly by your customers to write their own applications, some of the rules may not be important to you. Take the time to wade through the (often very large) set of problems reported by FxCop and decide if they represent issues that you care about. If they do not, you can exclude some rules from processing, or you can declare exceptions so that individual violations can be overlooked. Once you have cleared up all the warnings, either by fixing or excluding them, you will have a good baseline against which to measure future builds. If further violations come up, you may choose to fail the build, thereby calling attention to those potential problems early on.

What you add to your build process will depend on what metrics you think are important to your process. Some builds stop with compilation and unit test runs. Others add all the analysis and reporting tools they can find. These make the build process considerably more complicated and may require additional specialization in a "build master" to keep it all running, but they provide a much more detailed picture of your process and how your software is progressing. Those additional metrics may make the added complexity and time worthwhile.

Setting Up a CI Server

Once your automated build runs all the necessary steps, and produces the desired reports, it is time to set up a Continuous Integration server process. The CI server will become your "build server" of record and will be responsible for all the building, reporting, and executable packaging for your project. This ensures that your build process will be reproducible and that it will use the same sets of inputs for every build to produce the most consistent results.

There are several server platforms that can be used for establishing a CI server. Probably the most commonly used is CruiseControl (CC), a set of Open Source projects run by ThoughtWorks. There are Java, .NET, and Ruby versions of CruiseControl available, depending on your coding platform of choice. CruiseControl can be integrated with a large number of source control systems and build scripting tools.

The most useful way to set up CruiseControl is to have it watch your source control repository for changes. This is the best way to use CC to run a Continuous Integration project. On some rapid intervals, CC will poll your source control system to see if any changes have occurred since the last time it asked. If changes have occurred, then the build will be kicked off by the CC server. This provides the shortest feedback cycle for Continuous Integration, since you will find out if anything has been broken as soon as the potentially breaking changes have been checked in.

It is best to provide a slight delay between when changes are detected in the source control system and when the build kicks off. What you don't want is for a developer to be making several atomic check-ins in order to complete a specific task, only to have the build start (and probably fail) as soon as the first check-in is made. CruiseControl can be told how long to wait after all changes have stopped before starting the build process. For example, if your CC.NET server is set up to poll the source code system (SCCS) every 30 seconds for changes and it does detect a change, then it should wait an additional 30 seconds, and then repoll the SCCS. If additional check-ins have taken place within that window, then the clock gets reset, and the server waits another 30 seconds. If no changes have taken place after that, the build begins. A system such as this prevents (or at least lessons the chances of) builds kicking off too soon while one developer makes several check-ins to complete a task.

Once the build starts, CruiseControl keeps track of the process, and then bundles up a report to send out on success or failure of the build. This report can be configured as part of the CC setup, and additional elements can be added to create new report sections. It is a very flexible and easy-to-use mechanism for adding new data to the report. CruiseControl keeps track of the XML file(s) produced by the build system it is configured to use, and uses that XML file to determine success or failure. Once the build is finished, CruiseControl applies an XSL stylesheet to the build results to produce the report. To add additional sections, you just merge in additional XML data from other tools such as code coverage or unit testing results, and add additional stylesheets to add new sections to the report. You can add unit test, static analysis, code coverage, or other report sections so that the build report contains all of the information that you need for each build.

The report also includes what changes were detected in the source control repository and who made them, which makes it much easier to track down the culprit if the build should fail.

CruiseControl also supports very simple scenarios, and so can be used for personal or small projects as well as enterprise-level projects. In the following example, CC.NET is configured to use the "file system" source control repository, meaning that it will look at the time stamps of the files in a local directory and check them for changes. If changes are detected, CC.NET will launch Visual Studio .NET and build the solution file specified.

```
<cruisecontrol>
    <!-- This is your CruiseControl.NET Server Configuration file. Add your
projects below! -->
    <project name="SimpleTestProject" >
        <workingDirectory>d:\mvpsample</workingDirectory>
        <triggers>
            <intervalTrigger name="continuous" seconds="30" ↵
buildCondition="IfModificationExists"/>
        </triggers>
        <sourcecontrol type="filesystem">
            <repositoryRoot>d:\mvpsample</repositoryRoot>
        </sourcecontrol>
        <tasks>
            <devenv>
                <solutionfile>MVPSample.sln</solutionfile>
                <configuration>Debug</configuration>
                <buildtype>Build</buildtype>
                <executable>C:\Program Files\Microsoft Visual Studio ↵
8\Common7\IDE\devenv.com</executable>
                <buildTimeoutSeconds>600</buildTimeoutSeconds>
            </devenv>
        </tasks>
    </project>
</cruisecontrol>
```

This is certainly a simple example, but all of the pieces are in place. CruiseControl knows which repository to watch for changes, how often (specified in the "trigger" block), and what to do when changes occur. For a very simple project, this would provide all of the basic building blocks necessary for Continuous Integration to work.

The preceding build produces a report like this when it is complete:

```
<cruisecontrol project="SimpleTestProject">
  <request source="continuous" buildCondition="IfModificationExists">continuous
triggered a build (IfModificationExists)</request>
  <modifications>
    <modification type="unknown">
      <filename>MVPSample.Core.csproj.FileList.txt</filename>
      <project>d:\mvpsample\MVPSample.Core\obj</project>
      <date>2007-10-14 22:02:30</date>
      <user />
      <comment />
      <changeNumber>0</changeNumber>
    </modification>
    <modification type="unknown">
      <filename>MVPSample.Tests.csproj.FileList.txt</filename>
      <project>d:\mvpsample\MVPSample.Tests\obj</project>
      <date>2007-10-14 22:02:31</date>
      <user />
      <comment />
      <changeNumber>0</changeNumber>
    </modification>
    <modification type="unknown">
      <filename>MVPWinForms.csproj.FileList.txt</filename>
      <project>d:\mvpsample\MVPWinForms\obj</project>
      <date>2007-10-14 22:02:30</date>
      <user />
      <comment />
      <changeNumber>0</changeNumber>
    </modification>
  </modifications>
  <build date="2007-10-14 22:03:01" buildtime="00:00:05"
buildcondition="IfModificationExists"><buildresults>
  <message>Microsoft (R) Visual Studio Version 8.0.50727.42.</message>
  <message>Copyright (C) Microsoft Corp 1984-2005. All rights reserved.</message>
  <message>------ Build started: Project: MVPSample.Core, Configuration: Debug Any
CPU ------</message>
  <message>MVPSample.Core ->
d:\mvpsample\MVPSample.Core\bin\Debug\MVPSample.Core.dll</message>
  <message>------ Build started: Project: MVPWinForms, Configuration: Debug Any CPU
------</message>
  <message>MVPWinForms ->
d:\mvpsample\MVPWinForms\bin\Debug\MVPWinForms.exe</message>
  <message>------ Build started: Project: MVPSample.Tests, Configuration: Debug Any
CPU ------</message>
  <message>MVPSample.Tests ->
d:\mvpsample\MVPSample.Tests\bin\Debug\MVPSample.Tests.dll</message>
  <message>========== Build: 3 succeeded or up-to-date, 0 failed, 0 skipped
==========</message>
</buildresults></build>
</cruisecontrol>
```

This report contains all of the information about what the CC server did, why it did it, and what the results were. The report above states that the CC server detected a change in one or more of the files it was supposed to watch, that it decided to run Visual Studio .NET, and includes all of the output from that build process. Again, this is a very simple example. In an enterprise environment, the report would include the names of the files modified in source control, who modified them, and a detailed report containing the results of all the tools such as unit tests or code coverage that ran as part of the build process.

More than one project can be included in the same CruiseControl configuration, so the server can keep track of a number of different projects running at the same time. On the management side, the CC server also ships with a web "dashboard" (see Figure 3-2) that indicates the current status of all the projects it is managing, and allows a user to view the latest build report or to "force" a build (cause a build to start right away, even if no change has occurred).

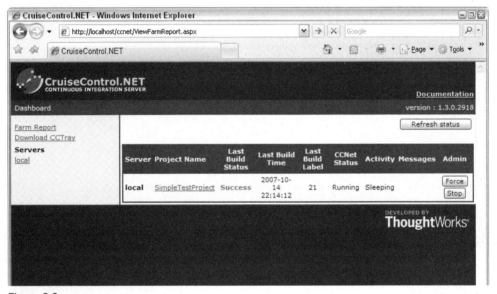

Figure 3-2

For an individual project, you can see when each build occurred, see whether or not it succeeded, and see all the details of the report. In this case, the report shows the same information as the XML report, only formatted in a way that humans can absorb more easily, as shown in Figure 3-3.

As you can see, along the left side of the report, CruiseControl.NET ships with stylesheets for formatting reports from tools such as NUnit, NAnt, FxCop, and Simian, which is a tool for detecting code duplication. Any of those tools can be very easily added to a CC.NET project, and the reports will automatically be included.

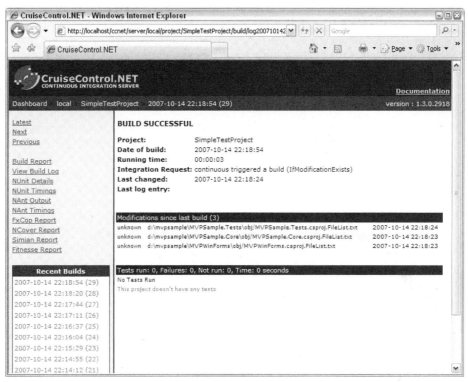

Figure 3-3

Multiple Builds of the Same Project

You might want to set up more than one build of the same project on your Continuous Integration server for different purposes. The basic CI build should run every time changes are checked in to the source control system. If you have extensive sets of integration tests that take a long time to run, you might consider running them on a fixed schedule rather than when check-ins occur. Or you might want to build a release rather than the debug version of the project once a day, rather than continuously. Those can be set up as different CruiseControl "projects" but run the same build file with different parameters, and so on. One thing to be careful of is potential conflicts accessing common files. Make sure that you won't have two builds going at the same time trying to build the same software. That can lead to all kinds of trouble with locked files or other cross-build conflicts. You can include exclusions in your trigger block that make sure one build will not start while another specified project is already running.

Coordinating Build Output

One part of the Continuous Integration process that often gets overlooked is repeatability. Just because you do lots of builds doesn't mean that you don't need to know what got built each time. It is critical to be able to link a single build of the software to all of the inputs that produced it. This is especially true once you have software in the field being used by customers. Those customers will report bugs, and install patches, and report more bugs. The only way for you to fix those bugs is if you can link the right versions of the source files to the version of the binaries your customer has installed.

To make that easier, part of the CruiseControl project definition is a "labeler." Other CI platforms have similar constructs. The labeler in a CruiseControl project defines the "build number" for each build. The default behavior, with no explicit labeler defined, is to start at 1 and increase monotonically. That means that build number 102 represents the 102nd time your CI server has (successfully) built the software. You can use that number to correlate your binaries with your source files. CruiseControl ships with a number of different labeler modules, or you are free to write your own. Included with CC.NET are labelers that use the date and time of the build, the contents of a file, or the version of another CC.NET project. Version numbers for .NET assemblies use a four-part numbering scheme, in the format *Major.Minor.Build.Revision*. The labeling scheme that has proved most useful to me has been to take a statically defined major and minor version number (e.g., 1.2) and append the last digit of the year followed by the ordinal of the current date (so January 4, 2007, would be 7004) and the number of seconds that have elapsed since midnight. So if you built version 2.3 of your software on January 7, 2007, you might end up with a version number like 2.3.7007.3452. There is no labeler that ships with CruiseControl to accommodate this format, but it is trivial to write your own. Version numbers in this format are very useful because they carry information about which version you built (you may be building more than one version at a time), the date on which it was built (in a format that is always unique and always increases for the sake of sorting), and even the exact time to the second the build label was created, although that is most useful just to distinguish two or more builds created on the same day.

You can use such a version number as the assembly version in all of your binaries. Alternatively, if you don't want to constantly change your assembly version numbers (this has consequences for dependency management), you can leave the assembly versions static and use the build number as the Win32 file version of the binary files. Those Win32 version numbers are easily visible in Windows Explorer and in other file tools, but they have no bearing on dependencies in the .NET runtime. This schema allows anyone to determine exactly which version of a specific binary they have.

The other half of the coordination comes about by using labels in your source control system. After a successful build is complete, use CruiseControl or the CI platform of your choice to label all of the source files used to produce that build with the same (or similar) version stamp as that you applied to the binaries. You may need to modify the actual string used for the label, as different version control systems have different restrictions on valid version strings. For example, CVS requires labels to start with an alpha character, and Subversion doesn't allow the "." character. You might have to use a label such as v-2_3_7007_3452 to match build number 2.3.7007.3452. Many of the source control blocks that ship with CC.NET provide for automatically labeling your source files on successful builds.

Once you have the version numbers and SCCS labels in synch, you will be able to reproduce any given build from the source code that originally produced it. This makes debugging problems much easier, since it is very simple to fetch all of the source to match whichever build is exhibiting the problem(s).

Notifying People about Build Results

The last major step in getting your CI process going is deciding who gets notified about build results and what that notification should communicate. This bears some thinking about, because notifying the wrong people, or notifying the right people too often or not often enough, will degrade the effectiveness of your CI process.

Not everyone on the team needs to know the results of every build. Different groups may need different sets of information, more or less frequently. CruiseControl by default provides five separate notification settings:

- ❑ **Always** — Sends notification every time a build completes regardless of success or failure
- ❑ **Change** — Sends notification only when the status changes from success to failure or vice versa
- ❑ **Failed** — Only notifies on failure
- ❑ **Success** — Only notifies on success
- ❑ **Fixed** — Sends notification when the build was failing, but a check-in caused it to succeed

Different groups on your team need different types of notifications. Managers may only need to know when the status changes, for example, so that they can keep track of how often the build is destabilized or fixed. Testers may only want to be notified on success so they can pick up new builds to be tested. The most useful setting for developers may combine "failed" with "fixed." That way the developers will know when the build breaks and how many tries it takes to get it fixed. The build master responsible for keeping the build server running should probably be informed of every build. That way it is easy to tell if the server is having problems. A whole day without a notification probably means that the server is down.

The key is to not overnotify each audience but to notify them often enough to give them the information that they need. If you notify every developer on every build, they will start to ignore the messages, and the messages lose their effectiveness. If you don't notify them every time the build fails, then they won't get a sense for how much "thrash" is happening. Ask each group which list they would like to be on. Individuals may want more or less information. Just be wary of sending out too many notifications. If people really want more information, it might be better to provide them with some other means of tracking build status, such as access to the dashboard web page, or CCTray, which is a small system tray application that pops up balloon notifications based on the user's preferences. That can be much more effective than email, especially since the CCTray icon turns red or green, depending on the failure or success of the build. That gives the developer using it an instant sense of how the build is doing without requiring much thought or attention.

The red/green light concept can be moved into the physical world as well. There have been numerous documented attempts to bring build status to the masses, including reader boards that announce the current build status, ambient lights that turn red or green to alert people to build status, and other tricks to make it obvious (painfully to some) if the build has been broken, as quickly as possible.

Fix a Broken Build before Integrating Changes

For Continuous Integration to work, it must be the primary goal of every developer to make sure that the build doesn't break. Seriously. Not breaking the build becomes the most important job of everyone on the project, all the time.

The whole point of CI is to reduce the integration work required for a project, and more important, the risk associated with that integration work. By keeping each integration as small as possible, and by completing those integrations early and often, the overall risk of any given integration cycle hurting the project schedule is vastly reduced. It also makes each integration cycle much easier for the developers involved. If the build is broken, then that cycle of integrations cannot proceed until the build is fixed. If the team can't count on the integrity of the source code at the "head" of the version control tree, then they cannot integrate with it. That means integrations they would otherwise be accomplishing smoothly get put on hold, and this costs the team time and money. If the team is serious about CI, then a broken build brings the entire team to a halt until that build is fixed.

This can be very difficult to communicate to a team that is just getting started with CI. It is one of the hardest behaviors to instill in a team, even one seasoned in Continuous Integration process. If developers don't take a broken build seriously enough, they will hold up the team or compound the problem by continuing as if nothing were wrong.

Once the build is broken, the only changes that should be checked in are those *directly* related to fixing the build. Anything else only compounds the problem and confuses the situation. If everything is working as it should, then your build notifications should include the changes that caused the build to proceed and who made those changes. In a perfect world, one and only one integration would be the cause of each build. That makes it very easy to determine which change(s) sparked a failure. If more than one integration is included in one build, then if it fails, it can be more difficult to determine the cause. Developers will have to sort through the error messages and relate them to the changes to determine the cause.

If people continue to check in changes once the build has failed, then you have a real problem. There are three potential causes:

❑　Your build is not configured properly. It could be waiting too long after a check-in before starting the build, or not checking for modifications often enough. Tighten up the intervals to make sure that fewer integrations are included in each build.

❑　Notifications aren't going out frequently enough, to the right people, or in the right format. If developers aren't getting the word in time that the build is broken, they may unknowingly check things in after the build breaks. Change how often people are notified or try other channels such as reader boards or tray icons.

❑　Developers don't care. This is the hardest one to fix. Checking in changes after the build is broken can mean that a) they aren't paying attention, or b) they aren't buying into the process. Either way there is a serious personnel problem.

Every time a check-in happens after the build is broken, it means not only that the cause of the failure will be harder to determine, but also that whoever checked in changes after it broke isn't following the right process. If everyone is checking out the latest changes and completing a build/test cycle before committing their work, then the build should never have broken in the first place. Occasionally, the build may still break because of timing issues, essentially source control "race conditions," where it is impossible to update to the latest source and complete a cycle before someone else commits work. With some SCCS, that simply isn't possible; with many others it is. If the build is broken, and then additional changes get checked in (ones not related directly to fixing the build), it means that those changes can't have been properly built and tested.

If changes aren't being properly built and tested before being committed, it means that the productivity of the team is being hampered by individuals being lazy or sloppy. This becomes a management problem rather than a development problem. Developers can do their part by heaping scorn and derision on the head of the build breaker. Dunce caps are an excellent deterrent. A few weeks of stigmatizing and humiliating the scofflaws in the group can be an effective catalyst for change.

Hyperbole aside, it is important that everyone on the team understand their role in the process, and how important it is for the build, and hence the integration branch of your code, to remain as stable as possible. That means that developers need to take personal responsibility for keeping the build succeeding. Nobody can check in changes at 5:00 p.m. on Friday before going on vacation. Making sure the build succeeds becomes an extension of the check-in process. If it fails, then either it needs to be fixed right away, or the problematic changes need to be rolled back until the fix is in place. In Chapter 6, we'll look at some source control strategies that make this easier to manage.

Summary

The point of Continuous Integration is to reduce the risks posed by integrating the work of many developers and to keep as many people working in parallel as possible. To that end, a CI process is designed to build software as often as possible. This is usually done by setting up a Continuous Integration server that builds a project automatically, without human intervention, preferably every time a change is committed.

This process provides testers with continuously updated versions of the software to test, and increases developer confidence in the integrity of the latest version of the source code, which makes it easier for them to stay up-to-date, and reduces the risk of integrating each individual change with the rest of the project.

The only way to gain full benefit from a CI process is if every developer takes it as a personal responsibility to keep the build from breaking so that other members of the team can keep working and integrating their changes as soon as they are completed.

Part II
Process

Done Is Done

One of the most important sets of rules to establish with your team are those defining when a given task is "done" and ready to be turned over to testing. Typically, "done" means that the developer has completed coding to his or her satisfaction, and feels that it is time for testing to have a go at it. Sometimes that works, and sometimes it does not. If that is the only criteria, it is easy for developers to become sloppy, which in turn makes quality assurance (QA) defensive, and no good can come of this.

So what does it mean to be done with a task, and how is that task defined?

How a task is defined depends on your project management methodology. If you are following a waterfall model, a task might be a task as defined by the project manager driving the schedule. If you are using Extreme Programming (XP), it might be a story or a task that supports a story; in Scrum, a backlog item or a specific task that is part of a backlog item.

Part of taking your project (and your personal skills) to the next level is raising the bar on what it means to be done with one of these tasks. So what kind of rules should you establish for your team (or yourself for that matter) to make sure that done really means done? We will examine a few rules that I think are important; you may have your own. Almost all of them come down to discipline in the end. "Done is done" means sticking to the rules, even if you don't think it's necessary in one particular case, or if you don't see the point in a specific instance. Come up with a set of criteria that should always be applied to finishing a task. There are inevitably going to be exceptions, but it is worth trying to apply all of the rules first to find cases that really are exceptional, not just the ones you don't feel like dealing with.

If you can come up with a solid set of criteria, and stick to them, you will end up with a much higher percentage of your work being accepted by QA. That means fewer defects due to oversight, omission, or just plain sloppiness. Fewer defects of this kind mean that you will spend more time doing productive work, and testers will spend less time chasing bugs that could easily have been avoided. Even if it feels like it takes you more time to stick to the rules, when you consider all the time you won't have to spend reading defect reports, trying to reproduce defects, and otherwise dealing with your defect tracking system, you will come out ahead in the end.

Whatever the set of rules you come up with, your whole team should be in agreement. There is no point in establishing rules that the team doesn't buy into because no one will follow them if that is the case. It is worth taking the time to drive consensus around the "done is done" rules so that everyone is equally invested (as much as is possible) in seeing the rules followed.

It is also important that each of your rules be verifiable, so part of establishing your "done is done" rules is formulating a way to validate that the rules are being followed. If you can't validate the rules, it will take a lot of extra work on the part of some person or persons to try and "police" the team's work, and that is not what you want. Nobody wants to play the role of team rules validation cop. It works best if you can validate the rules as part of your build process because the output of the build is visible to the whole team, and you can take advantage of the power of peer pressure to keep everyone on track.

This chapter presents a basic set of rules:

- ❑ Any significant design decisions have been discussed and approved by the team.
- ❑ Every class in your system should have a corresponding test fixture in your unit test suite.
- ❑ Each one of your test fixture classes should test the functionality of only one class under test.
- ❑ Code coverage should be 90% or better by line.
- ❑ Set your compiler to treat warnings as errors.
- ❑ Any static analysis tools that run as part of the build should generate no errors/warnings.
- ❑ Before committing anything to source control, update to the latest code and compile/test.
- ❑ Get your documentation in order.

You'll examine why these rules are important, what they mean to your development process, and how they can be validated.

Discuss Design Decisions

Any significant design decisions should be discussed and approved by the team. There is a fine line to be walked here between getting people's buy-in and the dreaded "design by consensus" syndrome, but I think it is an important rule to establish. Design by consensus cannot work and is never what you want your team to spend their time on. Everyone has opinions about how every piece of code should be designed, but at some point, there needs to be one hand on the tiller. The role of designer/architect is an important one, but "architect" doesn't need to be synonymous with "autocrat."

Personally, I favor an approach in which one or a small team of architects sketch out an initial design, preferably as part of a baseline architecture. That means building out as wide a solution as possible that touches all the riskiest parts of the design without going too deep. You want to prove that the solution is viable without spending much time building features. Once that initial work has been done, additional design work falls to the rest of the team. The architect should be responsible for the top-level design, but asking the architect to be responsible for designing every corner of the system is neither practical nor beneficial. That means that there will be some design work assigned to each member of the team as they build "down" or add features to the skeleton established by the baseline architecture.

That said, it is still the responsibility of the architect to make sure that the overall design expresses a consistent vision of how the system should work and how the code should be laid out. To that end, any significant design decision that is made during the course of building out the system should be raised with the group and discussed so that the architect can approve it. That doesn't mean that everyone on the team gets a vote. Nothing paralyzes a team faster than trying to reach consensus on every design point. No group of developers larger than one will ever agree on everything, and trying to get a team of 10–12 developers to reach consensus on design decisions will cause your project to bog down in short order.

However, if significant decisions get raised with the team and discussed, everyone benefits. The architect may be exposed to new ideas that he or she hadn't considered before, or specific aspects of the system's domain may come to light that make design changes necessary. If those decisions are raised in the context of the group, everyone learns from them, and you will have a better chance of staying consistent throughout the project and as a team. What you really want to avoid is any surprises that the architect might stumble across later during development. If parts of the system are inconsistent with the rest of the code or with the goals of the architect, then everyone's job becomes more difficult. You end up either just living with the inconsistencies or ripping out and redoing work that has already been done, which doesn't make anyone happy.

This is one of the harder rules to uphold, unfortunately. It really requires the architect to be involved at code level across large swaths of the software. Spot checking may be enough, although there are tools that will give hints as to where there might be issues. Using the source control system to track where changes are being made helps to identify "hot spots" where lots of changes are happening at once. Looking for new files being checked in can help find new areas of functionality being added. And occasionally generating artifacts like class diagrams may help highlight areas of interest.

The most important tool that the architect can employ is communication. Talk to your team and ask them what they are working on. Do they have questions? Do they need help? Are they unsure about anything? Do they understand how their work fits in to the system as a whole? Watercooler chat is a great way to identify which parts of the code may need extra scrutiny.

So how do you identify a "significant" design decision? Adding a new class isn't significant. Adding a new interface might need to be double-checked, but maybe not. Adding a new abstract base class probably bears looking at. Introducing a new third-party component or tool definitely is significant. As an architect, you really don't want to find out a month into development that one developer has introduced an inversion of control container (see Chapter 9, "Limiting Dependencies," for more on inversion of control) into their code independently of the rest of the team. Ultimately it is up to the team to decide what will constitute a significant change. Just make sure that everyone understands it in the same way, so no one is surprised.

To relate this back to "done is done": before any task can be "done," any design issues that are included in that task need to be brought to the attention of the team and the architect and signed off on before the task can be considered completed. If such issues are brought up on a task-by-task basis, there is less chance of things slipping in and persisting in the code for a long time before being noticed.

Every Class Has a Test Fixture

Every class in your system should have a corresponding test fixture in your unit-test suite. This is largely an organizational issue, but it is an important one. The easiest way to validate the fact that new code comes with tests is to look for a corresponding test fixture in your test suite. Of course, the addition of a new test fixture to go with a new class doesn't guarantee that the right things are being tested, or that the code is being tested thoroughly, but it is a starting point. This means that not only is at least some form of testing being included, but also that a particular organizational scheme is being followed. If you separate each fixture into its own file, and follow a convention for naming said files (see Figure 4-1), it becomes very easy for everyone on the team to find what they are looking for when correlating test code with code under test.

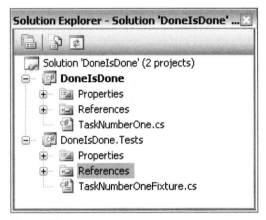

Figure 4-1

I prefer putting test code in a separate assembly/package/library so that it is physically separated from code under test. There is no reason to ship test code to a customer, and the easiest way to keep that from happening is to keep test code in a separate binary file, or however your executable code gets packaged for deployment.

The previous example shows how to consistently name both binary files and classes/files for maximum clarity. There is no need to speculate on what code is being tested in the DoneIsDone.Tests assembly. Or which class within DoneIsDone is being tested by the TaskNumberOneFixture class. Pick a naming convention that is easy to remember and easy to pick up on visually. If you can maintain a one-to-one relationship like the one shown in Figure 4-1 between test code and code under test, it will be very easy for developers to get a feel for where to look for code and tests, which means one less thing you will have to explain. The same sort of organization should be applied to the code itself. Looking inside the files shown in Figure 4-1, you'll see that the code under test:

```
using System;
using System.Collections.Generic;
using System.Text;

namespace DoneIsDone
{
    public class TaskNumberOne
    {
        public string FormatCurrencyValue(decimal money)
        {
            string result = string.Format("${0}", money);
            return result;
        }

    }
}
```

corresponds obviously to the test code that exercises it.

```csharp
using System;
using System.Collections.Generic;
using System.Text;

using NUnit.Framework;

namespace DoneIsDone.Tests
{
    [TestFixture]
    public class TaskNumberOneFixture
    {
        [Test]
        public void FormatGoodCurrencyValue()
        {
            decimal val = 4.99M;

            TaskNumberOne task = new TaskNumberOne();

            string actual = task.FormatCurrencyValue(val);

            string expected = "$4.99";

            Assert.AreEqual(expected, actual);
        }
    }
}
```

There are no surprises here. It is intuitively obvious which code is which. If you have lots of code that is similar, or handles similar cases, you may also want to establish a naming convention for test method names, although this can be a bit trickier. However, if you can come up with a scheme that makes sense, it adds that much more information to your code that developers can take advantage of when navigating through it. For example, if you have code that deals with input values in a consistent way, you might want to name test functions consistently to deal with all the possible input cases.

```csharp
namespace DoneIsDone
{
    public class TaskNumberTwo
    {
        public string FormatDoubleValue(double? val)
        {
            return string.Format("{0:#.##}", val);
        }
    }
}

namespace DoneIsDone.Tests
{
    [TestFixture]
    public class TaskNumberTwoFixture
    {
```

```
[Test]
public void TestGoodValue()
{
    double val = 1.222;

    string expected = "1.22";

    TaskNumberTwo task2 = new TaskNumberTwo();

    string actual = task2.FormatDoubleValue(val);

    Assert.AreEqual(expected, actual);
}

[Test]
public void TestBadValue()
{
    double val = double.NaN;

    TaskNumberTwo task2 = new TaskNumberTwo();

    string actual = task2.FormatDoubleValue(val);

    string expeced = "NaN";

    Assert.AreEqual(expeced, actual);

}

[Test]
public void TestNullValue()
{
    TaskNumberTwo task2 = new TaskNumberTwo();

    string actual = task2.FormatDoubleValue(null);

    string expected = string.Empty;

    Assert.AreEqual(expected, actual);

}
    }
}
```

It may not be possible or practical to come up with such a naming schema (i.e. TestGood ... TestBad ... TestNull ...), but if you can, it will make the test code easier to understand and to navigate.

This rule is easy to validate visually, but it would also be easy to write some sort of automated test that could be run as part of your build process to verify that the correct convention was being adhered to.

Each Fixture Exercises Only One Class

Each one of your test-fixture classes should test the functionality of only one class under test. If you have separated out your test code as indicated in Figure 4-1, each class MyClass should be tested by a corresponding `MyClassFixture` test class. That `MyClassFixture` test class should only test the code in `MyClass`, and nothing else. Furthermore, `MyClassFixture` should exercise *all* of the code in `MyClass`. That sounds simple at first, but it can be harder to achieve than you might think.

To make sure that you are testing all of the code under test, and nothing else, you have to carefully manage your dependencies. This is where a mock object framework can come in extremely handy. `MyClassFixture` needs to test only the code that lives in `MyClass`, and not code in other classes that `MyClass` might call. The very best way to assure that you achieve that level of test separation is to use dependency injection and an inversion of control container. By using those two technologies together, you can eliminate almost all runtime dependency issues and easily substitute test versions of all your dependencies at test time. Dependency injection and inversion of control are complex topics in and of themselves that are outside the scope of this book, but in summary, dependency injection means loading dependencies dynamically at runtime, using interfaces and runtime type creation (which means you don't have compile-time dependencies except on the interfaces), and an inversion of control system usually involves passing all of your dependencies to each object's constructor. By setting up constructors that take only interfaces as their dependencies, an inversion of control system can insert itself at runtime and automatically create classes that implement those interfaces based on declarative configuration. It takes real discipline and quite a bit of work to implement these technologies well, but if it can be done, it is very easy to remove any and all dependency issues at test time by providing test or mock versions of your interfaces.

Even if you don't go quite that far, many mocking frameworks provide support for creating runtime "mock" versions of your interfaces at test time. That keeps your test fixtures testing the code you want to test, and not the dependencies that should be tested someplace else.

Code Coverage Is High

Code coverage should be 90% or better by line. Yes, that is a tall order. Frankly, it's hard. It can take a lot of careful planning and work to get your coverage that high. But it is absolutely worth it. If you strive for such a large percentage of code coverage, you will be constantly thinking about how to make your own code more testable. The more testable code you write, the easier it will get. Once you have gotten used to writing highly testable code and good tests that exercise it, you will be turning out much higher-quality code than you did before and spending less time dealing with defects.

Getting to 90% coverage will also teach you things about your code and your coding style that you didn't know before. If you are consistently having difficulty testing all of your error handling code for instance, maybe you should change the way you are dealing with errors, or how you deal with dependencies. You should be able to generate all the errors that you intend to handle with your test code. If you can't, maybe you shouldn't be catching those exceptions.

If you have some file-handling code that catches file IO exceptions like the example below:

```
public class ErrorHandling
{
    public string ReadFile(string path)
    {
        if(File.Exists(path))
        {
```

```
            try
            {
                StreamReader reader = File.OpenText(path);
                return reader.ReadToEnd();
            }
            catch(UnauthorizedAccessException)
            {
                return null;
            }
        }
        else
        {
            throw new ArgumentException("You must pass a valid file ↵
    path.","path");
        }
    }
}
```

How will you test the catch block that handles the UnauthorizedAccessException? You could write
test code that creates a file in a known location and then sets access permissions on it to cause the access
exception. Should you? Probably not. That's a lot of work and fragile code to test the fact that accessing a
file you don't have authorization to access really throws that exception. Do you need to test that? Nope.
Microsoft is supposed to have done that for you already. You should expect it to throw the exception.

There are a couple of options that will provide you with an easier path to better code coverage. The first
is to factor out the dependency on System.IO.File:

```
public interface IFileReader
{
    StreamReader OpenText(string path);
    bool         Exists(string path);
}

public class FileIOReader : IFileReader
{
    public StreamReader OpenText(string path)
    {
        return File.OpenText(path);
    }

    public bool Exists(string path)
    {
        return File.Exists(path);
    }
}

public class BetterErrorHandling
{
    IFileReader _reader;

    public BetterErrorHandling(IFileReader reader)
    {
        _reader = reader;
    }
```

```
public string ReadFile(string path)
{
    if (_reader.Exists(path))
    {
        try
        {
            StreamReader reader = _reader.OpenText(path);
            return reader.ReadToEnd();
        }
        catch (UnauthorizedAccessException)
        {
            return null;
        }
    }
    else
    {
        throw new ArgumentException("You must pass a valid file path.", ↵
"path");
    }
}
```

Now rather than your code depending directly on System.IO.File, it depends on an implementation of IFileReader. Why is this better? Because now in your test code, you can implement a test version of IFileReader or use a mocking framework to simulate one that throws an UnauthorizedAccess Exception. Yes, it does mean writing more code, but the benefits are many. You can now test all of your code, and only your code, without relying on an external dependency. Better still, because the IFileReader interface has been introduced, if later on you have to extend your code to read files from an FTP site or over a network socket, all it takes is new implementations of IFileReader. If you decide later on to introduce an inversion of control container, the code is already prepared, because your dependencies get passed in to the constructor. Given the benefits, the extra code you have to write to make this work adds up to very little against the potential return.

The second solution is to get rid of your exception-handling code. If you can't get your test code to generate the exception you are handling, should you really be worrying about it? Maybe. But maybe not. Can you really do anything about an UnauthorizedAccessException? In the previous example, the solution is to return null, but in a real application, that would be misleading. It might be better to just let the exception go and let someone higher up the call stack handle it. You will examine that issue in more detail in Chapter 12, "Error Handling." Measuring your code coverage will bring such issues to light. You may find out that code isn't being covered by your tests because it isn't really necessary, in which case you can get rid of it and save yourself the extra work of maintaining it.

If your code is based in part or whole on legacy code, you may have a hard time getting your code coverage up as high as 90%. It is up to you to come up with a number that you think is reasonable for you and your team. Once you have arrived at a reasonable number, make sure that the whole team knows what it is and extend your Continuous Integration build to check code coverage and fail if it dips below your chosen threshold.

No Compiler Warnings

Set your compiler to treat warnings as errors. Before any task can be called done, it should generate no compiler warnings. Warnings are there for a reason, and every warning you eliminate ahead of time is one less potential problem to face later on. It is easy to ignore warnings when you are in the middle of trying to solve a particular coding problem. They can be difficult and time-consuming to track down, and after all, they are just warnings. However, those warnings may represent real issues. Just because code will compile doesn't make it a good idea. Warnings about unreachable code, unused variables, or uninitialized variables may not cause problems today, but they will surely cause problems tomorrow. If they don't turn into actual defects, they will hang around to confuse whoever comes along after you. Remember, you aren't just writing code that you will have to deal with. You are writing code that will be read, modified, and maintained by other developers, possibly for years to come. Every unused local variable is a potential source of confusion for someone who is less familiar with the code than you are.

Improve your code (and your legacy) by getting rid of all the compile warnings. It really doesn't take that much time, and it will make your code easier to read and less likely to exhibit defects later. It is true that there are some warnings that really are spurious. Sometimes you really do know better than the compiler (although not as often as most of us like to think). If that turns out to be the case, at least you will have thought about the warning and decided for yourself whether or not it represents a real issue. In most languages, you can apply a very specific way of turning off warnings. In C#, you can use the `#pragma warning disable` directive. That will turn off reporting of a specific warning until you re-enable it with `#pragma warning enable`. In either case, you follow the directive with one or more warning numbers. Make sure that you re-enable the warnings when you are done so as not to mask real problems.

Such directives need to be used with responsibility and honesty. If you sprinkle your code with `#pragma warning disable` directives just to avoid setting off the compiler (yes, I've seen people do this), you will be doing a great disservice to both yourself and your teammates. Again, warnings are there for a reason, and turning them off just so that you personally won't have to deal with them is asking for trouble. Also, it isn't as if the rest of your team won't notice. You will hear about it eventually, so it's probably easier to just fix the warnings.

The best way to check this rule is to set your compiler to treat warnings as errors, at least on your CI build machine. That will cause the build to fail if warnings aren't properly dealt with, making them obvious and easy to find.

Static Analysis Tools Generate No Errors

Any static analysis tools that run as part of the build should generate no errors/warnings. This one only applies if you are using such tools, but if you aren't, you probably should. Tools like FxCop (from Microsoft) or the static analysis tools of choice for your platform should generate no errors or warnings on the code you just finished. Static analysis tools (discussed further in Chapter 7, "Static Analysis") can be run as part of your build to detect problems with the code, such as excessive coupling, interface guideline violations, or other problems that can be detected by looking at your code while it isn't running.

If, for example, you are shipping a library that your customers will use to develop their own software, it is worth running a tool such as FxCop that checks to make sure that you are following best practices for naming your properties and methods, validating your input parameters, and for other aspects of the code that may affect the usability of your interface(s).

From an architectural perspective, you may want to run static analysis tools, such as NDepend from the NET world, which measures how loosely or tightly coupled your libraries are, how many dependencies your code has, or other design/architecture issues that may affect how easy (or not) it is to understand and maintain your code.

Other tools, such as Simian, check for code that is duplicated in more than one place, which may indicate a need for refactoring.

Whatever the tool, establish expectations about how compliant you want to be, and make it part of your build. If you want to make sure FxCop reports no critical errors in your code, put FxCop in your CI build, and fail the build if it generates a critical error.

Before Committing, Update

Before committing anything to source control, update to the latest code and compile/test. One of the most common reasons that builds fail is because developers don't update to the latest code before committing or checking in their changes. If you don't update before committing, there is no way to know whether or not you are checking in a breaking change. If someone else committed ahead of you, your changes may conflict with theirs and break the build. To keep any changes from conflicting, before you commit, make sure that you have updated to the latest (the tip) in the repository, run a complete build, and passed all the unit tests. Then and only then can you commit your changes and be sure that you haven't broken anything. This process is illustrated in Figure 3.1 in the preceding chapter.

Some source control clients will enforce this rule for you, but others will not. Most systems will prevent you from committing changes to individual files that haven't been updated, but they won't prevent you from committing changes to the repository when other files in the repository have changed.

This is probably one of the rules that is most often flagrantly disregarded. Developers may just forget, or be in too much of a hurry, or not bother to follow the right process. This can be particularly problematic if your build or unit-test process takes a long time or is hard to use. If it takes 20 minutes to do a build of your system and another 30 to run the unit tests, developers will simply not follow the right process. If you are having consistent problems with people not updating before committing, measure your build and test process. It's probably taking too long. Do whatever you can to limit the time it takes to build and test. Less than 10 minutes to build and test is ideal. That's long enough to go to the bathroom and get a fresh cup of coffee without sitting around feeling like your time is being wasted. Longer than that and developers start to feel like their time is being wasted for no good reason, and they will start committing changes without updating, building, and testing. Then the build will start to be broken more and more often, and your CI process will start to unravel, or at least be put under real strain.

If the build and test process is quick enough, there will be plenty of incentive for developers to make sure that they update before committing. No one wants to break the build, because everyone will know who did it, and updating first makes it much less likely that the build will break with your name on it.

Documentation in Place

The last step in ensuring that done is really done is putting your documentation in order. What that means in practical terms will differ, depending on what platform you are using to write your code. It might mean updating a word processing document with documentation about your new code, including how to use it and what problems consumers might encounter. It might mean updating formal electronic documentation such as a .chm compiled help file. Or it could mean updating a wiki or other interactive electronic source.

In .NET, it might mean making sure that your XML Documentation comments are properly in place. In C#, you can use comments with the marker /// and XML markup to embed documentation directly into your code. The following is an example of how to use XML comments to document a small class:

```
/// <summary>
/// This class demonstrates a better way of dealing with
/// dependencies and exception handling.
/// </summary>
public class BetterErrorHandling
{
    IFileReader _reader;

    /// <summary>
    /// Constructs a BetterErrorHandling class using
    /// the specified IFileReader interface.
    /// </summary>
    /// <param name="reader">An IFileReader for reading files.</param>
    public BetterErrorHandling(IFileReader reader)
    {
        _reader = reader;
    }

    /// <summary>
    /// Reads the file at the specified path as a single string.
    /// </summary>
    /// <param name="path">The path of the file to read.</param>
    /// <returns>A string containing the contents of the file.</returns>
    /// <exception cref="UnauthorizedAccessException">The current user does not
    have
    /// permissions to the file at <i>path</i></exception>
    /// <exception cref="ArgumentException">The file specified in <i>path</i>
    does not exist</exception>
    /// <example>string fileContents = ReadFile(&quot;c:\temp\file&quot;);
    </example>
    public string ReadFile(string path)
    {
        if (File.Exists(path))
        {
            try
            {
                StreamReader reader = _reader.OpenText(path);
                return reader.ReadToEnd();
            }
            catch (UnauthorizedAccessException)
            {
                return null;
            }
        }
        else
        {
            throw new ArgumentException("You must pass a valid file path.",
    "path");
        }
    }
}
```

If you turn on the XML documentation flag in the C# compiler, the compiler will output an XML file including all the comments in a structured way, like this:

```xml
<?xml version="1.0"?>
<doc>
    <assembly>
        <name>DoneIsDone</name>
    </assembly>
    <members>
        <member name="T:DoneIsDone.BetterErrorHandling">
            <summary>
            This class demonstrates a better way of dealing with
            dependencies and exception handling.
            </summary>
        </member>
        <member name="M:DoneIsDone.BetterErrorHandling.#ctor(
DoneIsDone.IFileReader)">
            <summary>
            Constructs a BetterErrorHandling class using
            the specified IFileReader interface.
            </summary>
            <param name="reader">An IFileReader for reading files.</param>
        </member>
        <member name="M:DoneIsDone.BetterErrorHandling.ReadFile(System.String)">
            <summary>
            Reads the file at the specified path as a single string.
            </summary>
            <param name="path">The path of the file to read.</param>
            <returns>A string containing the contents of the file.</returns>
            <exception cref="T:System.UnauthorizedAccessException">The current
user does not have
            permissions to the file at <i>path</i></exception>
            <exception cref="T:System.ArgumentException">The file specified in
<i>path</i> does not exist</exception>
            <example>string fileContents = ReadFile("c:\temp\file");</example>
        </member>
    </members>
</doc>
```

Using one of a number of build-time tools, that XML file can then be styled into human-readable documentation, much like the documentation that Microsoft generates for the .NET framework itself. A styled version of the documentation for the ReadFile method might look like Figure 4-2.

This particular example was generated using the "CR_Documentor" plug-in for Visual Studio .NET, which can be found at www.paraesthesia.com/archive/2004/11/15/cr_documentor---the-documentor-plug-in-for-dxcore.aspx. NDoc and the as-yet-unreleased Sandcastle project from Microsoft are alternative tools for generating human-readable documentation from XML comments.

In the case of .NET XML documentation comments, this rule is easy to check. When you turn on the documentation flag on the C# compiler, it will generate warnings for any elements in the code that don't carry documentation comments. If you are compiling with "warnings as errors," then missing comments will break the build. You will still have to double-check visually to make sure that developers are entering real comments, and not just adding empty XML to get rid of the warnings (this happens frequently) without adding real value.

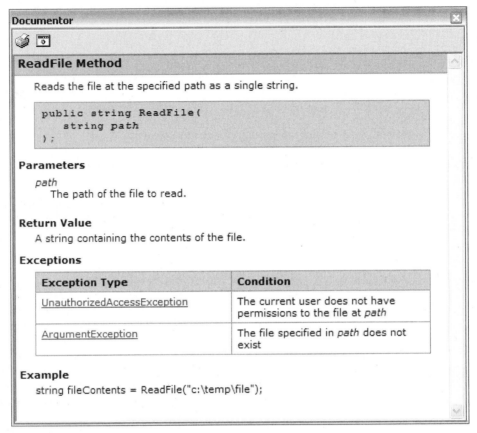

Figure 4-2

If you are using some other system for documentation, it may be harder to automatically validate that the rule is being observed.

Summary

An important part of a mature development process is the definition of what it really means for a developer to be "done" with each of their tasks. If you take the time to establish a set of guidelines for what "done" means and make sure that those guidelines are understood by the whole team, you will end up with code of a much higher quality. Furthermore, your developers will learn a lot about how they write code, and how it can be written more cleanly and with fewer defects.

It takes some extra effort to both establish the rules and ensure that they are being followed, but the return on investment will make it worthwhile. It will improve not only the output of your team, but also your coding skills and those of your team. Making sure that each task is really "done" will also mean less time spent in testing and fewer defects to deal with before your product can be shipped to customers.

5

Testing

Testing, often referred to as quality assurance (QA), is one of the most important parts of the whole software-development process. Unfortunately, most of the time testing gets the least consideration, the fewest resources, and generally short shrift throughout the development organization.

Every study ever done on the effectiveness of software testing has shown that the more time you spend up front on testing, the less time and money it takes to complete your project to the level of quality you want to achieve. Everyone in the industry knows this to be true. Yet most developers don't think about how they will test their software until after it is already written. Despite the fact that, time and again, all the evidence points to the fact that a bug found at the beginning of development is orders of magnitude less expensive and time-consuming to fix than one found at the end of the development cycle, and bugs are even more expensive and time-consuming to fix after the product has reached the customer.

Why should this be the case?

There are many reasons why developers don't like testing. Testing is perceived as less "fun" than writing "real" code. Most software-development organizations reward developers for producing features in the shortest amount of time, not for writing the highest-quality code. The majority (or at least a plurality) of software companies do not have a mature testing organization, which makes testing appear amateurish and as though it is not serious business to other developers. Because of the history of the industry, testing is often seen as an entry-level position, a low-status job. This causes testing to attract less-qualified or less-experienced developers, and many of them want to "get out" of testing as quickly as they can. Again, because most organizations favor and reward producing features over quality, testing usually receives the fewest resources and tends to get squeezed out of the schedule at the end of a project. This reinforces the impression that quality assurance is not valued.

The single most important thing that any developer can do to improve their skills and those of their team is to take testing seriously and internalize the importance of quality throughout their organization. Let me repeat that. The most important thing you as a developer can do to *Code Up!*, to take your skills to the next level, to increase your marketability, and to improve your job satisfaction is to embrace testing as a first-class part of the software-development process. Period.

Embracing testing won't just improve the quality of your code. It will also improve your design skills. It will bring you closer to understanding the requirements of your customers, both internal and external. It will save you time and hassle throughout the development process, and long after it is over. It will keep your phone from ringing on the weekends or in the middle of the night when you would rather be doing something besides providing support to your customers.

Best of all, it will make you a better developer.

Why Testing Doesn't Get Done

If everyone knows that testing early and often improves the quality of software and goes a long way toward making schedules more achievable, why does it never seem to happen that way?

> *I'm generalizing here. Many companies do actually have mature testing organizations, and many more developers understand the relationships involved here between commitment to testing and quality. You may be one of them. But if so, you are still in the minority.*

Most of the real reasons are psychological. The people who sponsor software-development projects (the ones who write the checks) don't care about metrics. (Again, I'm generalizing.) They care about features. Project sponsors want to see things happening in web browsers and on their desktops in ways that make sense to them and solve their business problems. The unfortunate reality is that unit tests do not demonstrably solve business problems. They improve quality, lower costs, and make customers happy in the long run. But they don't do anything. No project sponsor is ever impressed by green lights in a testing console. They expect the software to work. The only way to convince project sponsors that they should devote more rather than fewer resources to testing is to demonstrate that projects are delivered with higher quality and less cost, with real numbers. That takes time and commitment to processes improvement, and it requires that you record information about your process at every level.

Then there is the schedule. For a whole suite of well-known reasons, psychological, organizational, and historical, developers tend to underestimate how long their work will take, and testing organizations (in my experience, still generalizing . . .) tend to overestimate how long their work will take. This means that when push comes to shove, and schedules slip, developers are allowed more time (because they are busy producing features that project sponsors care about), and testing schedules are gradually squeezed tighter and tighter to make up for the shortfall.

In many organizations, if this continues too long, it enters a downward spiral. Testers feel undervalued because their schedules and resources are continually being cut. This causes them to become bitter and disillusioned, worsening relations between development and test, and leading to testers seeking other employment. That means you have to hire new testers, who have no understanding of your product and are often less experienced in general. This, in turn, leads to testing estimates getting longer and longer (because now you have nervous, inexperienced testers), and the cycle begins again.

Sure, I might be exaggerating this a bit, but not by all that much. I've personally experienced this cycle on more projects than not.

Many developers don't like writing tests. It can be tedious. More importantly, as mentioned previously, the whole software industry is designed to reward developers for producing the most features in the shortest amount of time, rather than for producing the highest-quality code. Traditionally, in any given group of developers, there is at least one who is widely known for turning out feature after feature to the delight of project sponsors, and at the expense of quality. You all know who I mean. The one you always have to clean up after, and who still manages to get all the kudos.

The fact is, improving quality is a long, hard process that requires commitment at every level in the development organization. Starting with the developers themselves.

How Testing Will Make You a Better Developer

If each and every one of us accepts personal responsibility for the quality of our code, most of these problems will go away. Granted, this is easier said than done. For all of the reasons previously discussed, it can be much more rewarding to write more features at lower quality and hope that either nobody will notice or that somebody else will deal with the bugs later. However, the rewards of taking responsibility for your own code quality are many and varied.

Your Designs Will Be Better

Writing tests, whether before or after you write your code (although before is still better; see Chapter 2, "Test-Driven Development"), will force you to use your own interfaces. Over time, the practice of consuming your own interfaces will lead you to design better, more usable interfaces the first time around. This is particularly true if you write libraries that are used by other people. If you write libraries that expose features you think are important but never try to use those libraries, the design will suffer. The way you picture the library working may not be the most practical way to write the code from your consumer's perspective. Writing tests will force you to see both sides of the equation, and you will improve the design of your code. If you write the tests first, you won't have to go back and fix your code later. If you wait until you are done before writing your tests, you may have to go back and make some changes to your interfaces, but you will still have learned something about interface design.

This process takes a while to get the hang of. It's easy to write interfaces in isolation, either in code or in a modeling language like the Unified Modeling Language (UML), but these interfaces may not be easy (or even possible) to use. If you are working in UML or another modeling language, you can find some problems by doing things like sequence diagrams. They provide you with some sense of how the interfaces will be used, but they don't necessarily give you a sense of how clean the code will be for the consumer.

The best way to really get a feel for how your code will be used is to use it. You could do that by writing prototypes or harness code, but if you do it by writing tests instead you'll also improve your quality and build up a suite of regression tests to ensure that you haven't introduced any problems down the road. You'll explore this in more detail about later when you look at unit versus integration testing.

You'll Have to Write Less Code to Achieve Your Goals

This is particularly true when you write your tests first. When you practice Test-Driven Development (TDD), you only write the code necessary to meet the customer's requirements. No more and, hopefully, no less, which is why you have tests. It is widely known that one of the constant problems plaguing software development is the YAGNI (You Ain't Gonna Need It) syndrome. You end up writing a lot of code that turns out not to be needed. Sometimes that is because requirements change, but more often it is because you jump ahead of yourself and make up requirements that aren't really there. Sometimes it is because you always wanted to try writing some particular code and think this would be the perfect opportunity to try it. Sometimes it is because you build out framework code in the attempt to create something reusable, only to discover that it will be used in just one place.

If you really practice TDD, however, it should never happen. If you write your tests first, then write only the code you need to make the tests pass, you will learn to write leaner code with less baggage to support later on. This is one of the hardest parts of TDD to really internalize. You are habituated to trying to pull out reusable code, or to follow some design pattern in cases where it's not required, or to plan for the future so that you won't have to revisit the same code again later. If you refuse categorically to write a single line of code that you don't need, you will start writing better code that will cost less to support.

That doesn't mean that writing less code should be a goal in and of itself. That way lies sloppiness and obfuscation. Writing less code doesn't mean you stop checking for error conditions or validating input parameters. When I say only write the code you need, those things are included in that statement.

What TDD really teaches you is how to avoid writing any code that doesn't directly provide business value. That should be your ultimate goal. If you stick to only writing code that supports your tests, and your tests reflect your requirements, you'll only write code that provides value directly to customers.

You Will Learn More about Coding

It's all too easy to fall into ruts when you write code, particularly if you write essentially the same kind of code over and over, or consistently work on solving the same kinds of problems. For example, you might be working on a web-based application that customers use to manage some resource, be it bank accounts, health care, insurance, and so on. Most of what you write probably centers around taking data from a database, showing that data to customers, and occasionally responding to their requests by saving some data back to the database, such as preferences or other details. It is easy to fall into less-than-optimal coding habits if that is the majority of the code that you write.

Testing can help. If you strive to write more tests, it may cause you to rethink your designs. Is your code testable? Is it separated properly from the UI? If you aren't writing tests, that separation is really only an academic concern, and that means that it doesn't get done. If you start really trying to test all the code that you write, you will come to see how important that separation is. It becomes worth your while to write better factored code, and in the process, you will learn more about writing software.

As you write more code, and develop tests for it, you may come to be more familiar with common patterns that can help you in your job. This is particularly true with negative testing. Writing negative tests, or ones that are designed to make your code fail, will teach you new and better ways of handling error conditions. It forces you to be the one consuming your error messages and dealing with how your code returns errors. This, in turn, will lead you toward more consistent and user-friendly error handling. One thing that happens quite often during negative testing is discovering that different parts of your code return errors in different ways. If you hadn't done the negative testing, you might never have noticed the inconsistency and so been able to fix it.

By learning to write only the code that makes your tests pass, you will inevitably learn to write tighter, more consistent code, with fewer errors and less wasted effort. You will also learn how to tighten up and normalize your error-handling code by doing negative testing.

You Will Develop Better Relationships with Your Testers

This is your opportunity to walk a mile in the shoes of your friendly neighborhood quality-assurance engineer. All too often, an antagonistic relationship develops between development and testers. Testers who constantly find the same defects over and over start to lose respect for developers who appear lazy and careless. Developers feel picked on by testers, who they feel are out to get them and make them feel bad about their mistakes. I've been on both sides of the fence and experienced both emotional responses. The reality is that all the engineers in a software-development organization, code and test, are working toward the same goal: shipping high-quality software. Developers don't want to go home at night feeling that they are writing low-quality software. No one derives job satisfaction from that. Testers also just want the organization to ship high-quality software. They don't want to "pick on" developers or make them feel bad. At least you hope that is not the case. If it is, you have some serious organizational problems beyond just the coding ones.

By embracing testing as a first-class development task, developers gain a better understanding of the problems and challenges faced by their testers. They will come to understand that quality is everyone's concern, not just the province of quality assurance. This leads to much less strained relationships between development and QA. Again, I'm generalizing here, but this has proven to be the case in more than one organization I have worked with personally.

One of the happiest outcomes of developers writing tests, from the QA perspective, is that those developers will start writing more testable code. Code that is well factored and designed to be tested. Code that has been subjected to negative testing, and edge case testing. Code with fewer defects for QA to find. Testers love to find bugs, but only ones that developers probably wouldn't have found on their own. Finding trivial bugs isn't fun for anyone.

Getting developers to write tests can also lead to dialog between developers and testers. Developers want to know what they should be testing and what the best way to go about it would be. QA can provide test cases, help define edge cases, and bring up common issues that they have seen in the past. Going in the other direction, developers can help QA write better tests, build test frameworks, and provide additional hooks into code for white box testing and test automation.

If developers and testers are getting along and working toward the common goal of shipping high-quality software, the result can only be increased quality and a better working environment for everyone.

Taken together, all these factors will help to improve your performance as a developer. You will learn better coding practices, build well-designed software that is easier to test, and write *less* code to solve *more* business problems.

You Will Make Your Project Sponsors Happy

As previously discussed, investing extra time and money in testing can be a very hard sell with project sponsors. What people who write checks for software development really want to see is the largest number of features that provide business value, developed for the least amount of money.

Testing in general, and particularly Test-Driven Development, directly supports your project sponsor's goals. Test-first development leads to less code being written that doesn't directly support requirements. That means not only less money spent on coding, but also a better understanding of what those requirements are.

Writing tests before code forces developers to clarify the project's requirements so that they know what tests to write. You can't write the appropriate tests unless you have a thorough understanding of the requirements of the project, which means that if you don't understand those requirements and still need to write tests, you will be forced to ask. This makes customers and project sponsors happy. They love to be asked about requirements. It makes them feel like you really care about solving their problems, which of course you do. Attention to detail is important here. As you work more with TDD, you will come to a better understanding of what questions you should be asking. Ask about edge conditions. Ask about use cases. Ask about data. One of the problems that often comes up during development is overcomplicating requirements. Most of us really like to put the science in computer science — to extrapolate, to consider all of the implications surrounding the requirements we actually got from the customer. This leads to developers not only making up requirements (which happens far more frequently than most of us like to admit), but also to making existing requirements much more complicated than they really are. If you always go back to your customer to *ask* about requirements, this escalation of complexity is much less likely to happen. In actual practice, most business problems are pretty easy to solve. As often as not, your customer will prefer a simpler solution to a more complex one. Get feedback as often as you can.

Get feedback on your tests as well. You can ask your customer or sponsor for edge conditions and use cases (which lead to more tests), and for elaboration on the requirements. This information leads to more and better tests that come closer to representing the customer's requirements. For example, whenever you test an integer field, ask the customer what the real range of the integer field should be. When testing string fields, find out if you should be testing very long strings, empty strings, or strings containing non-English or other special characters. You may find out that you only have to support strings of 20 characters or less, in English, and that empty strings are not allowed. That will allow you to write much more targeted and complete unit tests that test for the real conditions that your customer expects. You can also use that information to write better negative tests, and refine your error handling. In the previous example, you might want to write tests that disallow non-English characters, empty strings, or those longer than 20 characters.

As an example, let's say that you're testing a class that saves and reads customer names:

```
public class CustomerTests
{
  public void EnterCustomerName(string name)
  {

  }

  public string ReadCustomerName()
  {

  }
}
```

At the most basic level, you might use a simple test to make sure that the `EnterCustomerName` method really saves the right name:

```
[TestFixture]
public class CustomerNameTests
{
  [Test]
  public void TestBasicName()
  {
```

```
      string expected = "Fred";
      EnterCustomerName(name);
      string actual = ReadCustomerName();
      Assert.AreEqual(expected, actual);
    }
  }
```

That tests the most basic requirement. The method saves the customer's name in such a way that you can read it later and get the same string you sent in. How do you know how to test edge conditions with a method like this? Can customers have a name that is the empty string? Or null? Probably not, although there may be cases where it's OK. Perhaps the only thing you really care about is their email address, and the name is optional. In that case, null might be an OK value here. However, the empty string might not be OK because the empty string would result in something with no value being written to the data store.

```
    [Test]
    public void TestNullString()
    {
      string expected = null;
      EnterCustomerName(expected);
      string actual = ReadCustomerName();
      Assert.AreEqual(expected, actual);
    }

    [Test]
    [ExpectedException(typeof(ArgumentException))]
    public void TestEmptyString()
    {
      string expected = string.Empty();
      EnterCustomerName(expected);
      Assert.Fail("EnterCustomerName should not have accepted an empty string.");
    }
```

Now you have something more than just tests. You have requirements, and a way to validate those requirements. You have a way of further defining your code's contract and a way of communicating that contract to other developers (and yourself once you forget). Given the previous code, no developer would have to wonder about whether null or empty strings were acceptable. You could further elaborate on the contract and requirements with more tests:

```
    [Test]
    public void VeryLongStringIsOK()
    {
      string expected = "...very long string goes here...";
      ...
    }

    [Test]
    [ExpectedException(typeof(ArgumentException))]
    public void NoNonEnglishCharacters()
    {
      string expected = "Reneé";
      EnterCustomerName(expected);
      Assert.Fail("Non-English character should have been rejected.");
    }
```

The more tests you can develop along these lines, the better your contracts, the better your error handling, and the happier your customers will be that you have fulfilled their requirements.

Yes, the process takes time. Yes, it takes additional effort on your part. It may seem like busy work. Sometimes it is. But if you develop tests like the ones covered in the previous code before you write a single line of the implementation of `EnterCustomerName()`, your implementation will be exactly what is required as soon as all the tests pass.

This brings up a key question. Should you write all the tests first, then the code? Or should you write one test first, then some code, then another test, and so on.

In a strictly TDD world, you would write the first test, which in this example is the simple case:

```
public void EnterCustomerName(string name)
{
  Database.Write(name);
}
```

Then you'd write the second test, the null string test, which might not require any code changes. The third test for the empty string might lead to more changes, however. . . .

```
public void EnterCustomerName(string name)
{
  if(name != null && name.Equals(string.Empty))
    throw new ArgumentException("name cannot be empty");

  Database.Write(name);
}
```

Writing the tests one at a time will keep the resulting method as lean as possible. It is tempting to write all the tests first, and then make them all pass at once. This temptation should be resisted, however. If you try to make all the tests pass at once, you might overengineer the method and make it too complicated. If you take the tests one by one, the solution that results should be as close as possible to the simplest solution that meets all the requirements.

This works even better if you are pair programming. One partner writes the tests, and then passes the keyboard to the other partner to make the test pass. This keeps it interesting for everybody. It becomes a game in which creative tests get written, and clean, simple code causes them to pass.

Code Coverage

Code coverage, in the simplest possible terms, means how much of your code is actually executed by your tests. Code coverage analysis is the art of figuring that out.

Figuring out how much of your code is being covered by your tests is a key part of your testing strategy. It's not the most important part, or the least. After all, it's just a number. But it is a number that can help you figure out where to spend your testing resources, how much work you have left to do in terms of writing your tests, and where you might be writing too much code.

It is also a number that cannot stand on its own. You have to combine code coverage analysis with other metrics such as code complexity, test results, and plenty of common sense.

Why Measure Code Coverage

Code coverage is important for a couple of key reasons:

- ❑ If parts of your code aren't being covered by your tests, this may mean that there are bugs waiting to be found by your customers.
- ❑ If parts of your code aren't being covered by your tests, you might not actually need that code.

In a perfect world, you would write tests that exercised every line of code you ever wrote. Every line of code that doesn't get run by a test could be a defect waiting to appear later on, possibly after your software is in the hands of customers. As I said before, the earlier in the cycle you find a bug, the cheaper it is to fix and the less impact it has. So achieving a high level of code coverage as early as possible in your project will help you improve the quality and decrease the cost of your software.

There are lots of reasons why code doesn't get executed by tests. The simplest and most obvious is because you haven't written any tests. That seems self-evident, but unfortunately, by the time you get around to measuring code coverage, it is often too late to bring it up to the level you would want. The more code you have already written without tests, the less likely you are to go back and write those tests later. Resource constraints, human nature, and so on all make it harder to improve your code coverage later in the schedule.

There are other reasons why code doesn't get tested. Even if you have written tests for all of your code, you may not have written tests to cover every case, such as edge conditions and failure cases. The hardest code to get covered is often exception-handling code. As a matter of course, while writing code, you also write code to handle exceptions that might be thrown by various methods you call. It can be tricky, if not impossible, to cause all the failures that error-handling routines were meant to deal with during the course of your testing. In the next section, you'll see more about ways to generate those error conditions.

There are other measurements that need to be combined with code coverage analysis if you are to get the maximum value out of it. Possibly the most important one is *cyclomatic complexity*. Cyclomatic complexity is a measure of how many paths of execution there are through the same code. The higher the cyclomatic complexity is for any given method, the more paths there are through that method.

A very simple method is:

```
public void HelloWorld()
{
  Console.WriteLine("Hello World!");
}
```

This has very low cyclomatic complexity. In this case, it is one. There is only one path through the HelloWorld method used in the previous code listing. That makes it very easy to achieve 100% code coverage. Any test that calls HelloWorld will exercise every line of that method.

However, for a more complex method:

```
public void HelloWorldToday()
{
  switch (DateTime.Now.DayOfWeek)
  {
    case DayOfWeek.Monday:
      Console.WriteLine("Hello Monday!");
      break;
    case DayOfWeek.Tuesday:
      Console.WriteLine("Hello Tuesday!");
      break;
     case DayOfWeek.Wednesday:
      Console.WriteLine("Hello Wednesday!");
      break;
    case DayOfWeek.Thursday:
      Console.WriteLine("Hello Thursday!");
      break;
    case DayOfWeek.Friday:
      Console.WriteLine("Hello Friday!");
      break;
    case DayOfWeek.Saturday:
      Console.WriteLine("Hello Saturday!");
      break;
    case DayOfWeek.Sunday:
      Console.WriteLine("Hello Sunday!");
      break;
  }
}
```

The cyclomatic complexity is much higher. In this case, there are at least seven paths through the HelloWorldToday method, depending on what day it is currently. That means that to achieve 100% code coverage, you would need to execute the method at least once a day for a week, or come up with some way to simulate those conditions. To test it properly, you have to generate all the conditions needed to exercise all seven code paths. This is still a fairly simplistic example. It is not at all uncommon to see methods with cyclomatic complexities of 20–30 or higher. Really nasty methods may be well over 100. It becomes increasingly difficult to generate tests to cover all those code paths.

Cyclomatic complexity, then, becomes something that you can combine with your code coverage numbers to figure out where you should focus your test-writing efforts. It is much more useful than just code coverage data by itself. While it can be tricky trying to line up code coverage and complexity data, if you can correlate them, you will find out where the largest bang for the buck can be had, either by adding more tests to increase your coverage or refactoring to reduce the complexity of your code. Remember, TDD philosophy promotes a cycle of Red/Green/Refactor. If code isn't being covered because it is too complex to test properly, it may be an excellent candidate for being refactored into something simpler.

Another reason you may have low code coverage numbers is that you have surplus code that you don't need. Either you have code that is truly unreachable (although most modern compilers will flag that code as an error) or you have code that does not directly support meeting your customer's requirements. If the reason that you write tests is to express requirements and make sure that they are fulfilled, and after testing all your requirements there is still code left untested, then perhaps that code is unnecessary and you can get rid of it.

For example, if you add a default case to the switch statement in `HelloWorldToday`:

```
public void HelloWorldToday()
{
  switch (DateTime.Now.DayOfWeek)
  {
    case DayOfWeek.Monday:
      Console.WriteLine("Hello Monday!");
      break;
    case DayOfWeek.Tuesday:
      Console.WriteLine("Hello Tuesday!");
      break;
     case DayOfWeek.Wednesday:
      Console.WriteLine("Hello Wednesday!");
      break;
    case DayOfWeek.Thursday:
      Console.WriteLine("Hello Thursday!");
      break;
    case DayOfWeek.Friday:
      Console.WriteLine("Hello Friday!");
      break;
    case DayOfWeek.Saturday:
      Console.WriteLine("Hello Saturday!");
      break;
    case DayOfWeek.Sunday:
      Console.WriteLine("Hello Sunday!");
      break;
    default:
      Console.WriteLine("Unknown day of the week"):
      break;
  }
}
```

The new code will never be tested. The compiler is unlikely to flag this as unreachable, but no matter how many tests you write, the value for `DayOfWeek` must always be one of the enumerated values. It might seem perfectly reasonable to add a default case at the time the method is written (out of habit, if nothing else), but code coverage analysis would show it as code that you don't need, and can safely delete.

The same often ends up being true of error-handling code. It is very easy to write error-handling code (with the best intentions) that will never be executed. Keeping a close eye on your code coverage numbers will point out those areas where you might be able to get rid of some code and make things simpler and easier to maintain down the road.

Code Coverage Tools

The best way to get good code coverage numbers is to instrument your unit testing process by adding additional measurement code. If you can instrument that process, you should be able to capture a complete picture of which code gets run during testing.

There are two main strategies employed by tools for measuring code coverage: either your code is instrumented before it is compiled, or it is somehow observed in its unaltered state.

Many tools designed to work with traditionally compiled languages pursue the first strategy. Many C++ code coverage tools, for example, insert additional code in parallel with your application code at compile time, generating an instrumented version of your code that records which parts of it have been executed. This method tends to produce the most reliable results, because the inserted code can very carefully keep track of what code has been executed and what hasn't, because it runs in parallel with your application code. On the other hand, it tends to be time-consuming both at compile time and at runtime. Most important, the instrumented code is demonstrably different from your production application code, and so may throw other metrics (such as performance) out of whack.

In interpreted or dynamically compiled languages, another possibly strategy is for the code coverage tool to observe your code from the outside and report on its behavior. The example tool you will be looking at is the .NET tool NCover. Because .NET is a managed-execution environment, NCover can take advantage of the native .NET profiler interfaces to allow you to observe how your code executes at runtime. This means that your code does not have to be modified in any way to be measured. No code is inserted at compile time, so your code runs in its original form. NCover still has an impact on your code, however, because observing your code through the profiler interfaces also comes at an added cost, and may conflict with other tools that also make use of the profiler interfaces.

One thing to be careful of when dealing with any kind of code coverage tool is what metric is actually being reported. Code coverage is almost always reported as a percentage of code that is covered by your tests. However, that percentage may be the percentage of the number of *lines* of code tested or a percentage of *paths* through the code that are tested. The percentage of lines of code is usually easiest to measure, but is the more difficult to analyze. If you are measuring percentage of lines, numbers for smaller methods may be misleading. Consider the following code:

```
public string ReadFile(string fileName)
{
   if (fileName == null)
      throw new ArgumentNullException("fileName");

   using (StreamReader reader = File.OpenText(fileName))
   {
      return reader.ReadToEnd();
   }
}
```

If the file name is never passed in as null, the ArgumentNullException will never be thrown. The smaller the rest of the method, the lower the coverage percentage would be, even though the number of paths tested would remain constant if more lines of code were executed to deal with the open file. That can make your coverage numbers misleadingly low, particularly if you have a lot of small methods. In the previous example, the success case produces (in NCover) only an 80% coverage, due to the small number of lines. On the other hand, if you were measuring code path coverage, the previous method (in the successful case) might produce only 50% coverage because only one of the possible paths would be tested.

The important takeaway here is that coverage numbers are useful as relative, rather than absolute values. They are more important for identifying which methods need more tests than as an absolute measure of progress.

For the previous example, the test code might look like this:

```
[TestFixture]
public class CoverageTest
{
  [Test]
  public void FileRead()
  {
    Coverage c = new Coverage();
    c.ReadFile(@"c:\temp\test.txt");
  }
}
```

Using NCover to run your test code, you get a report like the following:

```
<coverage profilerVersion="1.5.8 Beta" driverVersion="1.5.8.0" startTime="2007-09-
25T23:39:27.796875-07:00" measureTime="2007-09-25T23:39:28.953125-07:00">
 <module moduleId="16" name="C:\TDDSample\TDDSample\bin\Debug\TDDSample.dll"
assembly="TDDSample" assemblyIdentity="TDDSample, Version=1.0.0.0, Culture=neutral,
PublicKeyToken=null, processorArchitecture=MSIL">
   <method name="ReadFile" excluded="false" instrumented="true"
class="TDDSample.Coverage">
     <seqpnt visitcount="1" line="13" column="13" endline="13" endcolumn="34"
excluded="false" document="C:\TDDSample\TDDSample\Coverage.cs" />
     <seqpnt visitcount="0" line="14" column="17" endline="14" endcolumn="61"
excluded="false" document="C:\TDDSample\TDDSample\Coverage.cs" />
     <seqpnt visitcount="1" line="16" column="20" endline="16" endcolumn="65"
excluded="false" document="C:\TDDSample\TDDSample\Coverage.cs" />
     <seqpnt visitcount="1" line="18" column="17" endline="18" endcolumn="43"
excluded="false" document="C:\TDDSample\TDDSample\Coverage.cs" />
     <seqpnt visitcount="1" line="20" column="9" endline="20" endcolumn="10"
excluded="false" document="C:\TDDSample\TDDSample\Coverage.cs" />
   </method>
   <method name="FileRead" excluded="false" instrumented="true"
class="TDDSample.CoverageTest">
     <seqpnt visitcount="1" line="29" column="13" endline="29" endcolumn="41"
excluded="false" document="C:\TDDSample\TDDSample\Coverage.cs" />
     <seqpnt visitcount="1" line="30" column="13" endline="30" endcolumn="45"
excluded="false" document="C:\TDDSample\TDDSample\Coverage.cs" />
     <seqpnt visitcount="1" line="31" column="9" endline="31" endcolumn="10"
excluded="false" document="C:\TDDSample\TDDSample\Coverage.cs" />
   </method>
 </module>
</coverage>
```

This is a report of how many sequence points (or unique statements from the compiled-code perspective) were visited by your tests. This provides the information that you need, but not in a format that is very usable to the average human being. What you really want to do is correlate the report with your source files, so that you can see in a more digestible way which code isn't being tested. Luckily, to go with NCover, you can get a copy of NCoverExplorer, which provides a much more user-friendly view of the NCover results, as shown in Figure 5-1.

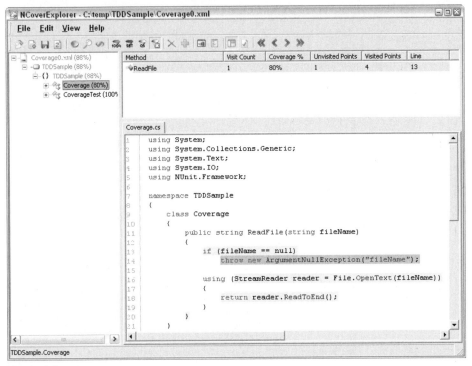

Figure 5-1

NCoverExplorer presents the report in a way that you can correlate with actual code. In the previous example, you can see that the one line that isn't executed is highlighted, providing a very visceral way of identifying the code that isn't being run. You also get a coverage percentage in the tree displayed on the left side of the screen. It shows a rolled-up percentage for each method, class, namespace, and assembly. Best of all, NCoverExplorer can provide fairly complex reports, tailored to your preferences, that can be delivered as part of a Continuous Integration build process.

One of the most useful knobs you can twist is the Satisfactory Coverage percentage, shown in the options dialog in Figure 5-2. That percentage determines what percentage of coverage you deem "acceptable." Any classes, methods, and so on with coverage numbers less than that threshold will show up as red in the UI and in any static reports you generate in NCoverExplorer. Again, this provides a very human-readable way of identifying areas of poor coverage and determining whether they are really problems.

These reports can also be integrated into a Continuous Integration process as discussed in Chapter 3, "Continuous Integration." NCover and NCoverExplorer in particular are easy to integrate with Continuous Integration tools like CruiseControl.NET. If you are ready to integrate code coverage analysis into your process, you may want to run coverage as part of your Continuous Integration build. You can use the Satisfactory Coverage % value to fail your build, if so desired. That way you can make code coverage an integral part of your CI process and demand that a certain level of code coverage be maintained.

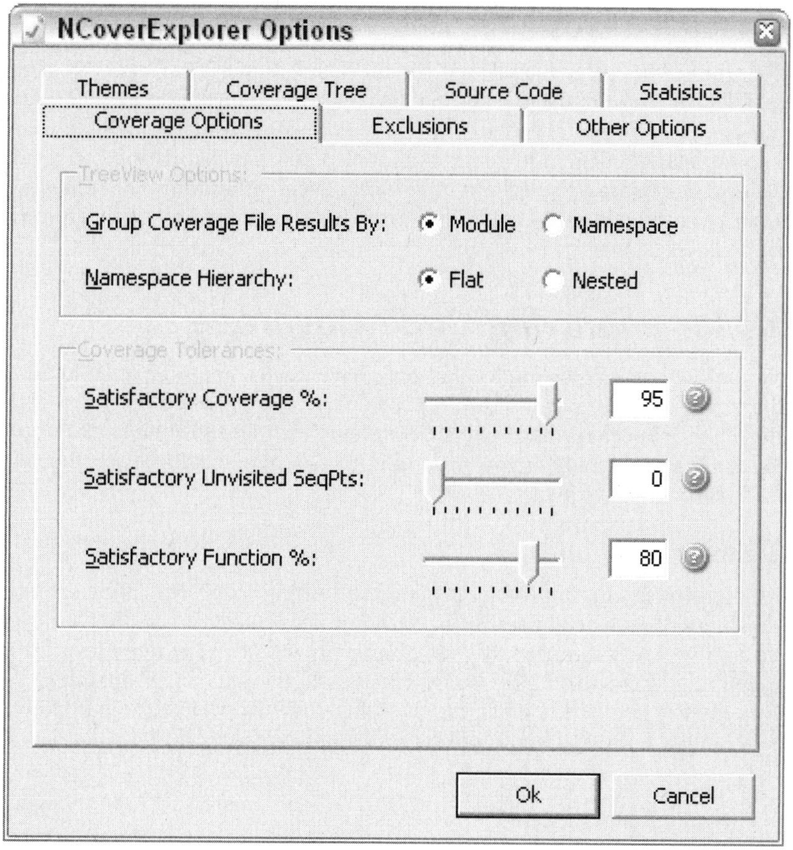

Figure 5-2

What is a reasonable expectation for code coverage? 100% code coverage is simply not a realistic expectation. In practice, anything over 60–70% is doing pretty well. Coverage of 85–90% is extraordinary. That doesn't mean that setting 85% as a goal is a bad idea. It forces developers to spend time thinking hard about how they write their tests and how they write their code to be tested. If you find out that your developers are having too hard a time meeting the coverage goal, you can either try to figure out why they are having difficulty getting their code tested, or you can revise your expectations. The former is much better than the latter. All code is testable. If you are finding it too hard to get good coverage for your code, it may be because your code is not well factored for testing. It might be worth reworking your code to be more easily testable.

For projects that are already under way before you start doing code coverage analysis, or projects that involve legacy code that did not have good coverage to start with, you may want to start with a baseline level of code coverage, then set that as your build threshold.

For example, if you have just started doing code coverage analysis on a project that involves a bunch of legacy code, and you find out that only 51.3% of your code is covered by tests, you may want to set your threshold value at 51% to start with. That way you will catch any new code that is added without tests, without having to go back and write a huge body of test code to cover the legacy code you have inherited. Over time, you can go back and write more tests against the legacy code and increase that threshold value to keep raising the bar.

Even if you aren't doing Continuous Integration, tools like NCoverExplorer can generate static reports that can be used to track the progress of your project. NCoverExplorer will generate either HTML reports that can be read by humans or XML reports that can be read by other programs as part of your development process.

Strategies for Improving Code Coverage

Once you find out what your existing level of code coverage is, you may want to improve that coverage to gain greater confidence in your unit test results. While there is some debate over this issue, it is my belief that the higher your percentage of code coverage, the more likely it is that your tests will expose any possible defects in your code. If you want to improve coverage, there are several strategies you can pursue to reach your coverage goals.

Write More Tests

The most obvious strategy for improving coverage is writing more tests, although that should be done carefully. It may not always be the best way, even if it is the most direct. This is a good time to look at your cyclomatic complexity numbers. If your complexity is low, write more tests. In the example of the file-reading method you examined previously, testing only the success case produced a coverage result of only 80%, even though only one line of error-handling code wasn't executed. In this example, the easiest fix would be to simply write another test to cover the failure case.

```
[TestFixture]
public class CoverageTest
{
  [Test]
  public void FileRead()
  {
    Coverage c = new Coverage();
    c.ReadFile(@"c:\temp\test.txt");
  }

  [Test]
  [ExpectedException(typeof(ArgumentNullException))]
  public void FileReadWithNullFileName()
  {
    Coverage c = new Coverage();
    c.ReadFile(null);
    Assert.Fail("Passing a null file name should have produced
ArgumentNullException.");
  }
}
```

This results in 100% coverage. However, this also exposes one of the dangers of relying on code coverage numbers without applying some human eyes and some common sense to the issue. Although you now have achieved 100% code coverage, you haven't eliminated sources of defects. A consumer of the ReadFile method could still pass the empty string, which is a case you don't have a test for and will cause an exception to be thrown. Having good code coverage just means that you've exercised all of the cases you've written code for, not that you have covered all the right cases. If you rely on code coverage alone, it could lull you into a false sense of security. You still have to make sure that you are testing for all of your application's requirements.

Refactor

Another way to get better code coverage is by refactoring. If you revisit the `HelloWorldToday()` example, you can make it easier to achieve full code coverage by refactoring. Without refactoring, you are likely to end up only covering one case out of seven, depending on what day it is when the test is run. If you refactor the code into something like this:

```
public void HelloWorldToday()
{
    Console.WriteLine(FormatDayOfWeekString(DateTime.Now.DayOfWeek));
}

public string FormatDayOfWeekString(DayOfWeek dow)
{
    switch (dow)
    {
      case DayOfWeek.Monday:
        return ("Hello Monday!");
      case DayOfWeek.Tuesday:
        return ("Hello Tuesday!");
      case DayOfWeek.Wednesday:
        return ("Hello Wednesday!");
      case DayOfWeek.Thursday:
        return ("Hello Thursday!");
      case DayOfWeek.Friday:
        return ("Hello Friday!");
      case DayOfWeek.Saturday:
        return("Hello Saturday!");
      case DayOfWeek.Sunday:
        return ("Hello Sunday!");
      default:
        throw new ArgumentOutOfRangeException();
    }
}
```

The code is functionally equivalent, and your original test(s) will still pass, but now it is much easier to write additional tests against the `FormatDayOfWeekString` method that tests all the possible cases without regard to what day of the week it is today.

This brings up some other interesting issues regarding code visibility. One of the common drawbacks to running any kind of unit testing code is that your test code can only test methods that are accessible to it. In the previous example, it would probably be advantageous from a design perspective to make the new `FormatDayOfWeekString` method private, because you don't really want anyone calling it except your own refactored `HelloWorldToday` method. If you make it private, however, you wouldn't be able to write tests against it because the test code wouldn't have access to it. There are lots of ways around this problem, and none of them (at least in the .NET world) is ideal. You could make the method protected instead, then derive a new test object from the class hosting the (now) protected method. That involves writing some extra throwaway code, and you may not actually want consumers to derive new classes from yours. In the .NET world, another option is to mark the new method as internal, meaning that only code in the same assembly can call it. Prior to .NET 2.0, that meant that you would have to put your test code in the same assembly as the code under test, possibly conditionally compiling it out in your release builds. Still a little unsatisfying. In .NET 2.0, you can use the new `InternalsVisibleTo` attribute. This attribute is similar to the C++ `friend` keyword, in that it can make methods and classes marked internal visible to other assemblies, but only to those that you specify. Again, this has implications. These and other choices related to accessibility have to be taken into account when refactoring to write more tests.

Introduce Mock Objects or Frameworks

We'll cover this in more depth in the next section, but another way of making it easier to write tests is to introduce some kind of mocking framework. Mocking frameworks allow you to simulate parts of your code to reduce dependencies. For example, in your `ReadFile` code, you might want to write tests against the `ReadFile` method without having to have actual files on disk present for the test to succeed. You could use a mocking framework to simulate the call to `File.OpenText()` at runtime, and return success even if no file is present, thus limiting your test's dependency on the file system. Mock frameworks can also be used to simulate error conditions or throw exceptions that your code needs to catch, without having to cause the actual error conditions.

Code coverage analysis can provide you with useful insights into how and in what contexts your code is being tested. This allows you to decide how best to achieve the quality you want by writing more tests, refactoring, or introducing mocking frameworks. However, code coverage numbers alone don't provide you with a complete picture of the effectiveness of your tests. They must be correlated with other information if they are to provide useful and comprehensive results.

Types of Tests

Testing is an integral part of any development process. That said, there are different kinds of tests, and each has its own distinct place in the development cycle. It is important to separate your testing into discrete segments, according to what you are trying to test and how you are trying to test it.

All tests are written to test some piece of code. That code may stand completely on its own, or it may have dependencies on other code, external systems, or resources of various kinds. Pieces of code with differing levels of dependency require different levels of testing, possibly with different tools.

Mixing different kinds of tests can cause confusion and consternation among developers, QA engineers, and potentially management as well. Different kinds of tests are meant to test different things, and to be written and defined by different people.

When writing any tests, you need to decide ahead of time what your intentions are. There are a number of questions to ask yourself, including:

❑ Are you writing stand-alone tests meant to prove the correctness of an algorithm?

❑ Are you writing tests to prove that two components are working together properly?

❑ Are you validating behavior that will be experienced by end users?

These situations demand different testing strategies and may require the use of different tools to achieve the results you want.

Here are some other questions to consider:

- ❑   Do you need to include performance testing for your application?
- ❑   When and how should performance be tested?
- ❑   Who should write tests?
- ❑   Who should run the tests?
- ❑   When should tests be run?

These are all factors to consider when designing your test plan and testing strategy. Any testing is always better than no testing, but testing the wrong things or in the wrong manner can lead to misleading results and problems left unexposed until it is too late.

For the sake of this discussion, tests that measure correctness can be broken up into unit, integration, and functional tests. You will examine each one in turn, than take a look at performance testing.

Unit Tests

Unit tests should be your first line of defense against defects. They are meant to work at the lowest level, against the simplest building blocks of your code: individual interfaces. For your purposes, "unit tests" are ones that test code that has no external dependencies. Unit tests should be able to run on any machine that can compile your code. They should run quickly, so that developers can run them continually without interrupting their work.

Unit tests validate the correctness of your interfaces, one at a time. You should strive to write your unit tests to be as atomic as possible, so that each test validates only one thing. This takes time and practice to achieve, but over time, this will yield the most useful results. It is much better to have large numbers of very small tests at this level than fewer tests that try to do too much.

Most unit tests are validated by using assertions. You run a part of your code, and then you assert that the results are what you expected them to be. When the results don't match your assertions, your tests will fail. While the details of how various test platforms achieve this pattern vary, the overall pattern itself is the same. Run some code, measure the results, assert your expectations.

One way to make your testing more effective is to limit your tests to a single assertion each. If each test method only makes one assertion, it is easy to discover which assertion failed without relying on messages or other data returned from the test.

If you are testing the `FormatDayOfWeekString` method previously described, you could write a test like this:

```
[Test]
public void TestProperDateFormatting()
{
  Coverage c = new Coverage();
  string monday = c.FormatDayOfWeekString(DayOfWeek.Monday);
  Assert.AreEqual("Hello Monday!", monday);
  string tuesday = c.FormatDayOfWeekString(DayOfWeek.Tuesday);
  Assert.AreEqual("Hello Tuesday!", tuesday);

}
```

The problem with this test is that it makes two separate assertions. The test asserts two different results for the method to return. If either fails, the test as a whole will fail. However, that means that when examining the test results, the actual failure message has to be examined to determine what path through your code caused the failure. If the result for Tuesday is incorrect, the result might be (as output by NUnit):

```
TestCase 'TDDSample.CoverageTest.TestProperDateFormatting'
failed:
 Expected string length 14 but was 13. Strings differ at index 6.
 Expected: "Hello Tuesday!"
 But was: "Hello Friday!"
 -----------------^
```

The message tells you which assertion failed, but it takes parsing by a human to determine which one of your two assertions failed and caused the test as a whole to fail. Better to break up your test code into two separate test methods, each with one assertion:

```
[Test]
public void TestProperDateFormatMonday()
{
  Coverage c = new Coverage();
  string monday = c.FormatDayOfWeekString(DayOfWeek.Monday);
  Assert.AreEqual("Hello Monday!", monday);
}

[Test]
public void TestProperDateFormatTuesday()
{
  Coverage c = new Coverage();
  string tuesday = c.FormatDayOfWeekString(DayOfWeek.Tuesday);
  Assert.AreEqual("Hello Tuesday!", tuesday);
}
```

This way, the failure is immediately apparent from looking at the name of the method that failed:

```
TestCase 'TDDSample.CoverageTest.TestProperDateFormatTuesday'
failed:
 Expected string length 14 but was 13. Strings differ at index 6.
 Expected: "Hello Tuesday!"
 But was: "Hello Friday!"
 -----------------^
```

This also requires you to pay attention to how you name your test methods. If you are careful about naming your test methods so that they reflect exactly what you are trying to test, the results will be easier to analyze when tests fail.

There are some cases where you may want to combine multiple calls to your test framework's assertion methods into one logical assertion. For instance, if the result that you are asserting the value of is a member of another object like this:

```
[Test]
public void CorrectRealPortionOfComplexNumber()
{
  Coverage c = new Coverage();
```

```
    ComplexNumber num = c.ReturnFavoriteComplexNumber();
    Assert.AreEqual(3.1415, num.RealPart);
}
```

what you are really asserting here is that `ReturnFavoriteComplexNumber` returns a non-null `Complex Number`, whose `RealPart` member is equal to `3.1415`. If `ReturnFavoriteComplexNumber` should return a null value for the `ComplexNumber`, the resulting message is:

```
TestCase 'TDDSample.CoverageTest.CorrectRealPortionOfComplexNumber'
failed: System.NullReferenceException : Object reference not set to an instance of
an object.
```

The name of the test implies that you are testing the real-number portion of a complex number, but the real portion cannot be a null value. It takes a moment's thought to discern that it is really the complex number itself that is null, not the real portion.

You can change your test code to reflect your real assertion, which is that `ReturnFavoriteComplexNumber` will return a non-null complex number whose real portion is 3.1415.

```
[Test]
public void CorrectRealPortionOfComplexNumber()
{
  Coverage c = new Coverage();
  ComplexNumber num = c.ReturnFavoriteComplexNumber();
  Assert.IsNotNull(num);
  Assert.AreEqual(3.1415, num.RealPart);
}
```

This leads to a better failure message on the off chance that you get back a null result:

```
TestCase 'TDDSample.CoverageTest.CorrectRealPortionOfComplexNumber' failed:
 Expected: not null
 But was: null
```

There is no ambiguity in this case as to what failed. You can tell at a glance that you received a null `ComplexNumber` where none was expected. This is a preference, and may be a point of disagreement. One could argue that it would be better to split up that test method into two separate test methods, each of which makes only one assertion. One test would assert that the result of the method was non-null, and the other would assert that the correct real-number portion was returned. That is a reasonable approach, but it relies on the assumption that test methods will be run in a particular order.

It is a common mistake to rely on test methods being run in a specific order. It is true that most TestRunners that execute NUnit tests run your test methods in file order, or the order in which the test methods appear in the parent test class, from top to bottom. However, there is no guarantee that all TestRunner implementations will behave the same way. Another implementation might run the test methods in alphabetical order or in some random order. Relying on tests being run in a particular order is relying on a side-effect behavior, which could change at any time and produce different test results. Each test you write should stand on its own, without regard to the other tests in its fixture.

The other feature that differentiates unit tests from other test categories is that unit tests should have no external dependencies. The value of unit tests is that they can be run very quickly, encouraging developers to run them as often as possible. To support the Red/Green/Refactor cycle, your tests need to run effortlessly. If it takes 5 minutes to run your unit tests every time you make a small change to your code, those tests will be run less and less frequently. Five minutes is long enough to forget where you were, get distracted by another task, and so on. To this end, every developer should be able to run all the unit tests without having to set up complex dependencies, install other pieces of software, or set up their development computer to be an exact duplicate of the machine on which the tests were written.

If you are testing code that reads a file from the file system, that file system represents an external dependency. That file must be present in the correct location for the test to succeed. That means you are testing more than just your code. You are also testing that the file system was set up correctly prior to the test being run. If your code relies on data in a database, tests for that code may require that the database server be present and available, and that it has been populated with the correct data. That represents a huge external dependency. In that case, a developer wishing to run such as test would have to either install database software or have a test database available at anytime. The database would have to have the correct table structures set up, and those structures would have to be populated with the correct test data. Such a test would not qualify as a unit test, because it has those external dependencies. That is not the kind of test that could be run quickly on any machine that can compile the code.

There are ways to mitigate some, but not all, of those external dependencies. In the file system example, the test code itself could write the necessary file to the correct place in the file system and then run the code under test that depends on that file.

> *For an example of how to deal with files as part of a unit test, see* http://www.cauldwell.net/patrick/blog/TestingWithExternalFiles.aspx.

By removing that dependency on the file system, the test qualifies as a unit test because it doesn't depend on any external agent to set up the file system.

Another way to reduce dependencies is to use a mocking framework. Because mocking (or mock object) frameworks work very differently depending on what language they target and how they are implemented, an in depth discussion on mocking is outside the scope of this book. However, to summarize, a mocking framework provides a way of creating artificial versions of your external dependencies. One common way to make this work is to factor out all of your dependencies behind interfaces and then create "test" implementations of those interfaces. You don't even need a full-blown mocking framework to make that approach work, although using one can greatly reduce the time it takes to implement.

As an example, let's say that you have a method that fetches a list of customer addresses from a database, then formats those addresses into a structured list of mailing addresses. The part of that method you would like to unit test is the formatting part. However, the database represents a pretty big external dependency. To solve the problem proactively, you can create an interface that represents the code that fetches the data from the database and then use the interface to fetch the data:

```
public interface IDatastore
{
    List<Address> GetCustomerAddresses(int customerId);
}

public string FormatCustomerAddresses(int customer)
{
    StringBuilder addressBuilder = new StringBuilder();
```

```
IDatastore datastore = new TestDatastore();
List<Address> customerAddresses = datastore.GetCustomerAddresses(customer);
foreach (Address address in customerAddresses)
{
  addressBuilder.AppendFormat("{0}\n{1}, {2} {3}",
    address.AddressLine1,
    address.City,
    address.State,
    address.PostalCode);
}
return addressBuilder.ToString();
}
```

For the sake of unit testing, you can create a test implementation (often referred to as a "mock" object) that returns exactly the data you expect for the sake of your tests. In this case, your mock object might be as simple as:

```
public class TestDatastore : IDatastore
{

  #region IDatastore Members

  public List<Address> GetCustomerAddresses(int customerId)
  {
    Address addressOne = new Address();
    addressOne.AddressLine1 = "111 2nd St.";
    addressOne.City = "Springfield";
    addressOne.State = "OR";
    addressOne.PostalCode = "99111";
    List<Address> result = new List<Address>();
    result.Add(addressOne);
    return result;
  }

  #endregion
}
```

This is a classic example of a "mock" object. Now you can test the proper formatting of the address string without depending on the database. The previous example is overly simplified. In practice, you would need to pass the class that implements the interface to the formatting method, or to the constructor of the object that implements the formatting method.

The drawback to this approach is that every time you come up with an interface that you need to test around, you have to implement a "mock" version of it. The service that mocking or mock object frameworks provide is that they can implement the interface for you and save you from having to write the extra code. This is often done by using reflection. At runtime, the framework creates a synthetic version of your interface and returns the values that you specify in your test code.

In several of the popluar mock frameworks, such as RhinoMock and TypeMock, those values are specified in terms of "expectations." This terminology is very useful here. By removing dependencies on actual implentations of your interfaces, and delegating to mock frameworks, you are specifying your "expectations" of those external dependencies. This helps to clarify the contracts you define between components. You can start testing your dependent code as soon as the interface is defined, before any concrete implementation exists. Your mocking code then sets expectations for that interface that can be very instructive when it comes time to implement the real thing. Your test code asserts your expectations for how the interface should behave. That communicates important intent to the ultimate implementer of the interface code.

If you reduce external dependencies, and write short, atomic test methods with very focused assertions, unit tests can provide concrete and rapid feedback about the state of your code. When you initially write your code, unit tests provide the lowest level of validation, letting you know that you are on the right track. When you are refactoring or making changes later on, unit tests provide you with the ability to make rapid incremental changes to your code, while continually validating its integrity.

Testing against Requirements

Unit tests provide the ability to verify that your code meets your customer's requirements at the interface level. These are often requirements that are not directly visible to the end user, so some thinking is required to determine what those requirements are and how best to test them. It is necessary to break down the functional requirements that a user would see into their component parts, and then write unit tests that validate those parts.

This is very easy to do when testing algorithms because the results are easy to quantify, and the processing of the algorithm is easy to factor out from user-level requirements. It is harder to do this when testing complex behavior or behavior that relies on a particular state. This is often the hardest part to learn. The process of turning requirements into tests can be time-consuming and challenging.

Unit tests express a developer's understanding of the requirements, and writing the tests forces developers to clarify the requirements. It is often an iterative process. Writing the tests brings up questions about the requirements. Understanding the requirements may prompt us to write more tests.

Test-Driven Development codifies this process and formalizes the relationship between writing tests and understanding requirements (see Chapter 2).

Defining and Testing Edge Cases

One of the areas that often gets overlooked when writing tests is the testing of edge cases or boundary conditions. Many methods are designed to work with parameters that fall within a very specific range. Developers implicitly understand that range and tend not to turn that implicit understanding into explicit test code.

If you are testing a simple Add method, for example:

```
public int Add(int op1, int op2)
{
   return op1 + op2;
}
```

your first thought is probably to test the most straightforward case:

```
[Test]
public void TestAdd()
{
   EdgeCases ec = new EdgeCases();
```

```
    int actual = ec.Add(2, 2);
    Assert.AreEqual(4, actual);
}
```

But this begs the question of what the boundaries are. In C#, `int` is an unsigned datatype. Are negative values OK? Are two negative values OK? What are the maximum and minimum values of each datatype? What happens if you try to add two values, each with the maximum value of an integer?

```
[Test]
public void OneNegative()
{
    EdgeCases ec = new EdgeCases();
    int actual = ec.Add(2, -3);
    Assert.AreEqual(-1, actual);
}

[Test]
public void TwoNegatives()
{
    EdgeCases ec = new EdgeCases();
    int actual = ec.Add(-2, -3);
    Assert.AreEqual(-5, actual);
}

[Test]
public void TwoMaxInts()
{
    EdgeCases ec = new EdgeCases();
    int actual = ec.Add(int.MaxValue, int.MaxValue);
    Assert.AreEqual(-2, actual);
}
```

The last test brings up a good example. Should that work? Intuitively, it doesn't make sense. It's a classic edge case. You shouldn't be able to add two copies of the maximum value for an integer without an arithmetic overflow. Instead, the behavior (in C# at least) results in a negative value. Should your `Add` method allow that counterintuitive behavior, or should you enforce your own behavior?

These are all common boundary condition tests. Another common boundary case is the maximum value for a database type. The maximum value of an integer, as stored in the database, may be smaller than the maximum value of the intrinsic `int` datatype in your programming language. That could cause errors when writing values to the database. Of course, in this particular case, you've gone beyond the bounds of unit testing, but you get the idea. The first time you get an error when trying to pass the value 65,536, you will start remembering to test those edge cases. Negative values will expose assumptions about signed versus unsigned datatypes. Null values should be passed for all reference types to test how your code deals with nulls.

Some testing frameworks provide shorthand for making this kind of edge case testing easier. MbUnit, which is derived from the NUnit code base and adds new features, provides what it calls row-based tests.

```
[RowTest()]
[Row(2, 2, 4)]
[Row(2, -2, 0)]
[Row(-2, -3, -5)]
```

```
public void BoundaryTest(int op1, int op2, int result)
{
  EdgeCases ec = new EdgeCases();
  int actual = ec.Add(op1, op2);
  Assert.AreEqual(result, actual);
}
```

Such a row-based test is called once for each [Row] attribute. It provides an easy way to run a large number of cases without writing a lot of extra code, and it is easier to read all the test cases at once by looking at the set of [Row] attributes. The preceding row-based test produces results like this:

```
Found 3 tests
[success] TestEdgeCases.BoundaryTest(2,-2,0)
[success] TestEdgeCases.BoundaryTest(-2,-3,-5)
[success] TestEdgeCases.BoundaryTest(2,2,4)
```

This makes it both easy to test the edge conditions and intuitive to deal with the results. Adding new edge cases is as easy as adding new [Row] attributes, without the need to write new test code.

MbUnit has a number of advanced features over and above what is provided by NUnit. If you are unit testing .NET code, it will be worth your while to check out MbUnit. It is a compatible superset of NUnit, so you can upgrade existing NUnit tests seamlessly just by changing your references.

Edge case testing is another area in which writing unit tests can help you clarify your requirements. The previous example, with the maximum value of an integer, begs the question of how is *should* work. Should negative values be allowed? Should nulls? These are questions that will come up during edge case testing and that may lead you to question your customer(s) to find out which cases you really *need* to support. Chances are that your customers haven't considered many of the edge cases either. Bringing up the questions will help to clarify everyone's thinking about requirements, and the edge case tests that you end up writing will codify your expectations and both define and document the requirements.

Negative Testing

One of the most difficult areas to cover with your unit tests is error handling. The whole point of error handling is that it is meant to deal with things that aren't supposed to happen. To test all of your error-handling code, you have to come up with ways to make those things that aren't supposed to happen, happen.

Like edge case testing, negative testing really helps clarify your requirements by bringing up questions. Is this really an error condition? What should the behavior be in case of an error? Should your code return an error or null, or throw an exception? By writing negative test cases, you define your error-handling policy and refine your code's contract.

If you have a method like the following:

```
public Customer LookupCustomer(int id)
```

what should the behavior be if you pass it the ID for an unknown customer?

```
[Test]
public void LookupUnknownCustomer()
{
```

```
        int badId = -1;
        NegativeCase nc = new NegativeCase();
        Customer c = nc.LookupCustomer(badId);
        Assert.IsNull(c);
    }
```

Should that test succeed? Should `LookupCustomer` return a null customer object if no customer with the specified ID is found? The previous test code implies that it should. But is that really the behavior you want? If it does, that means that the caller is responsible for checking the returned `Customer` object to make sure that it isn't null. Maybe an unknown customer ID should cause an exception instead. (More on this in Chapter 12, "Error Handling"; for now, it's just for the sake of argument.)

If an exception is the correct result, you can use test constructs to validate that behavior as well. NUnit/MbUnit use the `[ExpectedException]` attribute to specify that the test should cause an exception to be thrown. If the test completes without an exception being thrown, it will fail. If a different exception is thrown, it will fail as well:

```
[Test]
[ExpectedException(typeof(InvalidOperationException))]
public void LookupUnknownCustomerException()
{
    int badId = -1;
    NegativeCase nc = new NegativeCase();
    Customer c = nc.LookupCustomer(badId);
    Assert.Fail("Should have thrown an exception.");
}
```

In this very simple case, it is easy to provoke the errors you are trying to test for. It can be much harder to elicit all of the expected errors from a more complex method. It is particularly hard when dealing with external dependencies. When you need to test code that handles errors returned by external dependencies, it can be challenging to make them happen. This is another great place to use mocking frameworks. Using a mocking framework, it is often possible not only to simulate the external dependency, but also to simulate any errors or exceptions that might be returned by that code.

Who Should Write Unit Tests?

Developers should write unit tests. They should write them before they write their code. They should write them after they write their code. They should write them until they understand their requirements, and until they are convinced that they are validating all of their requirements properly.

Developers should write unit tests every time a defect is uncovered. This is one of the most important parts of defect resolution. When faced with a defect to fix, the first thing a developer should do is write a new test that causes the failure to happen and then make the test pass by fixing the defect. Not only does this make it easy to determine when the defect is fixed, but it also helps to determine the nature of the failure. The first step in understanding how to fix a defect is understanding what triggers the defect, and writing a test to exhibit the failure is the fastest way to do that. Once the test is written, not only can you exhibit the problem and verify that it is fixed, but you also have a regression test that will help you make sure that changes you make in the future don't cause the defect to reoccur.

That doesn't mean that developers are the *only* ones who can write unit tests. Testers can also write unit tests. Even if they don't write them, testers should read them. Testers should be responsible for making sure that the tests developers write represent the real requirements, and that all the right cases are being covered.

One area in which testers can have a huge impact is edge case and negative testing. Developers often get distracted, or bogged down in other things, and either forget or choose not to spend the time it takes to test all the edge conditions for a given piece of code. Testers can take up the slack by writing additional unit tests. This helps to clarify requirements, increase code coverage, and cover all the necessary cases. It also gets testers more deeply involved in the development process.

Testers can and should be responsible for understanding code coverage and using code coverage analysis to decide where there should be more unit tests. There is no reason why your testers can't also write the tests needed to achieve the necessary coverage.

Integration Tests

Integration tests are the next level up from unit tests. They involve more than one interface or rely on external dependencies that require some setup.

Unit tests should be designed to run on any machine that can compile the code, without requiring complex or time-consuming setup or software installation. But at some point, you will need to verify that the database server behaves the way you thought it would or that the third-party software product you purchased really meets your requirements. This is accomplished with integration tests.

Integration tests are very different in character from unit tests. They need not run as quickly, or as often, as unit tests. They can rely on services like networks, databases, file systems, or third-party code being installed. They still take place at the level of code interfaces, rather than user interfaces, but they may make use of more than one interface, unlike good unit tests.

If unit tests are meant to validate that your interfaces work the way they are supposed to, integration tests validate that your interfaces work *together* the way they are supposed to. Integration tests often end up dealing more with data flow than with calculations, although that is a generalization. Integration tests validate the kind of interactions that you write sequence diagrams to model, while unit tests usually validate the behavior of individual classes or objects. This may be less true if you are using integration tests to deal with external dependencies such as a database server. Testing your data access layer may only involve a single class, but it should be treated as integration testing because of the dependency on an external service.

Integration tests can be much easier to come up with than good unit tests. After all, you're moving up the stack, getting closer to code that solves business problems or causes things to happen at the user level. It is usually much easier to relate integration tests to user-level requirements than it is for unit tests. If you are testing a security system, your login method probably makes use of two different systems, one that looks up the user's credentials from your data store and another that validates those credentials against the ones that the user passed in. It can be difficult to write unit tests to test those two parts separately, but it is easy to test the combined login method because it is easy to understand the requirements at that level.

The same testing frameworks that are good for unit testing can also be used for integration testing because the environment is essentially the same. You can get the same familiar kind of feedback for your integration tests if you use the same testing framework to run them.

One major difference between unit and integration tests is how you use those tests to help frame your requirements. For unit tests, you might use boundary conditions to elicit questions about how your interfaces should respond to input. For integration tests, you might employ use cases to bring up questions about how your application should behave.

Rather than asking what a method should do if passed a null value, you should be asking what should happen if a user enters an incorrect password. That determination might require going to the database to look up the user's credentials, encoding the credentials passed in so that they can be compared, and then comparing encoded values to see if the user provided the right password. What should the application do if the user provides the wrong password? Throw an exception? Return a null value? Return some error code to explain what the problem is? Integration tests help us refine the contracts used between subsystems by forcing us to answer such questions. The answers to those questions may be dictated by more than just software. It may involve talking to business owners or project sponsors to flesh out the real requirements.

Integration tests may also depend on external software packages or services such as databases or web services. One common example is testing data access layers. Code that is meant to retrieve and save values to and from a database must be tested, but that code requires the database server to be running, to be properly set up, and possibly to have the right set of test data in it.

This brings up some additional issues around writing integration tests. Because they may require external dependencies or additional software installations, they may not run on every developer's machine. They may require network or server resources that have to be shared among several people. Those resources then have to be managed as part of writing and running those integration tests.

Unit-level tests don't typically involve having to set up preconditions or clean up state changes as part of the test. In integration testing, you may have to write extra test code to set up your preconditions and then more code to set up post conditions. This ensures that your test has the right initial state before running and that you have restored that state to its original condition once you are done. That makes testing cleaner and helps manage external resources. If you have multiple developers testing against the same database, for example, it is important that tests not interfere with one another by leaving "dirty state" in the database.

The following method demonstrates a highly simplified version of dealing with this kind of state. Before you can test the login method, the user you are testing with must exist in the database. First, you set up the right state in the database; next, you run your actual test code; then you clean up the state you changed in the database to prepare the database for the next test:

```
[Test]
public void TestLogin()
{
    Database.InsertUserCredentials("fred", "password");

    bool success = LoginUser("fred", "password");

    Database.DeleteUser("fred");
}
```

The goal is to make sure that after you run your tests, your database is still in a known, consistent state. That means that every record you add as part of testing, you must delete when you are done. There is some disagreement about the best way to achieve that, and there are several strategies. You can start your unit testing process by setting up all the right test data in your database, either by restoring a "canned" database backup or by programmatically adding all of the right data, using database APIs. The advantage to the "canned" database is that you don't have to worry about cleaning up after each individual integration test. You can just drop the whole database at the end of your test run and then restore it again at the beginning of the next run. During your test run, however, your database will be in an inconsistent state. If you go to the other extreme, you can set up all the right data for each test during the test itself, run your actual test code, then run more code to delete all the data you added at the beginning of the test. This can require a lot of extra code, and it is difficult to maintain, but if done properly, it means that your database is always in a consistent state during testing.

One compromise strategy is to use some kind of framework to help you manage what you write to the database. Some systems use database transactions to facilitate this process. You can create a "synthetic" transaction to represent all the database work you do to set up your test, and then use the framework to undo all the changes you made when the transaction is finished. This makes it easy to keep your database cleaned up, but it does have some overhead costs in terms of additional framework code you will have to maintain.

One antipattern to be aware of when writing unit tests, particularly ones that make use of external resources, is that of testing more than one part of your system at a time. If, for example, you are testing your data access layer against a real running database, you will need to test both the read and write methods. On more than one occasion, I have seen tests written to test the read method that then use the same read method to validate the write method:

```
[Test]
public void ReadFromDatabase()
{
    int customerID = 1;
    //write directly to database using low level api
    //to set up test data for that customer

    CustomerData data = myDataAccessLayer.Read(customerID);

    //validate that the values in the data object match what
    //you wrote using low level api

    //clean up database
}

[Test]
public void WriteToDatabase()
{
    CustomerData data = new CustomerData(1, "Fred", "Seattle");

    //testing the write method (OK)
    myDataAccessLayer.Write(data);

    //testing the read method! (not OK)
    CustomerData writtenData = myDataAccessLayer.Read(1);

    Assert.AreEqual(data, writtenData);
}
```

So what's wrong with this? The test for the read method is fine, but the test for the write method is using another method that you wrote to validate that the write happened correctly. This pattern is often defended by claiming that, because the test for Read() has already taken place and passed before the test for Write() runs, it must be OK. This is again banking on side-effect behavior, counting on the TestRunner to run your tests in the order you expect. What the test for the write method really ends up doing is testing both the Read() and Write() methods. What happens if a bug is introduced in the Read() method while you are refactoring? It is entirely possible for such a thing to happen, and for said bug to cause your test for the Write() method to fail, even though there is nothing wrong with the Write() method. It will take time, attention, and effort on the part of one or more humans to sort out that it was really a change to the read method that failed, not the write method. Those cycles could be spent more productively someplace else.

Why is this antipattern so popular? Laziness. It takes far more time to write low-level database API code to validate that the write method completed its work successfully. Far better to spend a few extra cycles (which *are* tedious, granted) writing the tests correctly than to spend them later on debugging your misleading test results.

It is true that integration tests are meant to test more than one thing. However, they are meant to test more than one *interface* and how those interfaces interact with one another — not how multiple methods on the same interface perform. The individual methods on one interface should be validated separately, in unit tests. It is important to narrow the scope of your tests such that you are only testing one thing at a time, although that one thing may be an interaction. Figuring out how to properly scope your tests is a learned skill, and takes time and practice to get the hang of. It is well worth your effort to practice because properly scoping your tests will provide you with the highest-value results.

When to Write Integration Tests

You should start writing integration tests as soon as possible. It may be tempting to put off integration testing until all of your components are finished and unit tested. It sounds like a more orderly process, and it probably is. If you start integration testing very early, you may have to deal with defects or incompleteness in the various components you are testing. The benefit of starting early is that you will be able to validate your overall design sooner. If you wait until all of your components are built and unit tested, and then start writing integration tests, you may discover that your components don't interact as smoothly as you thought they would or that one component isn't delivering all the data needed by another. In that case, you have to go back and change your components, change your unit tests to reflect the changes, and then continue writing your integration tests. In the long run, you will save time and effort by finding those design problems early on with early integration testing. You will catch design problems earlier, when they are cheaper to fix, even though performing integration tests on unfinished components may be a bit rocky at first. Those early integration tests will help you validate your baseline architecture.

Baseline Architecture

If you are following a Test Driven Development process and using your tests to help define and refine your requirements, you also have to consider some architectural issues. One of the early criticisms of "agile" methodologies was that they overlooked architecture. The argument runs that if you "just start coding" an application using TDD rather than following the old waterfall method to get every last requirement up front, you will build software without a consistent design or architecture. This is

---

certainly a danger if you don't manage your process carefully, "agile" or not. One way to mitigate this risk is by building out a "baseline architecture." By this I mean building out code that represents all the functional areas of your application, even if those areas don't do very much. The goal should be to build "wide" not "deep." Write code that touches all the various systems, third-party software packages, or dependencies your architecture requires. But not too much.

As an example, suppose that you are building a web application that displays weather reports. You know that you can get XML data about current weather conditions from a public web service. You also want to add additional value to your site by storing historical weather data and climate conditions for various locations. That additional data will be stored in your database. Your application will combine data from the web service with data from your internal database, and display that data on a web page. To build out your baseline architecture, you might build the simplest-possible HTML page with one button and a text field for submitting a zip code. On the server side, you could call the web service to get current conditions for that zip code, and look up the name of the town where that zip code resides. Then you can return a web page that simply displays the name of the city and the current temperature.

It's not pretty or fancy. It won't wow your project sponsors. But it will validate your assumptions about your architecture and prove that all the parts of the system interact the way they are supposed to. You will have greatly reduced your risk by making sure up front that your overall architecture is sound and that it will meet your needs.

Such a baseline architecture can often be built by a small team of one or two architects. Once the baseline architecture is established, more resources can be added to the project to build upon the skeleton put in place as part of the baseline. Those additional developers can build "deep" once the architecture is validated.

While unit tests are often focused on validating your *algorithms*, integration tests are used to validate your *assumptions* or *expectations*. You expect interfaces to work together in a certain way, and you assume that external systems will behave the way they are supposed to. You use integration tests to make sure that those expectations are reasonable, and that your assumptions are correct.

When to Run Integration Tests

Integration tests do not need to be run nearly as often as unit tests. You may wish to run them on a schedule, say once or twice a day, rather than every time you make any changes to your code. Because integration tests typically require more complex setup and involve shared resources like database servers, running them on a predictable schedule may be more practical. You looked at Continuous Integration in Chapter 3, and I talked about testing as part of that process. Integration tests should be run on some neutral machine, such as a build server or test box to make sure that they aren't dependent on features of one person's machine as opposed to another's. But while your CI build server might build and run unit tests every time a source file change is detected, it might only run integration tests at night, so that it can take maximum advantage of shared resources.

If your code is dependent on a number of external resources such as databases or web services, you may want to consider running your integration tests on a separate machine or set of machines. This means not only that your integration tests will be running in a more realistic environment, but also that your build server will remain as clean as possible. A clean build server is a happy build server. This works particularly well if your integration tests can be triggered remotely, so that you can deploy your code on a separate set of machines but run them from your build server, as shown in Figure 5-3. Your build server most likely already has the ability to collect test results, build reports, and send email, and you can take advantage of those capabilities when running your integration tests as well.

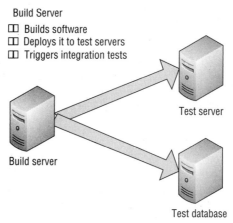

Build Server

⫿ Builds software
⫿ Deploys it to test servers
⫿ Triggers integration tests

Test server

Build server

Test database

Figure 5-3

Who Should Write Integration Tests?

Integration tests are best written by developers. If the point of integration testing is to validate your expectations and assumptions, those really are expectations and assumptions about how your code works, rather than about how the application as a whole works. Testers can write unit tests to flesh out edge cases, and they certainly should write functional tests (more on that in a bit) because those represent the requirements of the end user. But developers should write integration tests to validate that their interfaces work together and that their external dependencies behave as expected.

Functional Tests

Functional tests are intended to validate the behavior that the end user of your software will see. They represent the end user's requirements and are used to make sure that your customers will get the experience they expect from your application.

Functional tests can be the hardest to write and to validate automatically because of the difficulty of driving a full-blown end-user application without human intervention. In the past, functional testing was usually deemed too hard to automate, and it has traditionally been done by testers in a manual fashion. These are the tests that most people think of when they picture QA engineers testing an application.

Traditionally, functional testing was done by establishing a formal test plan. This usually takes the form of a document that describes how the application is expected to function, and how the testers should validate that functionality. Full-blown test plans might set out all the steps a tester should perform in the application, and the expected result. My very first job in the industry was testing an MS-DOS-based tape backup application. There was a team of 4–5 testers, and a test plan that ran fully 1,000 pages long. A test run involved going through each one of those thousand pages of test plan, pushing a series of buttons on the interface, and then validating by eye that the expected result had occurred.

To complete one test run took those 4–5 testers a full 40-hour week. Such test processes were very difficult to automate, because to push the buttons in the user interface, one had to simulate mouse movements and button clicks, and validation meant comparing an image of the expected screen to a captured version of the actual screen. This proved exceptionally error-prone because in many, if not most, user interfaces small details in the UI such as time stamps or other temporal data would change from run to run. That meant that bits of the image would have to be masked out and ignored for a successful comparison to take place.

Because of all these difficulties, and the relatively low cost of recent college graduates, not very many test processes were automated. Most functional testing remained the province of human testers, who had to personally validate that the application functioned as it was required to do. Any problems that were found had to be manually reported back to the developers, often resulting in details being lost in the process.

This kind of testing started to change once applications started moving from the desktop to the web. Because web interfaces ultimately break down to machine-readable HTML code, that HTML code can be parsed and validated by machines rather than by human testers. Better still, such TestRunners cannot only read HTML to validate results, but they can also simulate HTTP GET and POST calls, and drive the applications automatically without relying on simulated user interaction such as mouse movements and button clicks.

There were several attempts to make automating web application testing easier, including extensions for existing test frameworks such as JUnit and NUnit. The one that finally took off in the developer community was Watir (for Web App Testing in Ruby). Watir runs as a Ruby application, and provides a very simple and straightforward syntax for driving web apps and measuring the results that they return. Watir has gained great popularity among the tester community because it is easy to understand, and Watir scripts are easy to write and good at validating web application functionality. As an example, the following Watir script (from the samples available at http://wtr.rubyforge.org/examples.html) automates the Google.com search engine, and validates that the correct search results have been returned.

```
#----------------------------------------------------------------------
--------------------------#
# demo test for the WATIR controller
#
# Simple Google test written by Jonathan Kohl  10/10/04
# Purpose: to demonstrate the following WATIR functionality:
#   * entering text into a text field
#   * clicking a button
#   * checking to see if a page contains text.
# Test will search Google for the "pickaxe" Ruby book
#
#----------------------------------------------------------------------
-----------------------#

    require 'watir'  # the watir controller
```

```
# set a variable
test_site = 'http://www.google.com'

# open the IE browser
ie = Watir::IE.new

# print some comments
puts "## Beginning of test: Google search"
puts " "

puts "Step 1: go to the test site: " + test_site
ie.goto(test_site)
puts " Action: entered " + test_site + " in the address bar."

puts "Step 2: enter 'pickaxe' in the search text field"
ie.text_field(:name, "q").set("pickaxe")    # q is the name of the search field
puts " Action: entered pickaxe in the search field"

puts "Step 3: click the 'Google Search' button"
ie.button(:name, "btnG").click  # "btnG" is the name of the Search button
puts " Action: clicked the Google Search button."

puts "Expected Result: "
puts " - a Google page with results should be shown. 'Programming Ruby' should be
high on the list."

 puts "Actual Result: Check that the 'Programming Ruby' link appears on the
results page "
 if ie.text.include?("Programming Ruby")
  puts "Test Passed. Found the test string: 'Programming Ruby'. Actual Results
match Expected Results."
 else
  puts "Test Failed! Could not find: 'Programming Ruby'"
 end

 puts " "
 puts "## End of test: Google search"


 # -end of simple Google search test
```

The biggest advantage to Watir is that its scripting language is easy to write and easy to understand. Many organizations have adopted Watir as the standard way of automating their functional testing. Because Watir automates Microsoft Internet Explorer, it is running in the same context as a real end user running your application. The biggest drawback to Watir is that because it is written in Ruby, it requires the Ruby runtime and some additional libraries. If your web application happens to be written in Ruby, this is a no-brainer, but for developers working on other platforms, Ruby represents a new language to learn and a new runtime to install. Because Watir tests through the browser, however, it works with web applications written in any language. There is no requirement for your application to be written in Ruby.

The advantages of Watir encourage most organizations to overlook those drawbacks and take advantage of the excellent functional test features Watir provides, despite the extra overhead.

Relatively recently, efforts have been made to port Watir to other platforms so that Ruby is not required to run functional tests. One such effort for the .NET platform is WatiN (pronounced What-in), or Web App Testing in .NET. WatiN takes the same basic concepts regarding web app testing pioneered by Watir and implements them in .NET. The biggest advantage to WatiN is that for developers already working in .NET, there is no impedance mismatch between the code under test and the test code because both are written in .NET. Even better, the WatiN team has embraced the existing test paradigm established by NUnit/MbUnit, so that the WatiN tests follow the same pattern. Here is the WatiN version of the Watir script shown previously, taken from the front page of the WatiN home page at `http://watin` `.sourceforge.net`:

```
[Test]
public void SearchForWatiNOnGoogle()
{
 using (IE ie = new IE("http://www.google.com"))
 {
 ie.TextField(Find.ByName("q")).TypeText("WatiN");
 ie.Button(Find.ByName("btnG")).Click();

 Assert.IsTrue(ie.ContainsText("WatiN"));
 }
}
```

This test looks just like an NUnit test. It is marked with the `[Test]` attribute and uses the same assertion model to validate the expected results. This test code should look very familiar to anyone used to unit testing in .NET, yet it extends the reach of such test code to functional testing of web applications.

What this level of automation means is that it is no longer necessary to do all functional testing by hand. This makes functional testing faster and requires fewer resources to complete. Where once test plans had to be manually executed by hoards of testers and the results reported manually, now at least some percentage of functional testing can be done by machines on a regular basis, and the results can be reported and/or recorded automatically.

It is still difficult to run functional tests automatically on non-web-based applications. In many cases, the only way to automate desktop applications remains simulating user mouse movements and button clicks. However, by architecting your desktop applications correctly, you can run all but the most trivial parts of the application and get automated, functional testing. The key to making that work is the MVP pattern (or something similar), which you'll examine in more detail in Chapter 10, "The Model-View Presenter Model."

There is a third class of "applications" that should be considered for functional testing. Some applications have no user interface but can still benefit from functional-level testing. Examples are commercial software libraries, or web services applications that provide software services without an end-user-visible UI. These applications can be tested using essentially the same methods that you would use for integration testing, but with a greater eye toward usability and functional requirements.

The ability to automatically run and report on functional testing means that it can become part of a Continuous Integration process. Then you can get regular, automatic feedback about the state of your application at a functional level, which is the level that users will see. If defects are introduced that would affect end users, you will find out about it as soon as possible, when it is the least expensive to fix them.

What Is the Goal of Functional Tests?

Functional tests represent the interests of the end user. They validate the features and functionality that the application is designed to present to the people who use that application.

If the role of testers is ultimately to "represent the user" by making sure that the application behaves the way the user expects, then functional testing provides the means for them to play that role. For every user-level requirement in a software application, there should be a corresponding set of functional tests to verify that those requirements have been met. In a waterfall project, that is done by producing a test plan directly from a requirements document. For every individual requirement in the requirements document, there should be a corresponding section in the test plan that verifies that requirement. In an agile project, where there may not be a formal requirements document, the tests are written to validate "user stories" or "backlog items" or whatever name your agile process gives to the expression of user requirements.

For example, an XP-style user story for a payroll application might be "The application calculates FICA tax for each employee's payroll as 7.2% of the user's pretax wages." That user story might result in a functional test that reads a payroll statement and validates that the FICA tax withheld is equal to the correct percentage of wages. For a web application, that might be expressed concretely as a script to run the web site and read the results, then verify the numbers.

Such a test script would correspond directly to the user story and provide a good functional test for that requirement.

Who Should Write Functional Tests?

Functional tests should be written by testers, not by developers. Developers bring to the table too many assumptions about how the code works. That leads them (generalizing again . . .) to exercise the application only in the ways they expect it to work. It is the job of testers to represent the interests of the end user (among other things), and it is they who should be responsible for writing functional tests. Testers are more likely to test the application the way the user would expect it to work rather than the way the underlying code is known to work.

Developers may certainly be responsible for facilitating functional testing, however. They may need to add hooks to make the application more easily automatable, or structure the application in such a way (hopefully using the MVP pattern) that makes it possible to write functional tests at the code level.

There is a relatively new type of functional testing referred to as FIT (Framework for Integrated Test) testing. FIT testing was pioneered by Ward Cunningham with the intention of getting business users directly involved in functional testing. FIT employs a spreadsheet-like interface that allows nontechnical business users to define a set of inputs and expected results for doing functional testing. In FIT, developers and/or testers write supporting code to make FIT testing possible, and business users or product owners write the FIT tests themselves.

Performance Testing

Performance testing is possibly the least understood and most difficult subset of testing. It tends to be a bit of a black art. Performance (or "perf") testing requires specialized test-running applications capable of simulating high volumes of user activity and measuring the results. Those applications can be costly and difficult to learn. In addition, performance testing is best done on a hardware platform that resembles a production environment as closely as possible. This can be expensive as well because production web applications often require costly server hardware, network setups, and other infrastructure.

Because of these requirements, many companies have established performance testing labs that can be rented out to various customers, so that more people can take advantage of specialized hardware environments. For example, Microsoft has established labs all over the country that can be rented by customers for performance testing. Such labs come equipped with high-end multi-processor servers, clustered database servers running SAN disks, and other production-level equipment. They also have performance-testing software and enough client computers to simulate a very high load. Almost as important, they also provide consultants well versed in the dark art of performance testing.

Unless your company is willing to devote large amounts of time and money to performance testing, it is well worth your while to contract with one of these specialized labs to help you get the most out of perf testing.

Even if you do contract out your performance testing, you will still need to have someone in your organization who is familiar with the process, and can help establish baselines for how your application's performance should be tested. Those baselines should include what your expectations are and how they should be measured.

When Should You Do Performance Testing?

Some limited form of performance testing should be done as soon as you have a baseline architecture (see the sidebar on page 87) in place. It is important to get an early sense of how your baseline architecture performs. Carefully measure how long it takes to perform user-level operations. Then decide if that level of performance is acceptable or can be made so. If your architecture is incapable of meeting your performance goals, it is better to learn that sooner rather than later. That leaves you with time to make changes or pursue other options before it is too late.

Once your application is more fully developed, you might do some limited performance testing again to see where you stand. You shouldn't attempt to get a final set of numbers or test with a huge number of clients. You just want a ballpark result to make sure that you are on track.

When the application is in its final stages of development, it is time to do whatever final performance testing you want to do. This would be the time to contract with a lab and run your application on production-level hardware. Do not wait until you are ready to do customer-acceptance testing, however. One certainty about performance testing is that there will be tuning to do, and you will find problems that you didn't expect, especially if your production-style hardware is radically different from your functional QA hardware. Allow enough time to find problems and tune your application before sending it to customer testing.

How Is Performance Testing Done?

Performance testing is hard. It is difficult to set expectations, difficult to measure performance, and difficult to set up simulation environments. It requires a specialized skill set that many, if not most, developers are not familiar with.

The first step (and often the most difficult) is to set expectations. One thing that makes this hard is that many organizations and developers have a hard time differentiating between performance and scalability. Performance is how fast your application can perform certain operations. Scalability is how many times the application can perform that task at once before performance is degraded beyond an acceptable level. There is no way to intuit the relationship between performance and scalability. It requires testing and careful measurement. Your application may perform very quickly but degrade very fast under load. Or it may perform more slowly, but scale very well to a large number of users without loss of performance. The only way to know is to measure.

Performance testing can be done in a limited way as soon as your baseline architecture is in place. That is the time to start measuring how fast your application can perform a given task. Because you are unlikely to have access to production hardware, these measurements should be considered only as an order-of-magnitude approximation. If you are way off, you might want to reconsider your architecture or do a little tuning to see if you can get in the ballpark. Don't prematurely optimize. Measure twice, cut once. Or in the case of performance testing, measure several hundred times and then make as few changes as you can to achieve your goal.

The trickiest part of this early performance testing is setting your expectations correctly. What user level tasks should be measured? How fast do those operations really need to perform? As developers, you may want to optimize every part of your application to make it run as fast as possible. That costs time and resources that you may not need to spend. Ask your users what an acceptable level of performance is for your application. It may be slower than you would expect. It depends largely on user perception and expectations, and may vary wildly from application to application. If a user logs in to an online banking web site to check their balances, they expect those balances to be displayed very rapidly. They want information that they perceive to be readily available, and they want it right away. On the other hand, if they use the same application to apply for a loan online, they may not find it unreasonable to wait 1 to 2 minutes because applying for a loan is perceived as a "weighty" operation that takes time to complete. It is vital to understand what the expectations are before you spend time and money to make your application faster.

When the time comes to do final performance and scalability testing, there are two key things to focus on: modeling user behavior and measuring the results. When doing scalability testing, it is important to model the behavior of your users and find out how they really use your application. How long do they spend in each part of the application? How fast do they click from page to page? How often do they bring up the same page (important for caching)? If you understand how real users run the app, you can write performance-testing scripts that more closely resemble real conditions. Such scripts will provide you with more accurate performance and scalability data.

The other key area is measurement. When you do performance testing, you will also do performance tuning because the performance and scalability are seldom what you expect right out of the gate. To do that tuning, you must measure carefully. Don't guess. Huge amounts of time can be wasted by optimizing parts of the application that don't actually contribute significantly to your problem. Take the time to find out where the real bottlenecks in performance are first, and then tune only those parts of the application that will have the greatest impact. There are profiling applications for every coding platform that will tell you where the real issues in your code are so that you can address them properly when the time comes.

Performance testing is hard, but if approached carefully, it can be the factor that determines whether your users are happy or frustrated. Set your expectations before testing, and verify those expectations with real users to make sure that you aren't spending time and money where none is required, and everyone will come out ahead.

Test Automation

The time for test plans defined solely as Microsoft Word documents has passed. It may still sound like a good idea (to some) to hire a pack of recent college grads and set them to work manually testing your application. It might sound "cost-effective." It isn't. While creating an automated test suite takes additional work up front, it quickly pays off.

There are two main purposes for having a test suite, whether automated or manual. The first is to validate your code and your application to make sure that you are meeting your customer's requirements. The second is to provide an early warning system in case defects are introduced during development. The sooner you find out about defects, the easier and cheaper they are to fix, so finding out about problems as quickly as possible will save you money. If you are testing manually, the time it takes to get feedback is much greater. If you can automate as much of your testing as possible, you can shorten the feedback cycle enormously.

Shortening that feedback cycle also helps your developers work together in teams. From the perspective of Continuous Integration, a short feedback cycle is critical to enable developers to work together. By forcing constant building and testing of your application, Continuous Integration promotes the early warning system to a first-class part of your development process. When someone introduces changes that will cause problems for other developers, the Continuous Integration build breaks, notifications go out, and developers are encouraged (as highly as is feasible) to fix those problems. The sooner they get notified of problems, the sooner they get fixed, and the more time and money your organization saves.

The key to making this work is automation. You need to automate as much of your testing as possible, at all levels, from unit testing to functional testing and everything in between. It will take time, effort, and most importantly a clear plan, but the benefits of having good test automation far outweigh the costs.

Automating unit tests is fairly straightforward; integration tests are a bit more difficult, and functional testing is the most complicated to automate. However, because different parts of the organization work on different parts of the test suite, the work and responsibility for writing and maintaining test suites can be shared across teams.

If you can establish a solid testing plan, and get organized enough to bring it together, you can code away safe in the knowledge that you will deliver a high-quality product as soon as possible with a test suite to back you up.

Strategies for Test Automation

The most important part of test automation is having a solid plan for how you will go about it. You need to decide what will be tested, how much it will be tested, how often, and who will test it. You need to decide if you want rules for how much testing gets done and how you will enforce those rules. You need to figure out who will be in charge of managing the testing process at each level in your organization. You need to write down, or otherwise communicate, each of these decisions so that everyone is on the same page.

The first step is figuring out what you are going to test. Unit tests should be a given, but you need to decide how many resources you will involve in writing integration and functional tests. Once you decide which tests you will try and automate, you need to figure out how many tests you need. Set goals for code coverage at each level of testing. Establish procedures for measuring your code coverage.

If you decide not to automate functional testing, you might want to think about following design patterns (such as MVP) that make it easier to test your code below the user level.

One of the most important parts of your strategy should be to demonstrate progress as early as possible. As in other aspects of agile development, it is important to show progress in building your test suite as early as possible to keep project sponsors interested in funding it. That means that even if you don't have many tests, you should spend time making sure that your reports look good and that they get distributed to the right people. Project sponsors like to see lots of green lights, so write lots of little atomic tests, not fewer big ones. (This is important for other reasons as well, as previously discussed.) More tests mean more green lights, and more impressive reports. If you have functional tests that actually drive your application, show them off. Functional tests are good theater because to project sponsors they are very clearly doing the work of testers in a way they understand, only faster and cheaper than humans can do the same work.

Discuss your test plan with project sponsors. Explain to them what you are testing and how you plan to go about it. Don't expect them to be wowed, however. Test plans make people feel more secure if they are comprehensive and well crafted, but they don't *do* anything. If you are in an agile project and you do demos at the end of each of your iterations, demo enough of your test automation to show that you are doing it, but not too much or you will lose people's attention.

As mentioned previously, it is often difficult to get the resources you need to do the testing you want. Having a solid plan and figuring out how best to show progress to your project sponsors will go a long way toward getting you those resources.

Once you have a solid plan documented and in place, you can start building an automated test suite to achieve your goals. The first step in building such a suite is to pick tools that will allow you to achieve the level of automation set forth in your plan.

Testing Frameworks

Testing frameworks are libraries of existing code that provide a foundation for you to write tests on top of. They come in many forms, and for every coding environment. There are frameworks for unit testing that also work well for writing integration tests. There are frameworks for functional testing and tools for driving functional tests. There are also testing frameworks that seek to extend the reach of test writing to the business user, and allow nontechnical business owners to contribute to test automation.

Unit Testing Frameworks

Since the advent of the agile movement and Test-Driven Development, unit testing frameworks have sprung up for nearly every development environment, language, and platform.

The most popular and widespread are the XUnit frameworks. The original version, SUnit, was written in SmallTalk by some of the early XP advocates. Soon after, JUnit appeared for Java, and even VBUnit for unit testing Visual Basic 6 code. When .NET came on the scene, NUnit was soon to follow.

The X in XUnit is intended to represent letter substitution. At the time of this writing, a new testing framework for .NET called xUnit.net has been released.

While the implementation varies slightly from platform to platform, the overall idea remains the same. In each implementation, you write code that represents your unit tests and assert the results you expect.

The framework provides some method of identifying which code is test code, one or more TestRunners to run the test code, and a set of classes and methods to help you write your assertions.

The following examples use NUnit or MbUnit, both for the .NET platform. The code for JUnit or other unit test frameworks might look slightly different (for example, JUnit uses naming conventions rather than attributes to identify test code), but the pattern is equivalent:

```
[TestFixture]
public class SimplestTestFixture
{
  [Test]
  public void SimplestTest()
  {
    int x = 2 + 2;
    Assert.AreEqual(4, x);
  }
}
```

The [TestFixture] attribute marks the class as one that contains tests. The TestRunner uses the presence of the attribute to decide whether or not to run the class it is attached to. This is the basic pattern. Mark a method as test code, run your code, then assert the results you expect. In this case, you are asserting that $2 + 2 = 4$. The code under test here is the built-in addition operator provided by the .NET framework.

The TestFixture provides a grouping construct, and helps organize your tests. How you organize your test code should be part of your testing strategy. To get the most out of your test code, follow some convention for arranging and naming your test fixtures.

For example, if you write a class called StringCache, name the test fixture StringCacheFixture or StringCacheTestFixture in a file of the same name. Approach assemblies the same way. If your StringCache class resides in an assembly called MyCompany.Utilities.Caching, call the assembly containing the tests MyCompany.Utilities.Caching.Tests or something similar. If you establish and follow a pattern like this, it will be very easy for anyone coming on to the project to identify which tests go with which code.

A TestFixture can also provide some additional infrastructure for your tests. If you have a set of test methods that all need to take advantage of something that requires initialization, you can use a [TestFixtureSetUp] method.

```
[TestFixture]
public class SimplestTestFixture
{
  private string stringUsedByAllTests;

  [TestFixtureSetUp]
  public void FixtureSetup()
  {
    stringUsedByAllTests = "Hello World.";
  }

  [Test]
  public void LengthTest()
```

```
    {
        int x = stringUsedByAllTests.Length;
        Assert.AreEqual(12, x);
    }
}
```

The `TestFixtureSetUp` method will be run once before any of the tests in the fixture. Similarly, you can mark a method `TestFixtureTearDown`, and it will be run once after all the tests in the fixture to do cleanup.

For initializing before and cleaning up after each method in the fixture, use `[SetUp]` and `[TearDown]`:

```
[TestFixture]
public class SimplestTestFixture
{
    private FileStream stream;

    [SetUp]
    public void Setup()
    {
        stream = File.Open(@"c:\temp\test.txt",FileMode.Open);
    }

    [TearDown]
    public void Teardown()
    {
        stream.Dispose();
    }

    [Test]
    public void LengthTest()
    {
        StreamReader reader = new StreamReader(stream);
        string x = reader.ReadToEnd();
        Assert.AreEqual(12, x);
    }
}
```

This is very handy if you need to reinitialize for each test method.

One excellent feature of the MbUnit framework is the `FixtureCategory` attribute:

```
[TestFixture]
[FixtureCategory("unit")]
public class SimplestTestFixture
{
    [Test]
    public void SimplestTest()
    {
        int x = 2 + 2;
        Assert.AreEqual(4, x);
    }
}
```

You can use `FixtureCategory` to organize your test fixtures into multiple categories and instruct your TestRunner to treat them differently. You might use `FixtureCategory` to separate "unit" from "integration" tests. During your Continuous Integration process, you can run only tests marked "unit" on every build, and those marked "integration" once a night on a schedule. Using the attribute is much more flexible than trying to break up your unit and integration tests into separate assemblies or otherwise differentiate them.

When it comes time to run your tests, you have a lot of options. MbUnit, for example, comes with both console and GUI versions of its TestRunner, as well as report generation. The console version (see Figure 5-4) produces tried-and-true textual output to tell you how many tests were run, how many of them succeeded or failed, which ones failed, and why.

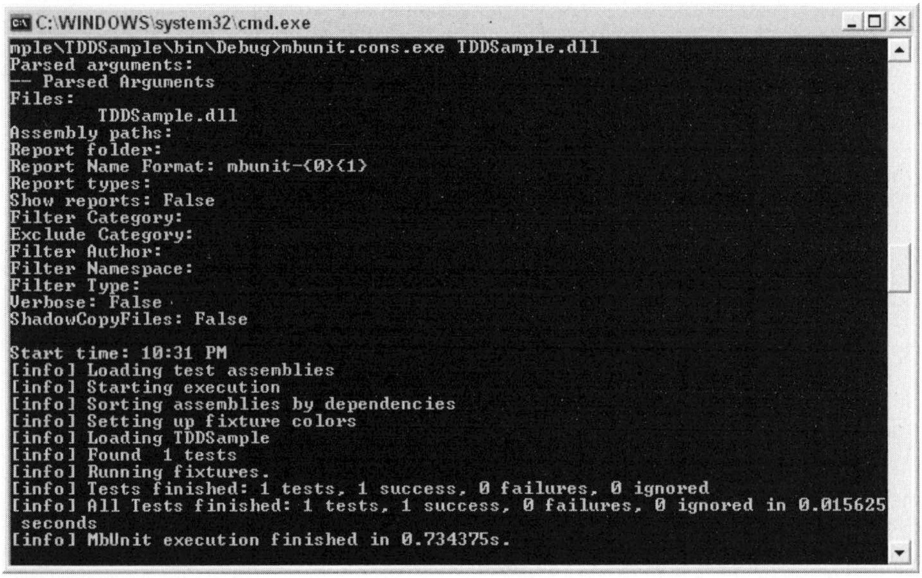

Figure 5-4

The GUI version (see Figure 5-5) displays the same information, with the addition of the infamous red-versus-green color scheme.

MbUnit also generates beautiful HTML reports that can be generated on your build server and distributed to your team, either directly over the web (as in Figure 5-6) or sent via email.

Any of these testing frameworks can also be integrated directly into your Continuous Integration process. For every testing framework, there exist plug-ins for CI platforms like Cruise Control (for Java and .NET) and build systems like Ant (Java), NAnt or MSBuild (.NET), and the various commercial build products such as MS TeamServer. By integrating unit testing with build or CI tools, you can cause your build to fail if any of your tests fail. Integration also provides the ability to report on unit testing along with the rest of your build process.

Figure 5-5

Figure 5-6

Functional Testing

For functional testing, there are two main categories of tools. Test frameworks such as Watir (written in Ruby) or WatiN (the .NET version) that allow you to write code in your language of choice to exercise your application. This is easy to do for web applications, and somewhat harder for desktop applications, although some solutions do exist.

TestRunner like Silk Test, Mercury TestRunner, or Rational Robot are designed to test desktop or web applications by simulating user-level interactions such as mouse movements and button clicks. These products are scriptable, so that test scripts can be written to drive your application and verify the results.

Let's focus on the former, rather than the latter, category. TestRunners tend to be expensive, temperamental, and to involve proprietary scripting languages that take time and effort to learn. They are also harder to integrate into an overall Continuous Integration or other test-automation strategy.

WatiN provides a set of primitives for running a web browser and parsing HTML that can be integrated into whatever testing framework you are already using. The following example uses MbUnit to define and run the tests, and WatiN to run IE (Internet Explorer) and validate the resulting HTML:

```
[Test]
public void ReadWebText()
{
   IE ie = new IE("http://www.cauldwell.net");


   Assert.IsTrue(ie.ContainsText("Patrick Cauldwell"));
}
```

This model provides a very handy way to integrate functional testing of your (web based) application with the rest of your unit and integration tests. You get integrated results and reporting across all types of tests. Because WatiN provides you with access to the underlying HTML document model, you can also do things like "push" buttons on web sites, or enter data in text fields:

```
[Test]
public void ReadWebText()
{
   IE ie = new IE("http://www.cauldwell.net");

   //finds the search text box
   ie.TextField(Find.ById("searchString")).TypeText("testing");
   //pushes the "Search" button.
   ie.Button(Find.ByName("_ctl133:Button1")).Click();

   Assert.IsTrue(ie.ContainsText("Patrick Cauldwell"));
}
```

By integrating with the rest of your tests, a framework like WatiN can provide a solid way of writing functional tests that provides you with consistent results and reporting, and a unified platform for all of your test automation.

FIT

FIT (Framework for Integrated Test) is a relatively recent attempt to bring functional testing to the business user. FIT uses HTML to define tests in terms of tables, where each table is filled with test input and expected results, as shown in Figure 5-7.

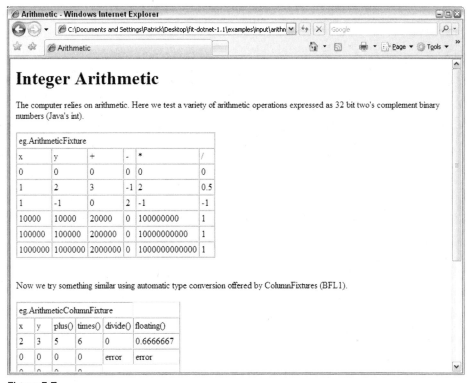

Figure 5-7

The intent is for business users to define these tables because it is the business users who know what the expected results should be.

This method is best applied to algorithm testing, rather than to more functional testing. The archetypal case for FIT testing is something like a payroll system. A business user would know what the expected results would be for each set of inputs, say calculating FICA tax from gross income. The nontechnical accountant can build a table of all the expected tax rates for each level of income, and developers can instrument their code and build the FIT infrastructure to run those tests.

While FIT testing is a very interesting idea, and applies well in a fairly narrow range of applications, it shouldn't be used outside of that range. Don't try to apply FIT to all of your unit testing, for example. Use it for what it was intended: getting business users to provide input and expected results to test your algorithms.

Automation and Your Organization

Test automation can be integrated with different parts of your organization. The biggest questions to answer are who writes tests, who runs them, and who gets notified of the results.

We've already talked about who should write which kinds of tests. Generally, developers should write unit and integration tests, while testers should write functional tests. But who writes the test plans? Who makes sure that the right testing is being done?

Developers may shoulder some of that burden, but ultimately testers should probably be responsible for overseeing testing as a whole, including testing done by developers. One approach is the buddy system. For each developer who is writing unit tests, assign a tester to review their tests and to help them establish good habits around test organization and code coverage. Before any developer declares their work done, they should have their body of unit tests finished and reviewed by their testing buddy. Collaborating in this way helps developers acquire good testing habits, and it gets QA involved in the development process early, so they can start developing their own testing strategies early.

Getting QA Involved

One common mistake that many organizations make is waiting too long to get QA involved in their development process. In the traditional waterfall model, because the testing phase occurred after most, if not all, development was done, QA often didn't get involved in a project until development was nearing completion. This is changing, even for waterfall projects today.

By getting testers involved as early as possible, you can take advantage of their expertise on a broader range of topics. Have testers review requirements before any code is written. That will help them become familiar with what your application will do, and they can start thinking early about how they will test it. Your project might involve new technologies they haven't tested before, such as web services, and they may need extra time to come up with a strategy for testing those new technologies.

Have testers review your design documents. They can provide feedback on how hard or easy your design may be to test and can familiarize themselves with how your application is laid out. By the time you start actually writing code, your testers will be in a position to start writing tests.

You may wish to assign some full-time testers to work with developers on unit testing, or you might farm out testing reviews to testers as they become available. Because testing resources are often scarce, assigning individual units of review across testers may be more effective.

Once your tests are written, someone must be responsible for running them. If you are using a Continuous Integration server, you may want the server to be responsible for running at least unit tests on a very regular basis. Integration tests may be run less frequently. Functional tests may be run by your CI server, or they may be run manually by testers on some schedule or as need arises.

Developers should be running tests as often as possible as part of their development routine. Make a change; run some tests. Make another change; run the same tests again. After integrating with another developer's work, run not only your unit tests, but also the full suite of integration tests to make sure that all the code works together correctly.

The last thing to consider is who will be notified of the results after tests run. For a Continuous Integration process, the best bet is to send out notification to developers and management only when the status of the build changes; for example, when a running build fails or when a failing build is fixed. You could send notifications on every build, but if you are building many times a day, that will generate a lot of extra email, and sooner or later people (particularly managers) will start to tune them out. If people are notified only when the status changes, they will be properly concerned when the build fails, and properly encouraged when it is fixed.

It may be a good idea to pick a few select people who get notified on every single build. If your build is broken and stays broken despite a whole series of check-ins, then something has gone wrong with your process. Developers are not taking responsibility for fixing the build. You might also be getting notifications of build failures due to network failures, or other infrastructure problems that need to be fixed. If you get a whole series of failures all at once, it can alert whoever is responsible for maintaining your build server that something is wrong.

Breaking the Build

Breaking the build is a serious problem. In a Continuous Integration setting, a broken build means that someone is not following the right development methodology. If the compiler fails, it means that someone didn't take the time to integrate all the latest changes on their own system before checking in their changes. If tests fail, it ultimately means the same thing. Every developer is responsible for managing the integration process before they check things in to the main code line (more on this in the chapter on source control), so that the burden of integration falls on those who make changes, not the rest of the team.

If every developer is updating their machine with the latest changes, building, and running all the tests before they check in their changes, the build should never break. If it does break, it means that someone has been lazy or inattentive, and that is a problem that needs to be dealt with swiftly because checking in breaking changes affects the entire team. The team as a whole should get in the habit of tracking down offenders and encouraging them to fix the build, and to change their evil ways if they are recidivists.

If people are constantly breaking the build, it could mean that your process is broken. If developers aren't running all the tests before checking in, why aren't they? Do the tests take too long to run? Do tests fail due to infrastructure issues like database servers going down? Are people writing incorrectly crafted tests that fail when they should be passing? If any of those things are true, developers may be tempted to skip proper testing before checking in. Sometimes that boils down to pure sloth, but sometimes it means you need to examine how your process as a whole is working for the team.

For functional tests, a more traditional feedback mechanism can be a good idea. If testers are finding defects with functional tests, they should report them as defects, which in most organizations involves a bug-tracking application. The fact that functional tests are failing should be tracked more carefully than the lower-level tests, and a defect tracker provides a persistent record of — and clearing house for — dealing with problems.

For a test-automation strategy to succeed, it must be well integrated into your organization. Everyone should understand their role in the testing process, as well as their responsibilities and the responsibilities of the other members of the team. It is important that people at every level in your organization be invested in testing, so that everyone contributes to the process, and the right resources are assigned at the right level and stage of the development process.

Summary

Testing is one of the most important parts of the development process, and yet it is often one of the most overlooked. People at all levels of the development organization need to buy in to the importance of testing, from requiring developers to meet code coverage targets to giving testers the time and resources they need to get their jobs done.

Testing early and often saves time and money by finding problems in code, design, and architecture as early as possible when they are easier and cheaper to fix.

Finally, as a developer, testing is one of the most important things you can do to improve your skills and those of your team. Creating a good testing strategy and practices help you learn to design better, code better, and work in a more integrated fashion with the other members of your team. No code can ever be defect free, but the more you test, the fewer defects you will write.

6

Source Control

For the vast majority of professional developers, source code control systems (SCCS or SCC) are a part of the landscape. Almost every serious development project relies on an SCC system to provide backups, version control, revision history, and archiving. Any source code control system (also known as version control or configuration management systems) will provide these basic features. However, very few organizations properly leverage their source control solution. A good SCC system can provide additional high-value features such as reporting, correlation with defect tracking, atomic commits, platform neutrality, and a host of others.

Not only can a good SCC system add a lot of value, but even a basic solution can be used to do much more than simply store multiple versions of the same files. If used properly, features such as branching, tagging, and merging can provide a new level of capabilities that your project and team can take advantage of.

At its most basic, the primary purpose of using a source control system is to make sure that changes to your source code take place in as orderly a fashion as possible. SCC systems help to coordinate and integrate the work of multiple developers, so that each developer can make changes freely and rely on the SCC system to coordinate their changes with the changes of other developers working on the same code. As a secondary benefit, SCC provides a historical record of all the changes that have taken place since the project was started, and allows you to retrieve specific versions or roll back to previous revisions if changes turn out to be unfortunate.

How much benefit your team or your project will get from source control will depend on which system you use, and how well you use it. Not every source control platform supports the same feature set or working model, but almost any system can be used to great benefit if used properly.

Source control is one of the cornerstone tools in any good Continuous Integration (CI) process. For CI to work properly, it must be easy for developers to update to the latest changes in source control, and just as easy for them to merge and check in their changes. SCC systems that do atomic check-in operations are even better for use in a CI process, since each integration can take the form of a single atomic check-in operation. Checking in files in an atomic batch provides better change tracking because all the files associated with a single change are grouped into one change set.

Such an atomic change set also makes it easier to speed up how often your CI server checks for changes. If your CI server can be assured that all the files necessary for a given feature or integration will be checked in as a batch, building from incomplete source is less of a concern. That means your CI server doesn't have to wait as long after changes are detected before starting a new build.

A comprehensive branching strategy (which you'll learn about in more detail later in the "Making the Most of Branching" section) can make your CI process easier to manage from a team perspective because it allows developers to continue to check in incremental changes without affecting the rest of the team using the integration branch.

A good source code control system can be just as important for developers working alone as it is for a team. Even if you don't have to worry about coordinating source code changes with other developers, you can benefit from a source code control system. It is very valuable to keep a historical record of changes you have made during development. You might find yourself wanting to roll back to a previous version if a refactoring goes awry, or you might just want to be able to experiment, secure in the knowledge that you can easily get back to where you started without having to manually backup your files, and so on.

Even if you are working alone, you may want to keep a historical record representing versions of your software already released to customers. Keeping multiple versions of your source in an SCC system is much more efficient than keeping flat file copies, and the SCC front end provides additional features such as branching and merging that would be difficult to do with file copies. If you have already shipped software to customers and they find bugs, you should have a simple way of correlating the version of the binaries they are using with the source that produced it. That is much easier to do with an SCC system than if you tried to maintain that information in a file system.

Some Source Control History

One of the earliest source control systems to become widely used was the RCS (Revision Control System) platform that shipped as part of many (if not most) UNIX systems. Because such systems were meant to be used by a number of people at the same time and software development became a common task, RCS played a vital role in making development easier. RCS had a simple command line interface, and used the UNIX file system as its storage mechanism. RCS worked by using pessimistic locking. If a developer needed to work on a file, that developer would "check out" the file. RCS would mark that file as "locked," and not allow anyone else to check it out until the first user checked the file back in, thus releasing the lock. This kind of locking was easy to understand and made it very difficult for two users to make conflicting changes to the same file or set of files. Because developers usually checked out all the files they needed to make a change to at once, it prevented any other users from changing those same files, protecting the integrity of each developer's changes. RCS stored all the versions of each file in a single node in the file system, using a diff format to represent the incremental changes to each unique version. Those diffs allowed any previous version to be recreated by assembling the appropriate series of diffs to make the right version of the source file.

The biggest advantage of RCS was its simplicity. Pessimistic locking is easy to understand, as is the file-based storage model. The fact that all the revisions of each file were stored in a single text file made that source code easy to recover if anything went wrong with the system, since everything was stored as human-readable text in the file system. The command-line-based interface employed by RCS was easy to use, and represented the common user paradigm at the time.

So successful was the RCS-style model that it became the dominant model used by source control systems for much of the early history of software development. Numerous commercial and freely available tools sprang up, each with a slightly different feature set, but all built along the same lines. When the first GUI-based source control tools started to appear after the advent of windowing systems, they, too, mostly followed the familiar RCS model. One of the most popular (or at least widely used) of these was Source Safe. Source Safe was an innovative Windows application that provided a very user-friendly GUI on top of the familiar pessimistic-locking model. It became sufficiently popular that Microsoft purchased it and bundled it, essentially for free, with its Visual Studio development environment, renaming it Visual Source Safe, or VSS. VSS was so widely used and so well integrated with Microsoft's IDE that it largely dominated (and continues to dominate in some circles) the SCC niche for Windows developers despite its (many) drawbacks.

All of these tools relied on pessimistic locking to prevent conflicting changes from being introduced into individual source files. Many added the ability to tag or label versions with arbitrary text so that disparate versions of various files could be semantically linked. Many also supported "branching" or the ability to fork off separate revision trees from a common ancestor, and later "merge" changes made in one branch back into another branch. This allowed different teams of people to develop different revisions of the same software simultaneously from a common ancestor or set of ancestors.

The pessimistic model has some drawbacks, however. Most importantly, pessimistic locking, by its very nature, means that only one developer can work on any give file or set of files at any one time. While that is good at preventing conflicts, it's bad at maximizing the productivity of a team. Just because two developers are changing code in the same file at the same time doesn't mean that they are working on the *same code*. If two developers are changing the same method at the same time without talking to each other first, then your team has a management and/or communication problem, not a problem with source control. Pessimistic locking slows teams down.

If two developers (let's call them Frank and Bob) are working in the same area of the code, and Frank has all the files checked out, then Bob can:

❑   Ask Frank to make his changes for him, or

❑   Wait for Frank to check the files back in and lose productive time, or

❑   Make changes to another copy of the files and try to merge them later.

That last option is the least attractive, since it almost always leads to more trouble at merge time than it is worth. An even bigger problem occurs when Frank checks out all the files and then leaves town on vacation. The only options then are either to wait (which is likely unacceptable) or to "break the lock," meaning that an administrative user unlocks the files, allowing Bob to get to work but probably leaving the code in an unknown and possibly inconsistent state.

As development teams grew larger and larger, and projects were often distributed across teams and across physical sites, the pessimistic-locking model became increasingly prohibitive. With the advent of the Internet came widely distributed projects that had contributors from all over the world, most of whom had never even met. Sites like SourceForge began hosting Open Source projects that required coordinating development work done by semi-anonymous users working from fully anonymous locations. In that situation, a pessimistic-locking model simply wasn't practical. If an anonymous user could check out and lock source files and then disappear off the face of the Internet, productivity would be seriously at risk.

Concurrent Versioning System (CVS)

The solution was what became known at the concurrent versioning system, or CVS. CVS changed the model from pessimistic to optimistic locking. In CVS, no user could check out and lock any file. (Actually, CVS does support pessimistic locking, but it is deprecated and should never be used.) In the concurrent model, users "updated" to the latest version of the source code. That update process would merge any changes that had been made in the code since the last update into the developer's local "working copy." If the changes couldn't be merged automatically, those files would be flagged as "in conflict," and the developer would have to manually merge the changes. When the developer was finished with the changes, those changes could be "committed" back to the repository. The changes thus committed became the latest version of the code.

CVS represented a major shift in the way that source control worked. The new model placed the burden of merging changes on the developer making the changes. Back to Frank and Bob. Frank updates to the latest version of the source and starts making changes. Meanwhile, Bob makes his changes faster and gets them committed. When Frank tries to commit his changes, he will be informed that he is not working on the latest version and so can't commit. Frank will have to update to the latest code that Bob committed, resolve any possible conflicts, and then commit his changes. The CVS model got rid of the locking model in favor of a model in which the first one to commit changes always wins.

The concurrent model makes it much easier for large teams of developers to work in parallel. The only time that they need worry about conflicts is at merge time, and often those conflicts never come about. As long as no two developers are changing exactly the same code at the same time, CVS will be able to handle all the merging automatically. This optimizes for developer productivity, since most of the time everyone can work in parallel without having to wait for locks to be released, and dealing with conflicts only affects those who cause the conflicts and not the rest of the team.

With the rise of Open Source and the ascendancy of SourceForge as the platform of choice for hosting Open Source projects, CVS has become more and more widely used. The concurrent model has become more and more popular in other SCC systems, including Subversion and other popular tools. Many, if not most, of those tools still allow the use of pessimistic locks, but they make it clear that such functionality is deprecated. Commercial products like Vault, ClearCase, and others support either model.

So which platform is best for you and your team?

Picking the Right SCCS

There are a number of things to consider when picking a version control system for your team, and each one of them should be carefully weighed. Almost any system will give you basic SCC functionality such as version history, merging and branching, and some limited reporting. Many systems have much more advanced features such as custom reporting and statistics, integration with other tools such as defect tracking, and the ability to replicate source code repositories across widely distributed sites over the WAN.

Before choosing an SCC platform, decide how many people you need to support working concurrently, what level of reporting you want, which locking model will work best for you, and whether or not the SCC system needs to be part of a Continuous Integration process or integrate with other tools as part of your development process. Are there rules that you want to apply to source control, such as "no empty comments" or "no code without unit tests"? How will you enforce those rules? Through tools, or process? How much money do you have to spend? Do you have someone dedicated to administering a source control system? These are all factors to take into account before settling on a platform.

Performance and Scalability

How many developers will be using the same SCC system, and how many of those will be working on the same project? Different SCC systems use different storage mechanisms and transport protocols, and those methods may have an impact on how many concurrent users can be supported comfortably. Some tools work directly against files in a file system, such as RCS. If multiple users are accessing the same files, they are relying on the underlying file-system-locking mechanism to handle the synchronization of changes. Everyone using such a system has to have access to the same file system, and so must be on the same network, and so on. Other systems such as Visual Source Safe use ISAM (Indexed Sequential Access Method) database files to store incremental version information. Again, those files must be accessible to all users of the system, and you are relying on file locking to keep two or more writes from conflicting. VSS is notoriously prone to file corruption problems for this very reason. For a small team working on the same LAN, VSS may perform just fine, however.

Many of the more recently developed SCC systems are client-server applications. The client sends and receives files to and from a central server that deals with the actual repository on the client's behalf. Those systems tend to be much more scalable, since all of the file I/O can be managed at the server rather than relying on file system locking. Some client-server systems rely on the file system on the back end (such as CVS), but many use SQL databases, which allow them to take advantage of indexing and other database features for better performance and more features.

Among client-server systems, some make more efficient use of network bandwidth than others. For example, if you commit a change to a CVS server, the entire text of the changed file is sent across the network to the server, which can be prohibitively expensive over a slower WAN connection. Subversion, by contrast, sends only deltas across the network, and so performs much better over the WAN by making much more efficient use of the bandwidth.

Some systems are designed to scale to large numbers of users distributed across physical sites by relying on replication. Separate servers at each physical location replicate copies of their repositories across the WAN to keep versions in synch. Some systems offer such a feature out of the box, and many others require add-on products for replication. Replication makes it more efficient for highly distributed teams to work on the same code, since local performance is optimized for speed and replication is relied upon to keep the teams in synch. These systems work particularly well when dealing with two or more teams in widely separated locations, as is often the case with outsourcing or offshoring. Teams in widely differing time zones can use their local repositories, and the replication tends to take place during times when no one is using the system in the other location(s). Such systems can be difficult and time-consuming to set up and maintain, however, as well as relatively expensive.

You will need to pick a system that will scale to meet the requirements of your team. A poorly performing SCC system is more a hindrance than a help, and keeps a team from working at peak performance.

Locking Models

You have already learned the differences between pessimistic- and optimistic-locking systems earlier in this chapter, so I won't reiterate the details here. In summary: the time for pessimistic locking has passed. A team of experienced developers starting a new project should be using a concurrent versioning system.

Concurrent versioning means that each developer spends less time waiting for other people to integrate their changes and more time making progress.

If you are planning on following a Continuous Integration process, then pessimistic locking is out of the question. You cannot support a good CI practice using exclusive checkouts. Developers need to be able to integrate their work early and often, as soon as each new feature or function is completed. If they have to sit around waiting for someone else to check in their changes first, everyone's time is being wasted. Many popular systems support both locking models. CVS, Vault, ClearCase, and others allow users to obtain exclusive locks, although that can usually be turned off at the server level. You should never allow exclusive locks, even if your tool supports it. It is never necessary (except possibly when working with binary files) and often is a major hindrance. Come up with a good solid integration routine using branches (details to follow), and you will never want to go back to exclusive locks.

Cost

How much money do you have to spend on a source control system? They range from freely available (free as in puppy, not free as in beer) to staggeringly expensive. If you have the budget and you want the features, it might be worth shelling out big bucks. This is particularly true if you want tight integration between source control and other tools in your process, such as defect tracking. If you want tight integration, you may have to purchase a bundled commercial tool suite such as those available from Serena, Rational/IBM, or Microsoft. These systems offer very good integration between source control, defect tracking, modeling tools, and requirements management tools. The cost of these features can quickly run into hundreds of thousands of dollars.

By contrast, you can get excellent source control systems that are freely available. The two most popular are CVS and Subversion. Both of these tools are Open Source projects maintained by very active development communities, and both are available at no cost. However, they may not integrate as tightly with other tools, or additional tools may have to be purchased to achieve that integration.

Another factor to consider when looking at the cost of source control is the administrative overhead. Some source control systems effectively require a full-time administrator to keep them up and running, and to keep them properly configured. Several of the commercial packages require specialized training to administer and maintain, and they require constant supervision if they are to function reliably. The cost of the training and administration has to be figured in to the total cost of ownership (TCO) of any system you might consider.

Atomic Commits

An important aspect of any source control system is how it deals with change sets. Some systems deal with every check-in of every file as a completely separate event, unrelated to any other change. When checking in large batches of files at once, those systems essentially check in each file separately in turn, as if it were the only file being checked in. If you check in 100 files, and number 50 fails, you will be left with 49 files checked in, and 51 files not checked in, potentially leaving your repository in an inconsistent state.

At the other end of the spectrum, some systems make use of change sets and atomic commits. That means that if you check in 100 files at the same time, all of those changes are tracked as an atomic change set. You can go back later and see which files were checked in together, and relate all the changes made at the same time. Plus, either the entire set of 100 files is committed to the repository or none are. The repository is never left in an inconsistent state. This is enforced by using transactions on the back end, so that if anything goes wrong during a commit, all the changes are rolled back together. Subversion was designed to be an improvement on CVS, and one of the largest improvements made in Subversion was the ability to do atomic commits. There is no way to leave the Subversion repository in an inconsistent state, which makes it much easier to use with a Continuous Integration server. A CI process works much more smoothly if changes are checked in as change sets. If you are lucky and configure your servers properly, each build should be the result of one change set. That makes it very easy to relate changes to the success or failure of any given build.

Change sets are also very handy when integrating with a defect-tracking (issue tracking for the politically correct) system. You can relate a single change set with a bug fix, so that you can go back later and see all of the changes that were made to fix a single defect. Testers love this feature. Some integrated systems such as ClearCase support this correlation internally (when used with the ClearQuest tracking system). When committing a change set, ClearCase can be configured to require correlation with a ClearQuest issue report. If you are using freely available tools, you can still correlate them with defect tracking. For example, you can check in a change set that fixes a defect and put the defect-tracking number in the comment associated with that change set, or you could label the files in that change set with the defect number, or use a separate branch for each bug fix where the branches are numbered to match the defect-tracking reports.

Branching

Branching is something that tends to be overlooked as a part of an everyday working model. Many, if not most, organizations branch only when they need to release one set of code as a product or "release" and then continue working on the next version. However, as you'll learn later in this chapter (see "Making the Most of Branching"), branching can be a very useful part of any development process on a day-to-day basis.

In order to make that daily use of branching work, however, it needs to be a relatively "cheap" operation from the perspective of your source control system. If branching needs to be done once or more a day, for example, it shouldn't take more than a minute to create the new branch even for a very large source base. This is something to consider when choosing an SCC platform. If you are shopping for a new SCC system, give the branching operation(s) a thorough workout in each platform you are considering and see what the performance is like. How long it takes to create a new branch can vary widely across systems, with some taking a very long time (essentially N * number of files) for large source bases, and some remaining nearly constant despite large numbers of files. In CVS, for instance, branching is done by attaching a special label to every file that needs to be branched. For very large source bases, that may take quite some time. In Subversion, on the other hand, branching is a trivial operation that takes a very short and nearly constant amount of time to finish, even for very large repositories. If you are going to integrate branching into your daily work process, you should choose a system that will make it easy and efficient to do, without making developers wait too long to complete branching operations.

Branching should also be easy to understand. Depending on the source control system, branching can be an easy operation conceptually, or it can be more difficult to get the hang of. Because CVS treats branches as a special kind of label, it can be confusing to first-time users when trying to understand the differences between labels and branches, and what the limitations of each are. Visual Source Safe treats branching as a very heavyweight operation that should be done as infrequently as possible since it is time-consuming and results in a structure that can be confusing to developers.

Merging

With branching comes merging. Merging operations is another thing to explore when choosing a new system. Some source control systems come with very reliable and feature-rich merging tools, others do not. Some treat merging in a way that is easier to understand than others. In some platforms, merging is a server-side operation; in others, it is handled client side. Server-side operations can be easier to understand, since they typically behave just as you would expect. You pick a source and target branch, and the results of the merge end up in the target branch. That isn't necessarily the best way to do it, but it is simple in concept and easy to visualize. By contrast, the client-side merge in Subversion is very difficult to conceptualize for many developers, which makes it harder to use. In Subversion, two source trees are merged into a working copy on the developer's local drive, which then has to be committed back to the repository. It is a safer operation, since everything is visible in the working copy and can be rolled back without affecting the source tree in the repository at all. That means that if a merge isn't as successful as you hoped, or if it merged the wrong things, it is easy to recover from, since nothing has been changed in the server-side repository. It does prove much harder to understand, however, and requires a good deal of training before it can be done reliably by the whole team.

Integration with Other Tools

If you have a team that is relatively inexperienced or a very large team with members from disparate parts of your organization, you may want to look for tools that will help you enforce your process. It is easy to integrate source control with other tools, using a manual process. For example, you can check a change set into your source control system, and in the comments put the number of the defect from your defect-tracking system that the change set addresses. When someone goes back to look at that defect later, they will be able to manually correlate the files that changed and the changes that were made to each with the defect that was (supposedly) addressed. Or a task branch can be named after the activity/backlog item/story that is being worked on in that branch. These are manual processes that cannot be enforced automatically. You can't "make" developers name branches correctly or use the right defect-tracking numbers in their comments. This isn't a problem with a small team of experienced developers who can work with a high level of discipline, but if your team lacks experience or discipline or if it is very large and difficult to manage, then you might have better luck with tools that enforce the correct process.

Many of the major source control systems can be integrated with a larger suite of tools, often consisting of defect tracking, modeling, requirements-gathering, and testing tools. The IBM Rational Software Delivery Platform and Microsoft's Team System are good examples of such integrated suites. It is possible to set up rules in such systems that can be enforced at the software level. For example, you can make it a requirement in IBM's Rational ClearCase source control system that every change set committed to the repository must be associated with an "activity" or a defect record in the ClearCase defect-tracking system. The tools simply will not let your developers get away with not following the process. That can be very valuable in situations where the whole team doesn't physically work together or when the team has a hard time communicating.

That integration comes at a cost, however. Such integrated systems tend to be costly and take a high level of expertise to configure and maintain. You may find yourself needing one or more full-time administrators to keep the system running from day to day. However, admins trained in the complex inner workings of your system may be hard to find and difficult to replace. A complete toolset may be just what your organization needs, particularly if your company is new to the idea of structured development processes. Some organizations may successfully develop and release software for years without relying on a structured process involving source control, defect tracking, unit testing, or requirements management (in a formal sense), let alone integration between those tools. If such an organization decides that the time has come to adopt a more structured approach, it can be much easier to start with an integrated toolset that makes it easy to follow the rules. When the cost of such a change is measured in terms of developer time, the $100K+ it may take to buy all of the tools may be comparatively small. It is up to each organization to balance the pros and cons of such an integrated suite, based on the nature of the organization and the projects that it is working on.

Another aspect of integration to consider is how well (if at all) your source control system fits into your IDE. One of the reasons that Visual Source Safe became so popular among Visual Studio users was because it was very tightly integrated into the Visual Studio environment. When using VSS with Visual Studio, you can easily see from within the project window which files are checked out and which files have been modified. You can check files in and out directly to and from your development project without resorting to external tools, which makes source control operations easier to understand and easier to complete successfully. Many other SCC tools are built to take advantage of the source control interface provided by Visual Studio. For other tools, it is possible to use third-party solutions to integrate with Visual Studio, such as the OSS project Ankh that can be used to integrate Subversion with Visual Studio.

Many other IDEs have good source-control integration as well. The Eclipse IDE, popular among Java and web developers working on OSS platforms, can be integrated with any number of SCC systems using readily available plug-ins.

Reporting

As a tech lead or manager of a software development team, you may need to know how your source control system is being used by the members of your team. Are they following the process you have established correctly? Are they using adequate comments? Are they associating change sets with defects properly? How often are branches being created and merges completed? How many times a day are people checking in changes? These are all questions that you may need to be able to answer about your source control system. Different SCC systems have different levels of built-in reporting capabilities. You may be able to rapidly and easily create complex reports using the SCC tool itself, or you may need to rely on a third-party package for such reporting. When picking an SCC tool, consider what information you need from the repository and how easy it will be to get out.

Extensibility

There may come a time when you want to extend the capabilities of your SCC system, using either code you write yourself or third-party products. That can be more or less difficult, depending on the system you choose. If you want to enforce complex rules regarding commits, branching, or other features of the system, you may need to write custom code to make that happen. Many systems support some kind of plug-in architecture that makes this possible. It is worth taking a look at the extensibility features of the systems you are considering, although it probably is not the highest priority. You should choose a system that meets your needs on day one, but take into consideration how hard it will be to extend as your process matures.

Making Your Choice

Given all of the preceding considerations, picking a source control system to meet your needs can be quite a daunting task. Everyone has a favorite system, every vendor wants to sell you a solution to all of your problems, and cost and feature sets vary wildly among the contending platforms. The best place to start is by making a list of the features that you absolutely need and ones that you think would be beneficial. Use the classic "must have"/"like to have"/"nice to have" ranking for each feature. Then decide how much you are willing to spend. If you have a lot of requirements around integration and process control, you may need to spend more. If you are willing to put the burden of following the process on individual developers, you may be able to use a freely available system.

After assessing requirements and cost, make a list of the 3–4 top contenders, and try them out for yourself. Setting up the OSS platforms like CVS or Subversion can be done quickly and with little experience. Vendors who want to sell you a commercial platform will happily help you get set up with a test system or provide access to one that is already set up. Try them out! No sales brochure or web site can give you a real sense of how hard or easy any given system is to use. Try to accomplish the same tasks on each system. For each of the systems you are considering try:

❑ Setting up a new repository. How hard is it? Will it take someone with special training?

❑ Importing some existing source code. Is it hard? Is it easy to understand?

❑ Checking code in and out. Do a series of updates and commits using multiple copies of the same repository, or different machines. How easy is it to update to the latest code? How long does it take? Is it easy to understand the process? How much training will your developers require?

❑ Creating some branches. Create 3–4 task or version branches. Is it hard? How long does it take? Is it conceptually easy to follow? How error-prone is the process?

❑ Merging. Make changes on one or more branches and then merge between them. How hard is it to understand and to complete successfully? How much training will be required?

❑ Integrating with other systems (if that's what you want to do). How hard is it to integrate source control with defect tracking? Does the model make sense?

If you can answer all of these questions, you should have all the information you need to make a good choice.

My own personal choice when working with an experienced team is Subversion. Subversion provides atomic commits, is relatively easy to set up, is freely available (not the same as free, remember), and performs branches and copies in constant time. Best of all, for use with a Continuous Integration process, Subversion versions the entire repository at the same time, rather than keeping separate version numbers for each file. For a CI process that means that each integration has to include a complete update to the latest version of the repository before being committed. Also, if you are working over a WAN, Subversion makes very efficient use of network bandwidth, which makes it much easier to use and faster over a slow network connection.

Subversion does have some cons, however. Merging in Subversion is very flexible and a powerful tool for working with multiple branches. That power comes at the cost of being difficult to understand. Subversion's merge feature works quite differently from other tools many developers are familiar with. Even for experienced coders, it can prove challenging to learn to use effectively. Plan for extra training time and reference materials relating to merging if you decide to adopt Subversion for your team. Furthermore, a full server installation of Subversion requires setting up an Apache web server, which may be unfamiliar to teams working on non-Apache platforms. Subversion's access control mechanism requires updating text files on the server and relying on Apache's built-in security facilities, which takes some time to get used to and requires an administrator with access to the file system on the server to make changes.

Subversion does not come with much in the way of reporting tools, and if reporting is a requirement, you may have to purchase and integrate a third-party solution.

For a less experienced team, or one requiring a high level of integration across tools, Subversion may not be the best choice, given the considerations above.

Organizing Your Source Tree

Once you have chosen your SCC system, it is time to think about how to organize your source code to take the best advantage of the system you are using. Spend some time thinking about how you will work with multiple branches or versions, and how different projects throughout your organization may need to be integrated.

Some of the issues involved in picking a layout will be determined by which SCC tool you pick. Different tools have different requirements and leave a different "footprint" on your local system. However, the basic concepts translate well across tools.

Using TreeSurgeon

A great place to start if you are using Visual Studio .NET is with a tool called TreeSurgeon. TreeSurgeon creates a starter project and directory structure that works well with a Continuous Integration process. Even if you aren't working with Visual Studio, TreeSurgeon's model is a good one to use with any development tools or IDE. TreeSurgeon creates three separate folders, lib, src, and tools. Figure 6-1 shows a top-level structure created by TreeSurgeon.

Figure 6-1

The lib folder should be used to store any libraries your project needs compile time access to. These should only be files that are necessary for the linker to get its job done. The tools folder contains all of the tools required during the build process, such as:

❑　The build tool itself (NAnt/Ant/MSBuild)

❑　Your testing framework (NUnit/JUnit, etc.)

❏   Code coverage tools

❏   Anything else that is related to the build process but not needed directly by the compiler/linker

The src folder is where your application's source goes. You may end up with a very complex structure under src, or you may choose to keep it very simple. Much of that depends on the size and complexity of your project.

TreeSurgeon also lays down a default NAnt build file and a batch file to run the build file. These portions are specific to .NET, of course, but the idea applies to any development environment.

By separating the lib, src, and tools parts of your tree, you can choose to version them separately. You may want to share tools across different projects, in which case your tools folder may point to a different source control repository than the one containing your source. In larger organizations, this makes good sense, as it helps the organization standardize on a common toolset, and version that toolset by using such a common repository. Because each project can pull a different version of the toolset from the tools repository, updating the tools in the repository doesn't necessarily mean all the projects in the organization have to be updated. When they are updated, however, that becomes as simple as pulling a different set of tools from source control and changing your build process to take advantage of the new toolset. By versioning the toolset in source control, you can make sure that each set of tools works well together. Teams updating to the latest version may have to change their source and or build to match newer versions of the tools, but they won't have to worry about whether or not the versions of different tools in the toolset will work well together.

Figure 6-2 shows TreeSurgeon's default tools folder.

Figure 6-2

Similarly, inside your lib folder you may need to create a set of subdirectories corresponding to different third-party products you are linking to, or to other projects built by your organization. If you have a dependency on another project inside your company, create a separate folder for that project under lib so that you can associate it with a different source control location. This is something that Subversion in particular facilitates well, because Subversion allows you to create "external" links to other repositories. If the other project you depend on publishes its public interface as a set of libraries in source control, you can link to its repository to pull either a specific version or the latest version of the libraries you depend on.

What goes into your source (src) folder can be harder to organize. Think about how you want to version your project, how projects have to work together, how they will be built, and what will make the most sense to your developers. The default structure laid down by TreeSurgeon is shown in Figure 6-3.

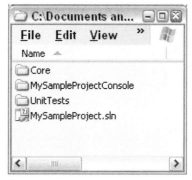

Figure 6-3

This structure separates the core features of your application from the application itself. The Core folder contains a library with common code in it, or code that is decoupled from the nature of the application, and the application folder (MySampleProjectConsole in this case) contains the code associated with the application itself that isn't common, such as user interface or other code that won't be shared by another project. The third folder is UnitTests. It contains all the unit test code to test the other projects.

Folder naming may seem like a trivial part of setting up a new project, but it can make a big difference in how easy it is to bring new developers onto your project. Think carefully about how you name your folders. Avoid ambiguous or indeterminate names. "Common" should be avoided at all costs. Code that ends up in a folder called "Common" often ends up not being very common nor being used by multiple projects in the way the name suggests. What does "Common" really mean in this context? Does it mean shared? That is usually the intent. However, that is the only thing that the name "Common" implies. Right after "Common" comes "Utils." Avoid names like these that express some nonconcrete intention. If you have code that will be used by multiple projects or applications, be explicit about what it does when choosing a name, not how you hope it will be used. "Core" is slightly better than "Common" but not by much. A better choice might be a top-level structure like the one shown in Figure 6-4.

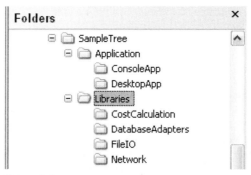

Figure 6-4

Name your folders based on what they mean to the functioning of your application, and what the code inside really does, not on how you hope those projects will be used down the line. If you name projects "Common" or "Core," they will end up being the dumping ground for everything that nobody wants to own later on.

One strategy that is worth considering is common in the Java community. Java projects are often organized by namespace, with the most specific part of the namespace farthest down the tree. In the traditional Java model, the namespace includes the URL of the company, probably stemming from the earliest use of Java for web-based applets. So if you have code in a namespace like com.*mycompany*.web.controls .buttons, you would end up with a folder structure like the one shown in Figure 6-5.

Figure 6-5

In this case, each level of the folder structure corresponds to a level in the namespace hierarchy. Many .NET projects follow a similar scheme, starting with the top-level namespace for the assembly in each project, then one folder for each subnamespace. The URL portion is typically omitted in .NET, so a similar hierarchy in a .NET project might look like the one shown in Figure 6-6.

Figure 6-6

These are by no means hard-and-fast rules, and just because it is the common style doesn't mean that's the way you should structure your project. It does, however, provide a solid jumping-off point to start from. The most important thing is to keep it as simple and easy to understand as you can. Avoiding overused and meaningless names like "Common" or "Core," and keeping the hierarchy simple and shallow will go a long way toward making your project easier to understand. The easier it is to understand, the faster you will be able to spin up new developers and make them productive in your environment.

It is also important to avoid repetition in naming wherever possible. If you end up with two projects that are named "Web.Common.Buttons" and "Common.Web.Buttons," you are asking for trouble. It is very difficult for new members coming onto the team to figure out a) why there are two separate projects in the first place, b) where they should go to find what they are looking for, and c) to which project they should add new code relating to web buttons. Such naming repetition often comes about because of historical accidents or through merging the products of multiple teams into a single tree. If you find duplication like this, stamp it out as quickly as possible to avoid the loss of time incurred by developers trying to muddle through a confusing structure.

Packaging

When doing an initial layout of your source tree, spend some time thinking about how your code will be packaged for deployment. The unit of deployment is different, depending on what platform you're writing your code in, but whether you are deploying .NET assemblies, Java packages, or groups of Python scripts, the basic issues are the same. It is important to separate logical units from physical ones when planning deployment packaging.

To examine a case from the .NET world, one trap that is easy to fall into is assuming that every namespace needs its own assembly, and every assembly should contain only one namespace. This particular example relates directly to source control. I believe this pattern came about because many, if not most, early .NET development teams were using source control systems that relied on pessimistic locking. In that case, it feels most natural to create one assembly per unit of work done by one developer, so that each developer can check out all the files relating to that assembly at the same time, in order to avoid conflicts. The result is a large number of assemblies, each containing a relatively small amount of code. This has real consequences in a number of areas. From an organizational perspective, it means a proliferation of projects, directories, and assemblies that are hard to keep track of. From a performance perspective, it means additional assemblies that have to be loaded, which carries a cost both in memory usage and in computing cycles. If you are using an optimistic-locking system, there is no need to split up each developer's work into a single assembly, and you can focus on what the real requirements are for packaging. The question to ask when setting up your projects (and thus your source tree) is "Is there ever a case where these two pieces of code won't be deployed together?" If the answer is no, then there probably isn't a good reason for having two separate assemblies/packages/zip files for deployment. Your source tree will be easier to understand and to manage. You may still want to create one subdirectory per level in the namespace hierarchy, since it lends additional meaning to your source tree and makes it easier for developers to find what they are looking for.

Adding Folders to Work with Source Control

Depending on what source control system you are using, you may need to add some additional directories to your tree to be able to take full advantage of the features of your SCC system. In some source control systems such as Subversion, branches and labels are represented as copies of other folders in the repository. Branching or labeling in Subversion looks just like making a copy of your source folder(s). To add additional meaning to those copies, you may need to add some extra folders to the tree. Figure 6-7 shows additional folders added to the Subversion hierarchy to attach additional semantics.

The only way for users to differentiate between a branch and a label in Subversion is by convention. Copies placed in a folder called "branch" represent branches and are intended to be treated as branches. Copies placed in a folder called "tag," on the other hand, are treated as tags or labels, and those copies are not intended to be modified. They exist only to associate a semantic label (the folder name of the copy) with a version of the repository. You may also want to create a separate folder called "task," which can be used to represent specific task branches. You'll learn more about task branches in the next section. By convention, the copy that represents the "tip" or "head" revision in any given repository is called "trunk," although you can pick any name that works for your organization as long as everyone understands what it represents, that is, the latest version of the source into which people commit their changes.

One of the great joys of working with Subversion is that making copies takes almost no time at all, and it costs next to nothing as far as the repository goes. Each copy is essentially just a pointer in the

Subversion database. Nothing actually gets copied. The upshot is that you can feel free to make as many copies as you need without worrying about it affecting the server. That allows you freedom to create as many semantic labels as you want for a specific version of the repository. You can add labels for build numbers, labels for tasks or progress markers, and labels for each iteration or demo you prepare for. You can add a great deal of additional information to your repository by using such labels, in a way that is quick and easy to accomplish. The more information you have in the repository, the easier it will be for people to find their way around, assuming that such information is well organized and communicated to the whole team/group/company. Write up a formal (short) document that lays out your scheme for branching/labeling so that it will be clear to everyone and easy to disseminate to new team members. One page or less is a perfect size. That is long enough to contain all the information you need if things are well thought out, and not so long that developers won't be willing to read it.

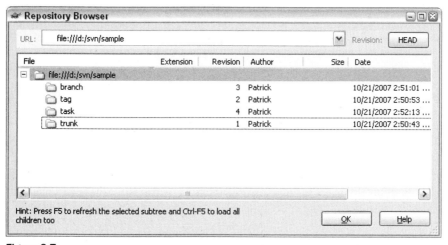

Figure 6-7

If your source code is organized properly, both on disk and in the repository, it will be much easier for new team members to get up to speed, particularly if you establish a corporate policy for how the source should be organized. New team members coming from other groups should have no trouble in quickly discovering how your application's source is laid out if they are already familiar with the schema. Experienced developers will also find it simpler to keep track of where everything is if they are comfortable with the pattern you establish.

Making the Most of Branching

Branching is the one aspect of source control that is most often overlooked, underappreciated, misunderstood, or abused, depending on the environment. To create a "branch" (sometimes referred to as a "codeline") in a source control system is to split a source tree in two (or more) "branches," each of which descends from a common ancestor. Changes made in one branch are not reflected in the other branch(es). This means that you can split one project into two or more projects simply by creating new branches in your source control system. This is most often done for the sake of continuing work on the latest code (the "tip" or "head" revision) while preparing to ship an earlier version in which changes need to be restricted. These "version branches" are the kind most often encountered in software shops, and the most readily understood by developers.

There are several other very good reasons for branching, however, that are less widely known. "Personal branches" allow developers to continue to check in incremental changes without affecting the integration branch. They provide an excellent place for developers to experiment, try out ideas, and work on XP-style "spike solutions." "Task branches" can be used to identify all of the work that went into a single task/backlog item/story. They serve as a macro-level change set, grouping together a set of changes that span multiple commits to the repository that are all related to a single task.

An "integration branch" serves as a way for developers to express the "done-ness" of their work. Such a branch should always contain the latest version of the code that is known to compile and pass all of its tests. A Continuous Integration server is likely to use such a branch as the basis for continuous builds. If it is managed properly and using the right tools, the integration branch also serves as a historical record of each integration activity that can be useful later in the project cycle.

Version Branches

Version branches are the ones that most of us are familiar with in everyday corporate software development. Say that your team is working on the very first version of your product, the 1.0 version. Typically, because of schedule and resource constraints, the 1.0 version doesn't contain all of the features and functionality that you would have liked to put into it. Nonetheless, you still have to ship something, and that something needs to come from a stable source code base if it is to be tested properly before being sent to customers. One way to achieve that is to simply stop development until the 1.0 version ships. The only things that are checked in or committed to your repository are defect fixes found during testing. Unfortunately, that tends to leave most of the team sitting on their hands until the product ships. It would be better if the team could continue working on the features that didn't make it into the 1.0 version, and continue to commit those changes to the repository. Enter the version branch. At the time that it is necessary to start stabilizing the 1.0 version, you create a branch that will become the 1.0 branch. The branch might actually be called 1.0, although various source control systems have various naming restrictions, so it might actually end up being called v-1_0 or something similar. In any case, defect fixes needed to ship the 1.0 release can be checked into the 1.0 branch, and additional features can continue to be checked in to the "tip" or the latest version of the main branch. The 1.0 version can be stabilized successfully without requiring anyone to stop working or making progress.

Creating Version Branches

How you create a version branch depends on the source control system that you are using. In Subversion, it is as simple as making a copy of your current *trunk* folder in the branch top-level folder. The copy (in this case called "1.0") is show in Figure 6-8.

Subversion knows which revision was copied to create the new branch and can report that information later on. It is important to know what version the branch was made from so that changes made on the new branch can be merged into future branches, or vice versa. Using TortoiseSVN, a freely available extension for Windows Explorer that is a full-featured Subversion client, you can look at a "revision graph" of the repository. Figure 6-9 shows a TortoiseSVN revision graph.

This graph shows that the new 1.0 branch was created from the /trunk folder at revision 4. Subversion, unlike many other SCC systems, versions the entire repository at once, rather than maintaining separate version numbers for each file. Every time an atomic commit is made to the Subversion repository, the version number of the repository is incremented. To talk about a specific file's version, you would speak of the version of file x from revision y. If you look at the history for any given file, you will see in which revisions of the repository that particular file was changed.

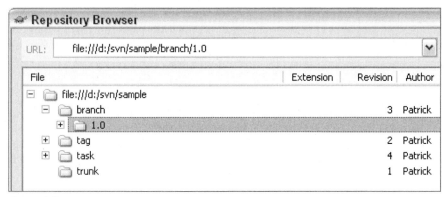

Figure 6-8

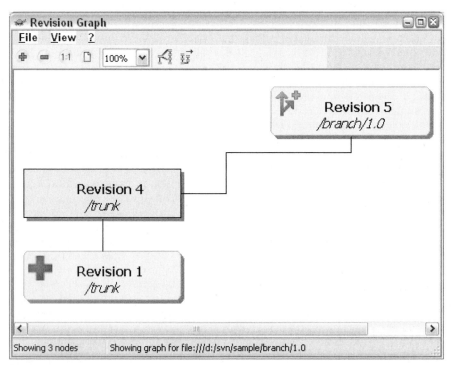

Figure 6-9

In CVS, you would apply a special branch label to the revision that you wanted to become the 1.0 branch. CVS treats branches as a special kind of label or tag, and they are created in the same way with the addition of the -b switch if you are using the command line client, or a "create new branch" check box in most graphical clients. The difference between labels and branches in CVS is that you can check out a copy of the source based on the branch tag, and then commit changes back to the repository. Those changes will be committed to the branch that you checked out. If you check code out based on a regular label, you will receive an error if you try to commit changes. This distinction is imposed by the CVS client itself. In Subversion, no distinction is made by the tool between a branch and a label. Both are copies from the perspective of the tool. By convention, copies made in the branch folder are updatable, while copies made in the tag folder should not be committed to. The tool will do nothing to prevent changes being made to "labels," however, so it is a matter of training and consensus to keep the two kinds of copies semantically consistent.

CVS keeps separate version numbers for each file in the repository and uses those file versions to keep track of branches as well. If a particular file in the newly created 1.0 branch has a version number of 1.2, the first time a change to that file is checked in to the branch, its version will be 1.2.1.1, or the 1st revision of the first branch created from the 1.2 version of the original file. The next commit would result in version 1.2.1.2, and so on. If another branch is created from the 1.2 version, its first new version would be 1.2.2.1. The version number of each file can be used to trace its branching history.

Other source control systems have similar ways of dealing with branching from the user's perspective, but they all achieve the same thing. Two or more forks of development that all spring from the same common source.

Managing Version Branches

Once you start creating version branches, or even better, before you start creating version branches, you should have some scheme in place for how you will manage the various branches. How often do you need to create a new version? How often are you likely to come back to a branch to make bug fixes? At what level do you need to create branches? These are all issues that you should have a clear plan for.

Typically, the time to create a new version branch is when you need to stabilize one release while continuing development on the next release. The first time that any developer wants to check in a change that isn't going to ship in the current release, you need a branch. One thing that makes this a bit easier is that in almost every SCC system, it is possible to go back and create a new branch from something other than the head revision. That means you can potentially put off the decision about when to branch until the last responsible moment. You can always decide a week or a month later that you really should have branched earlier. That is better than branching too early in anticipation of needing it. If you branch too soon, you will have to spend more time merging later. Any fixes that you make to stabilize one version will more than likely have to be merged into other branches that also need the fix in place. Merging shouldn't be a scary operation as long as you know what you are doing, but there is no need to create extra work for yourself if you don't have to.

Part of the decision to branch or not, and when to branch will be based on how your organization releases new code. If your business involves a hosted web site that you sell to customers as a service, then you may be freer to make frequent releases and branch less than a product company. If you can upgrade all of your hosted customers to the latest release at the same time, then you will have far fewer issues that require making fixes to old branches. In this case, you may only need version branches for your "major" releases, say 1.1, 1.2, 2.0, and so on. If, on the other hand, you are a product company that has to support multiple versions of your software and service packs, patches and/or hotfixes to your various product versions, then you will need to lean much more heavily on version branches. You might need to create a separate branch for every service pack or patch, so that you can go back later and make changes to only that branch to fix a customer's problem. Such a scenario requires much more careful management of your branches, and a consistent way of naming and dealing with such branches.

If you have to manage a complex series of version branches, establish a naming schema that will make sense to everyone in your organization and that matches your release model. If you are working with an SCC system that treats branch names like labels, such as CVS, you might end up with a series of labels like:

```
b_1_0
    b_1_0_sp1
        b_1_0_sp1_p1
b_1_1
    b_1_1_sp1
    b_1_1_sp2
        b_1_1_sp2_p1
...
```

Such a scheme makes it clear which branches belong to which releases. If you tie branches to internal code names, or some other less orderly scheme, developers will be forced to use some sort of lookup to map a branch to the version of the software that was released to a particular customer. You may still need to keep a mapping of which customers have which software version/service pack/patch level, but you won't have to dereference a separate list to find the right branch.

In Subversion, you can use folders rather than labels to achieve the same effect. A 1.0 release branch is shown in Figure 6-10.

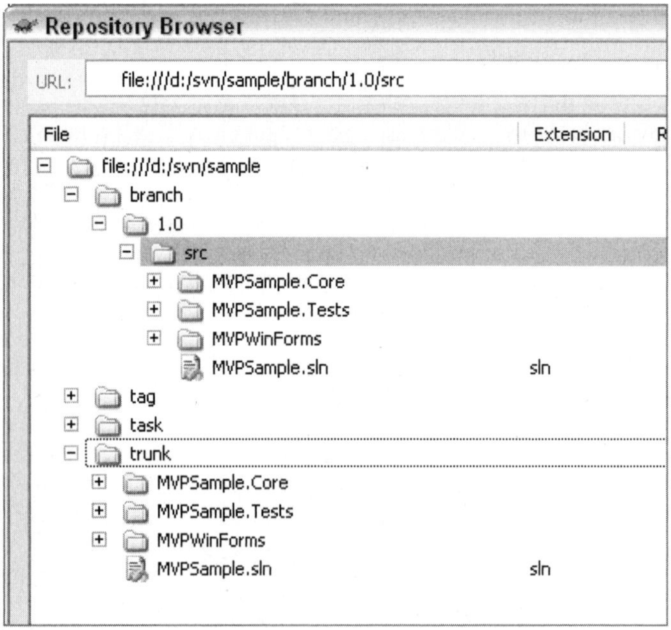

Figure 6-10

By using a folder called `src` or something similar under the `1.0` folder, you can add additional levels to the hierarchy for service packs or patches later on. Figure 6-11 shows service pack branches organized under major version branches.

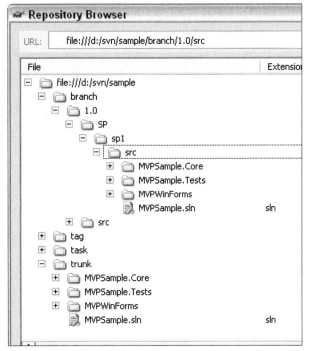

Figure 6-11

Keep in mind that additional copies cost essentially nothing in Subversion, so you can keep as many branches are you need to organize your versions properly.

Once you come up with a scheme for managing version branches, publish it within your organization and try to get all the developers to understand and agree to it. If every project uses the same system, it is much easier to move developers from one project to another as resource needs dictate and to have those developers be productive as quickly as possible.

Integration Branches

The branch that plays the most vital role in any Continuous Integration process is the integration branch. The integration branch is the one that the CI server will pull from to do its continuous builds. That means that whatever is in the integration branch should represent the latest source that builds and passes all of its unit tests. In most organizations, the tip/trunk/head also serves as the integration branch, but that may not be the most efficient way to organize things. If you make good use of personal and task branches (more on that to come), then it may be perfectly acceptable to use the tip as the integration branch. However, if you are not using branches in that way, then you might want to create an independent integration branch that represents the code that compiles and passes all the tests, rather than making that a requirement of the trunk.

If you are using a CI server, then whatever is in the integration branch should always build so that QA gets new versions to test and developers get feedback about the quality of their integrations as regularly as possible, without being hampered by a broken build. To that end, it is important that every developer take care to make sure that the integration branch will always build. Doing so becomes much easier if it isn't the same as the tip. Developers can feel free to check in as many changes as they want on the tip, whether they will build or not. When their task is complete, they can then merge the totality of their changes in a batch to the integration branch, properly updating, building, and testing before committing the batch. This cycle is shown in Figure 6-12.

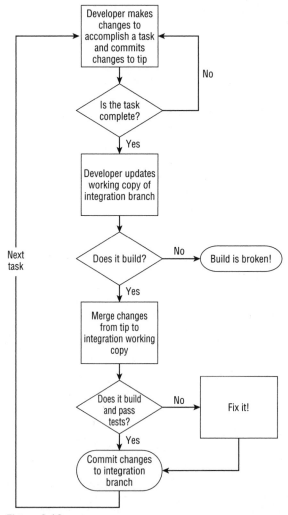

Figure 6-12

Using a separate integration branch in this way accomplishes two things:

1. Developers can check in as often as they like to the tip without fear of breaking the build.
2. By merging whole tasks into the integration branch at once, a record is maintained of all the changes required for a given integration.

The build is less likely to break because every integration is tested against the integration branch before being committed, so the Continuous Integration server stays happy, and the CI process rolls along unhindered.

The biggest drawback to this method is that each developer must keep track of all the changes they make to complete each task so that those changes can be merged as a unit into the integration branch. There is a better solution that accomplishes the same goals. Using separate personal and task branches and allowing the tip to be used for integration is easier to manage and groups together all the changes needed to complete any given task.

Personal Branches

While some developers tend to resist frequent check-ins, others may revel in them. Personally, I like to check in changes as soon as I make them and prove that they compile and pass tests. I might commit 7–10 or more times a day. However, it would be unfortunate if each one of those commits sparked a CI build, since it causes unnecessary churn on the build box for little additional benefit. Optimally, you want your CI server to build only when a complete integration has been committed to the repository.

One way to make this happen is to use "personal branches." A personal branch is essentially a private sandbox, where an individual developer can check in as many changes as desired without affecting the integration branch. The history of all those changes is preserved, and any of them can be rolled back at any time if a particular line of code doesn't work out or a radical new direction needs to be taken. Or if you just get in over your head and need to start over. There is a great deal of utility in being able to go back to an older revision without causing any additional churn in the integration branch.

Creating a personal branch may be as simple as creating a new folder named for each developer, as shown in Figure 6-13.

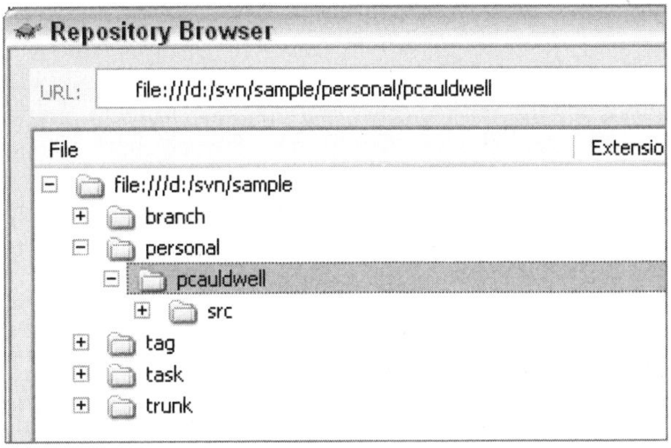

Figure 6-13

Once the source is copied into the new personal branch, it can be modified as often as is necessary, committed to, updated, and so on, without having any effect on the trunk. Once all the desired changes have been made in the personal branch, they can be merged into the trunk to constitute a single integration. The same scheme works in other source control systems using standard branching techniques.

Some SCC tools even support this concept as a first-class feature. In certain configurations of IBM Rational ClearCase, all check-ins are made locally in the working copy, and the "personal branch" is actually kept on the developer's hard drive. You can check in, check out, roll back, and so on, and it all occurs locally. At some point you then "integrate" up to the ClearCase server, which involves taking a diff of the tip in the working copy and merging that into the server's integration copy. That means that the copy on the server is always serving as the integration branch, and each developer's working copy is playing the part of the personal branch. This makes the process very clear, even using "integration" as a first-class part of the nomenclature.

In Microsoft's Visual Studio Team System, a developer can "shelve" his or her work, which in essence automatically creates a personal branch for that developer. However, you cannot commit multiple change sets to one "shelveset," so shelving a set of changes is a one-time operation that does not carry history or allow rollbacks. Shelving is most useful when you want to store a set of changes someplace that isn't just local to your hard drive, but don't want to risk breaking the integration build.

Subversion, as seen above, doesn't have any native notion of a personal branch, but because Subversion makes branching so simple and easy to organize, personal branches are trivial to create and manage. Subversion also makes it easy to see other user's personal branches, so work can be shared or reviewed without interfering with the integration branch.

However your SCC tools support them, personal branches allow developers to continue committing or rolling back changes without affecting the integration branch or the CI process.

Task Branches

Perhaps the most useful way to use branches to support a CI process is the *task branch*. Task branches represent a single branch for each integration. That integration might be equal to one task/backlog item/story, one spike solution, or one bug fix. Creating a separate branch for each integration makes it very easy to keep track of all the changes necessary to complete that integration, because looking at the history for the branch will reveal all the changes made on that branch.

Just as with personal branches, task branches provide a way of dealing with multiple commits that compose one integration, without having those commits affect the integration branch monitored by the CI server. In addition, task branches provide that extra history about what changes were necessary to complete each task. By batching up multiple commits into one merge operation, task branches provide a sort of mega-change-set when finally committed to the integration branch. If you commit all the changes from one task branch into the integration branch in one commit operation, the resulting change set should represent all the changes needed to complete the task.

Creating New Task Branches

In Subversion, creating a new task branch can be as simple as making yet another copy of your trunk folder. In this case, the new task branch is called task-bl102, for a backlog item numbered 102, as shown in Figure 6-14.

Naming your task branches after the tasks themselves provides not only a useful way of figuring out which branch is which, but also provides a link to external systems. If you are using a spreadsheet or tracking tool such as VersionOne to track SCRUM backlog items, you can use the numbers assigned to those backlog items as names for task branches. This gives you a direct correlation, albeit a manual one, between backlog tracking and source control tools. The same applies to defect-tracking numbers. If you use ClearQuest, for example, to track your defects, you might name a task branch task-cq7654 to denote the task associated with fixing ClearQuest defect #7654. Branch labels can provide additional semantics that you otherwise wouldn't get without an integrated toolset like the Rational Suite or Microsoft Team System.

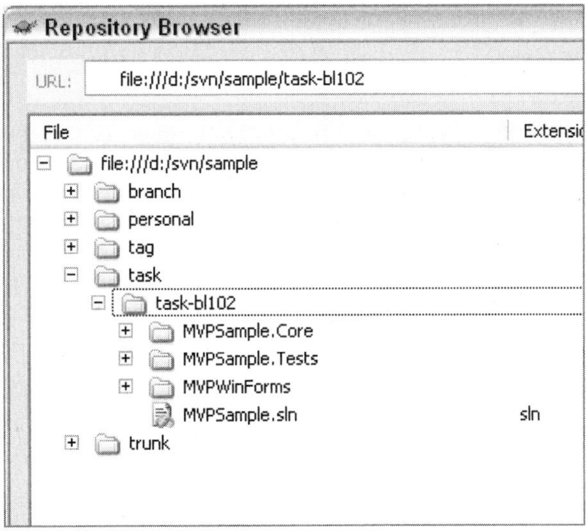

Figure 6-14

Once the task is complete, all the changes made on the task branch are merged back into the integration branch, preferably as a single change set. That way it is easy to later look up all of the changes that are associated with a given task. If you use comments when committing to the integration branch, such as "merging from task-bl102," then when someone comes back later, he or she will see the change set associated with that comment and understand that it represents all the changes needed to complete backlog item 102. Take full advantage of the added semantics you get from branch names to inject additional information into your SCC system that will prove useful later on.

Merging Branches

Merging is the act of applying changes made in one branch to another branch on which those changes have not yet been made. Task branches provide a simple example. You create a task branch to fix a defect, make all the changes to fix the defect, and commit those changes back to the task branch. Once you are satisfied that the changes are correct and complete, you must merge the changes made in the task branch back to the tip or integration branch. The way the merge works depends on which SCC system you are using. Each has its quirks, and each platform handles merges slightly differently. The basic principle remains the same, however. You compare a starting and ending revision to produce a set of diffs, and then apply those diffs to a working copy. Once the changes are made in the working copy, they can be committed to the integration branch, or whatever your working copy points to.

Merge conflicts occur when changes have been made in both versions being compared that cannot be reconciled automatically. If I create a branch based on a 1.0 release version, then make changes both to the 1.0 version and the branch, a merge conflict may be the result. Again, different tools treat merge conflicts slightly differently, so there is no definitive guide to dealing with them. See your SCC system's documentation for the best information. One thing that is constant across platforms is the necessity of having a good diff/merge tool. Some SCC platforms come with adequate or even good graphical diff/merge tools; others do not. Try out as many as you can until you find one that you like and that is easy to use. For resolving merge conflicts in particular, look for a three-pane solution that presents your local copy on one side, the latest copy in the repository on the other, and the merge result in the center. This is the best way of visualizing which changes were made where and what the resulting file will look like.

Using Labels to Simplify Merging

One thing you can do to make merging less complicated is to use lots of labels. You can label the original tree before branching and then the branch before merging. This makes it much easier to know which revisions to select as the starting and ending revisions for your merge. Before creating the new task branch task-bl102, the trunk folder is first copied to a tag called trunk-task-bl102-branchpoint. That tag signifies the point at which the task bl102 branch was created from the trunk. When all of the changes have been made to the task branch, it is tagged with task-bl102-trunk-mergepoint0 to signify the point at which task bl102 is to be merged back into the trunk. These two folders are shown in Figure 6-15.

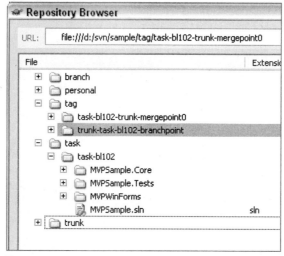

Figure 6-15

These two tags can then be used when the time comes to merge. In TortoiseSVN, you would specify the resulting merge as shown in Figure 6-16.

The alternative to using the tags is to try to remember or to otherwise track the starting and ending revisions for the branch, and use those revision numbers for the merge process. The tags provide an easy way of adding semantics that help keep track of which revision was used to create a branch, and which revision was used to merge that branch's changes back to the trunk.

A very similar scheme can be used in CVS or other label-based SCC systems. Rather than copying folders as you would in Subversion, you apply labels to your various branches that look much like the tags previously shown in Figure 6-15.

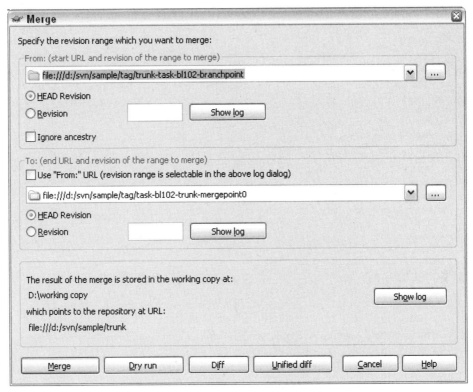

Figure 6-16

Summary

Source code control plays a vital role in any development process, and particularly in a process following the Continuous Integration model. There are many different SCC platforms to choose from, and you should carefully describe your organization's requirements and expectations before choosing a source code control system that meets those requirements.

Once your SCC system is in place, take the maximum advantage of it by organizing your source code in ways that make it easier to use with source control, and by taking full advantage of branching. Branching can provide much-needed organization to your source control system. It can be used for separating work done on different versions or done to accomplish specific tasks, and isolate that work from the integration branch used by your Continuous Integration server. You can also use branching to provide additional semantic data that otherwise would not be represented in your source control system, such as links to external systems or relationships between different branches.

Because SCC plays such a vital role in a CI process, it is important that you and your team understand how to use the system properly and how to use it to best advantage to get your jobs done.

7

Static Analysis

Put simply, static analysis means "stuff you can learn about your code without running it." There is a whole group of other tools — profilers, debuggers, memory mappers, code coverage analyzers, and the like — that fall under the heading of dynamic analysis. They all require that your code be running to do their work. Static analysis tools look at the code itself, either using reflection in languages capable of using it or by reading source files much as a compiler would.

Using Static Analysis Tools

Static analysis tools can provide you with a great deal of information about your code, such as how well you are following style or interface guidelines, how complex your code is, how loosely or tightly coupled your libraries are, and how similar various blocks of code might be. That knowledge comes at a cost, however. It is easy to gather more information than you know what to do with using such tools. To make the best use of static analysis tools takes time and study — time to get to know how to use the tools properly and study to figure out what the information they provide you really means to you and your team.

While static analysis tools can prove quite valuable in the right hands, they can also pose some risks. Results can easily be misinterpreted if you aren't familiar enough with what they mean. There is also a danger of "coding to the numbers," or changing your code to make metrics look more favorable without adding any real value. In addition, sometimes tools produce "false positive" messages (or false negative messages), which take time and good judgment to sort out.

Different static analysis tools provide different sorts of information about your code. Some look at metrics like the complexity of your code or how tightly coupled your various libraries are. Tools such as these provide information that can be vital in deciding which parts of your application need the most testing or how making changes to one part of your application will affect the rest.

NDepend

One excellent example of such a tool from the .NET world is NDepend (www.ndepend.com) written by Patrick Smacchia. NDepend measures things like the following:

- ❏ **Cyclomatic complexity** — The number of possible decision points that exist in a given method. Branching statements like `if`, `case`, `while`, and `for` (in C#) all add to the cyclomatic complexity metric. The higher a method's cyclomatic complexity, the harder it is to adequately test and to maintain. High cyclomatic complexity often points out code that needs to be refactored.

- ❏ **Afferent coupling** — The number of types outside one assembly (library) that depend on types inside that assembly. If a library has high afferent coupling, making changes to that library can have a large impact on other libraries.

- ❏ **Efferent coupling** — The number of types from other libraries that a type in one library depends upon. A library with high efferent coupling tends to be fragile because it has a wide range of dependencies that could change.

- ❏ **Instability** — A metric derived from coupling that indicates how likely a library is to be affected by changes elsewhere.

- ❏ **Abstractness** — The ratio of concrete to abstract types in any given library.

These are just a few of the metrics that tools such as NDepend can measure. There is a great deal to be learned about how such metrics should be applied and what they really mean at a practical level. Some of them are much easier to understand than others. Cyclomatic complexity (CC), for example, is a fairly simple metric that is readily understood by most developers. The more possible paths there are through any particular method, the harder it is to understand, to test, and to maintain. A formal CC metric just quantifies what most developers understand intuitively, and gives you a basis for comparison. To make your application more testable and less prone to maintenance problems, run some CC metrics and start your refactoring efforts with the most complex method. Testers also benefit from looking at CC numbers because they provide a sense of where to focus testing efforts. When combined with code coverage results, CC metrics should point to hot spots where more unit testing is required. If you have a particular piece of code with high cyclomatic complexity and low code coverage, you are asking for trouble. That's the first place to start when adding extra unit tests.

Unlike cyclomatic complexity, which is a fairly "tactical" metric, many of the other metrics reported by static analysis tools have a more strategic scope. Looking at metrics like afferent versus efferent coupling doesn't usually lead to obvious refactorings or point to specific "trouble spots." Such metrics are more likely to point to a strategic direction such as splitting up or combining libraries, or introducing more interfaces to decrease coupling. Those tend to be goals that take weeks to achieve, rather than the kind of quick refactorings or test writing that CC numbers point to.

NDepend also includes a built-in query language that enables you to write your own rules about what you think is important to measure on your particular project. That is especially useful if you want to integrate NDepend into a regular build process because it is easy to flag problems.

The danger with any static analysis tool is getting too much information. It takes time and research to learn to make proper sense of the metrics and decide what to do with the information you have obtained. The tools themselves can be quite "dense." When faced with the visual part of the NDepend tool, for example, experienced developers may run in terror. Figure 7-1 shows the NDepend user interface.

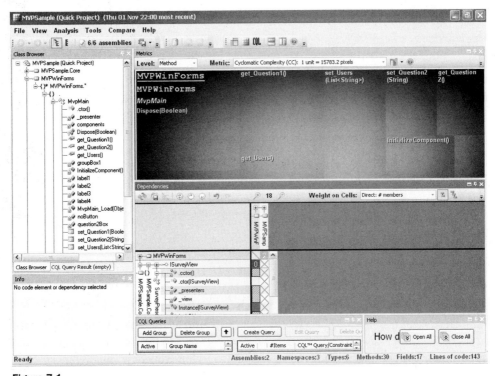

Figure 7-1

The interface is very informationally dense. If you know what you are looking at, there is a huge amount of information presented here in a very accessible way. If you don't know what you are looking at, it can appear confusing or overwhelming to the point that many people might just shut it down and never look back. That has much less to do with the tool (which is fantastically useful) than with the nature of the data it presents. One of the hardest aspects of using static analysis tools can be deciding who should use the tools and how often.

FxCop

There are other tools that measure things like interface guidelines, parameter validation, and other "best practices" issues. One such example from the .NET world is FxCop, a tool freely available from Microsoft. FxCop comes with an extensive set of built-in rules and provides interfaces for writing custom rules as well. Some of the built-in rules report issues like public members that have misspelled names, code that is not properly localizable due to improper string handling or formatting, and public methods that do not properly validate their input parameters. Figure 7-2 shows an FxCop run on a very simple assembly.

As with many of the other static analysis tools, the biggest danger in using FxCop is too much information. It takes time to learn what all of the rules mean, why they might or might not be important to your projects, and what the best way to fix them is. Figure 7-3 shows an example message with description from FxCop.

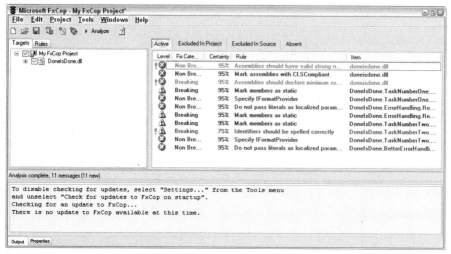

Figure 7-2

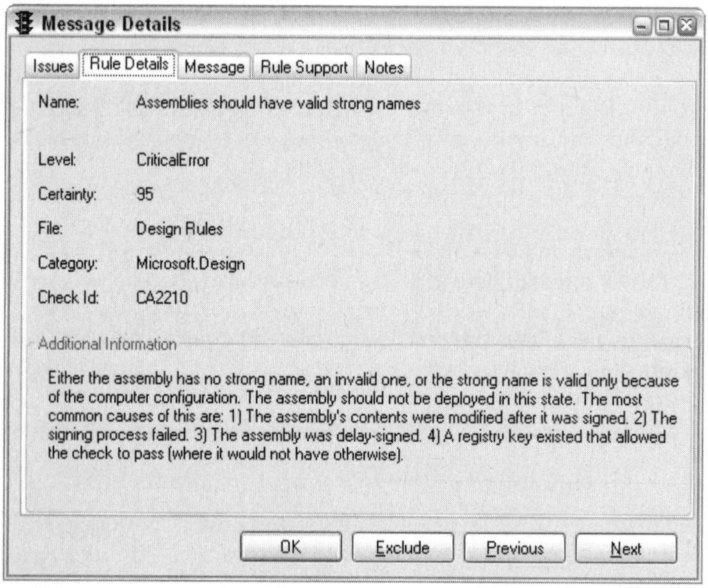

Figure 7-3

FxCop comes with pretty good documentation, and tends to provide reasonable descriptions of and solutions to most of its built-in rules. It still takes time to wade through them and decide whether they are really important. In the example in Figure 7-2, only 11 messages were produced, ranging from "critical" to "warning" in their severity. On even a moderately sized .NET project, a first-time run of FxCop might report messages numbering well into the thousands. That can be overwhelming for whoever is assigned to dealing with those messages, many of which tend to be false positives that require time to weed out.

Simian

Another interesting static analysis tool is Simian (http://redhillconsulting.com.au/products/simian), which analyzes similarities between different sets of source files. Why is that interesting? Because it provides an automated way to detect areas of code duplication by reporting similarities between different pieces of source code. It might indicate "copy-and-paste" reuse (code that is copied from one place and pasted somewhere else). If changes need to be made to the original block of code, they will also need to be made in all the places where that code was copied, which can be difficult to track down. It would be preferable to replace such copy-and-paste reuse with binary reuse (using code from a common assembly rather than copying it) by separating such repetitive code into new methods that can be called from multiple places, thus reducing maintenance problems. Simian runs on an impressive array of language files, including Java, C#, C, C + + , COBOL, Ruby, JSP, ASP, HTML, XML, and Visual Basic, which makes it useful across a large percentage of projects. In its current form, Simian spits out textual reports that are a little tedious to deal with but not difficult to understand.

These are just a few examples of common .NET tools. Similar tools are available for just about any language platform or OS and many, if not most, of the metrics and concepts apply to any code.

Who Benefits from Static Analysis?

Who will benefit from static analysis depends on what kind of data is gathered and the tools used. Choosing who should see what data is, I believe, an instrumental part of using such tools. Again, the biggest risk to introducing these tools is information overload, so making sure that the right level of information gets to the right people is an important part of their use.

Some metrics such as cyclomatic complexity can be useful to every developer. CC metrics can be distributed to your whole team. Every coder can benefit from understanding where code may be too complicated so that it can be simplified either right away or as time allows. If you are following a red/green/refactor style of Test-Driven Development (TDD), running a CC report after making your tests pass can point to the best places for refactoring. Correlating cyclomatic complexity with code coverage is a great way to target your unit-testing efforts.

For some of the more obscure metrics, however, such a wide distribution may not be a good idea. Trying to get every member of your team to understand the difference between afferent and efferent coupling, and training them to know what to do about either of them may be more trouble than it is worth. The more widely you distribute those kinds of metrics, the more likely that developers will start coding to the metrics, or changing code just to make the numbers change without a proper understanding of why or what they are doing.

Such relatively abstract metrics are more important to an architect or designer than to the rest of the team. Measuring instability or abstractness provides insight into how your application as a whole is laid out, and how changing some pieces will affect others. That data helps to drive strategic rather than tactical decisions about where your application is going in the longer term. Even for an architect, gathering those metrics is only worthwhile if he or she takes the time to learn what they mean and what to do about them.

FxCop-style coding issues are certainly relevant to every developer, but you have to be careful about how you introduce such a tool and how it fits into your development process. It often falls to a technical lead or architect to decide which rules are important for the organization, and which additional custom rules may be worth writing to get the maximum value from such a tool. You don't want to overwhelm developers with too many warnings, especially ones that aren't very important for your particular project. For example, if your interfaces are filled with trade names, having FxCop report them all as misspelled may not represent the best use of your resources. To prevent such problems, you can either turn off whole rules or establish exceptions so that the same problems won't be reported over and over again.

Some teams establish very formal policies around such exceptions, defining a finite set of acceptable rules to create exceptions for, as well as a fixed set of reasons for granting such exceptions. The advantage to such rules is that they help limit the number of exceptions by forcing anyone setting an exception to think about whether it is really an exceptional case and if he or she has an appropriate reason for ignoring the error or warning. If you want to set up such rules, make sure that they are simple and easy to understand so that they will be easy for developers to comply with them. There is no point in establishing rules too complicated for anyone to follow or to use effectively.

The biggest benefit to exposing the whole team to FxCop style reports is that it encourages group learning and continuous improvement. Rather than being forced to deal with errors and warnings in FxCop reports, developers will start to fall into the habit of doing things the right way the first time, which makes everyone's job easier and everyone's code better. This is particularly true for topics such as localization. FxCop has a complex set of rules that catch potential problems for localization, such as string literals in code, not passing format providers to string formatting methods, improper date and currency formatting, and other issues that can become problems when translating your software into another language. Many developers are not familiar with these concerns, and FxCop provides not only a way to flag issues, but also a way for your team to learn and become familiar with such rules, and to learn how to avoid localization problems in the future.

A tool such as Simian can provide both tactical and strategic value. There is value for every developer in knowing that there is code duplication going on related to their code so that it can be factored out and reused properly. There is additional value for a team leader in knowing how much duplication is going on and whether it is being addressed. If code is regularly being duplicated by copy-and-paste reuse, perhaps your team needs some instruction in constructing reusable libraries, or perhaps they just aren't communicating well enough, and multiple developers are writing the same code independently to solve the same problem. Either way, work is being done that is counterproductive for the team as a whole.

Getting the right metrics in front of the wrong people can cause confusion and wasted work, so be careful about which things you measure and whom you tell about them.

How to Integrate Static Analysis into Your Process

A number of static analysis tools (and all of the specific ones discussed previously) are built to be integrated into an automated build process. However, you need to think carefully before you take that step. To integrate a tool like NDepend into a Continuous Integration build process, you must be cautious about which metrics you include. Will a report from every build on afferent versus efferent coupling be useful? Or confusing? Is every member of the team likely to benefit from the information? Will you fail the build if afferent coupling gets too high? Probably not.

Other metrics, such as cyclomatic complexity or percentage of comments, might make more sense to include as part of a CI build process. It is perfectly reasonable to set a threshold for cyclomatic complexity and fail the build if that threshold is exceeded. You want the whole team to be alerted if a method with a CC number of 50 suddenly shows up — that is something that is worth reporting and failing the build on, in order to draw immediate attention to it and get it fixed. The same might be true of percentage of comments. That is a measure of how many lines of comments your application contains in relation to the total number of lines. If that number suddenly declines, it means that your developers have stopped commenting their code. Better to know about it right away and get it fixed.

Another thing that can form a useful part of a CI build report is an NDepend-generated graph that shows the ratio of abstractness to instability (see Figure 7-4).

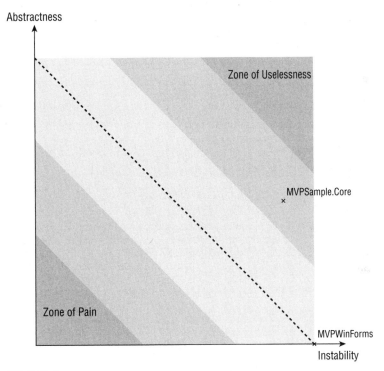

Figure 7-4

In one corner of the graph lies the Zone of Pain, which indicates libraries that are fragile and easily broken by changes in other components. In the opposite corner lies the Zone of Uselessness, which indicates libraries that are not used and so should not be maintained. A library consisting entirely of abstract base classes from which nothing actually derives would fall squarely in the zone of uselessness. The goal is to have all of your libraries lie along the line between the two danger zones. As part of a continuous build, the graph is more useful as a measure of change over time than it is at any given instant. It is very instructive to learn if your libraries are moving closer to or farther from that median line as your project progresses.

Metrics can play an important part in a CI build process as long as you pick the right metrics to display and set your thresholds to reflect your goals for the project. Once those goals are set, make sure that every developer on the team is aware of them and the metrics that measure progress against those goals.

Code-cleanliness tools like FxCop make a useful addition to a CI build process, as long as you start from the beginning of the project. It is very difficult to introduce FxCop late in the process and have developers suddenly faced with 3,000–4,000 messages that they are supposed to correct. Anything more than a few hundred messages is likely to just be ignored, negating the usefulness of the tool. Start early in your development cycle, and get all of the initial messages cleaned up — either fixed or added to your FxCop project as exceptions. Once that is done, you can start failing the build when new messages appear because that means that developers are not following the "done is done" guidelines by cleaning up errors and warnings before committing their tasks to the source control repository. If you are going to add FxCop to your build process at all, make it fail the build. Simply presenting a report full of errors with every build only encourages people to ignore them.

FxCop is very easy to integrate into a continuous build process because it outputs an XML report format that can readily be read by other applications or styled into something human readable. Here's an example FxCop report:

```xml
<?xml version="1.0" encoding="utf-8"?>
<?xml-stylesheet type="text/xsl"
href="http://www.gotdotnet.com/team/fxcop//xsl/1.35/FxCopReport.xsl"?>
<FxCopReport Version="1.35">
 <Targets>
  <Target Name="$(ProjectDir)/Visual Studio
2005/Projects/DoneIsDone/DoneIsDone/bin/Debug/DoneIsDone.dll">
   <Modules>
    <Module Name="doneisdone.dll">
     <Messages>
      <Message TypeName="AssembliesShouldDeclareMinimumSecurity"
Category="Microsoft.Usage" CheckId="CA2209" Status="Active"
Created="2007-11-02 05:52:54Z" FixCategory="Breaking">
       <Issue Certainty="95" Level="CriticalError">No valid permission
requests were found for assembly 'DoneIsDone'. You should always specify
the minimum security permissions using SecurityAction.RequestMinimum.</Issue>
      </Message>
      <Message TypeName="AssembliesShouldHaveValidStrongNames"
Category="Microsoft.Design" CheckId="CA2210" Status="Active"
Created="2007-11-02 05:52:54Z" FixCategory="NonBreaking">
       <Issue Name="NoStrongName" Certainty="95"
Level="CriticalError">Sign 'DoneIsDone' with a strong name key.</Issue>
      </Message>
      <Message TypeName="MarkAssembliesWithClsCompliant"
Category="Microsoft.Design" CheckId="CA1014" Status="Active"
Created="2007-11-02 05:52:54Z" FixCategory="NonBreaking">
       <Issue Name="NoAttr" Certainty="95" Level="Error">'DoneIsDone' should
be marked with CLSCompliantAttribute and its value should be true.</Issue>
      </Message>
     </Messages>
     <Namespaces>
      <Namespace Name="DoneIsDone">
       <Types>
```

```
        <Type Name="BetterErrorHandling" Kind="Class" ↵
Accessibility="Public" ExternallyVisible="True">
        <Members>
          <Member Name="ReadFile(System.String):System.String" ↵
Kind="Method" Static="False" Accessibility="Public" ExternallyVisible="True">
            <Messages>
            <Message ↵
Id="System.ArgumentException.#ctor(System.String,System.String)" ↵
TypeName="DoNotPassLiteralsAsLocalizedParameters" ↵
Category="Microsoft.Globalization" CheckId="CA1303" Status="Active" ↵
Created="2007-11-02 05:52:54Z" FixCategory="NonBreaking">
              <Issue Certainty="95" Level="Error" Path="C:\Documents and ↵
Settings\Patrick\My Documents\Visual Studio 2005\Projects\DoneIsDone\↵
DoneIsDone" File="ErrorHandling.cs" Line="93">BetterErrorHandling.ReadFile↵
(String):String passes a literal as parameter 1 of a call to ↵
ArgumentException.ArgumentException(String, String). Retrieve the following ↵
string argument from a resource table instead: 'You must pass a valid file ↵
path.'</Issue>
            </Message>
            </Messages>
          </Member>
        </Members>
        </Type>
...
</FxCopReport>
```

These XML reports contain all the information needed to report and describe how to fix each issue. Popular CI platform CruiseControl.NET comes with built-in style sheets for FxCop output to include them in Cruise Control's build reports. The latest versions of Cruise Control also include style sheets for Simian reports, so those can also be added to continuous build reports.

Summary

Static analysis tools can be an important tool for improving the quality of your code. They can help you identify hot spots in the code that need more testing or refactoring, or help an architect determine strategic changes that need to be made across the entire product.

The biggest cost of such tools comes in the form of the additional time and training needed to bring the team up to speed on what the reports mean and how issues they bring to light should be dealt with. If the wrong metrics are published or too much information is added to the build process by analysis tools, the information will cause more problems than it solves. It will lead to time wasted on chasing the wrong things, or writing code just to change the results of the metrics being measured. Take every metric with a grain of salt, and apply some real effort to making sure that you get the right ones to the right people.

Any static analysis tools should be integrated into your process as early as feasible so that problems they uncover can be fixed a small number at a time, and new problems will be obvious and not get lost in the noise of too many errors going unaddressed. Pick carefully which metrics you want to report to the whole team as part of a CI build, and make sure that the ones you choose are relevant to everyone and can be addressed by every member of the team.

Part III
Code Construction

8

Contract, Contract, Contract!

What does it mean for software to have a contract? There turns out to be no hard-and-fast answer to that question. It can mean something very formal in some situations. Some programming languages such as Eiffel have raised the notion of a software contract to the level of a first-class language feature (meaning that the ability to define a complete contract is part of the language). In other languages, contracts have to be defined in less formal ways. Is it possible to write software without a contract? Not really. It is, however, possible to write software with a poorly defined or misunderstood contract.

In the simplest terms, having a contract means promising to do something. Software can have contracts that are explicit or implicit. The more explicit your contract is, the easier it will be for people who consume your software. Having an explicit contract means communicating in no uncertain terms what your software will do, and promising to do it. Implicit contracts are often defined by class/property/method names. Let's take a look at a `Calculator` class:

```
namespace ContractsInCSharp
{
    public class Calculator
    {
        public double Add(int op1, int op2)
        {
            return op1 + op2;
        }

        public double Divide(int divided, int divisor)
        {
            return divided / divisor;
        }
    }
}
```

In this case, the `Calculator` class establishes an implicit contract through naming. The name `Divide` implies a division operation, and since its arguments are named divided and divisor, you can assume that divided will be divided by divisor to establish the result. That implicit contract works because the English words used to name the method and its arguments have semantic meaning (to an English speaker) that you can understand. However, there is no programmatic way of establishing what that contract is. By looking at the code above for the `Divide` method, you can see the contract really goes deeper than that. Because of the way the method is implemented, the implicit contract extends to the fact that divisor must be non-zero. A divisor with a value of zero would result in a `DivideByZeroException`, which breaks the implicit contract that the `Divide` method will return a result that is a double value. By throwing an exception, the implicit contract is broken because no result is returned.

Naming is an important part of making your contract clear. I believe that the best way to make sure that your naming conventions support strong contracts is to think in terms of nouns and verbs when designing interfaces. This practice coincides well with the "domain driven design" approach, which focuses on real-world objects and processes when designing software. If you create method names that are verbs, your contract will be much clearer to callers. For instance, if you have a method named `Transfer` in a banking application, which takes two account numbers and an amount as parameters, it isn't too much of a leap (at least for an English speaker) to assume that the method will transfer money from one account to another. Because the method name is a descriptive verb, it makes the pre- and postconditions the author expected much clearer.

This is the part of establishing a software contract that is often overlooked and misunderstood. A contract runs two ways. In a real legal contract, one party agrees to perform a service or provide some goods, and the other party agrees to pay or trade for those goods or services. In a software contract, the caller has to pay for the services received by passing the correct arguments and establishing any required preconditions. Passing a non-zero divisor is the part of the contract that the caller must adhere to if the `Divide` method is to perform its service correctly. Unfortunately, in most programming languages, those expectations are difficult to communicate to the caller. Traditionally, that has meant relying on written documentation that describes the necessary preconditions or argument formats that the software contract is expecting. Additionally, written documentation about error messages lets the caller know in what way the implied contract has been violated.

Even in a language like C#, which does not have a first-class notion of contract in the Eiffel sense, you can both make the contract clearer and take steps to enforce that contract. There are a variety of ways to make the contract clearer. One way is to use comments:

```
/// <summary>
/// Divides the first argument by the second.
/// </summary>
/// <param name="divided">The argument to be divided.</param>
/// <param name="divisor">The divisor to divide the first argument by.
Must be non-zero.</param>
/// <returns>The number of times divided is divisible by the divisor.</returns>
/// <exception cref="DivideByZeroException">divisor is zero</exception>
public double Divide(int divided, int divisor)
{
    return divided / divisor;
}
```

Because the C# compiler carries such comments around in metadata, the documentation above will stick with the method and be accessible to consumers. When formatted into user-readable documentation, the preceding comment results in documentation like that shown in Figure 8-1.

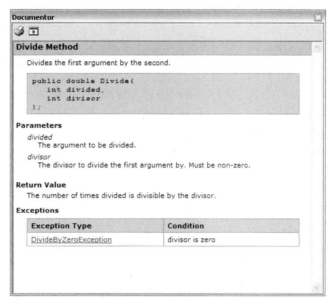

Figure 8-1

Another good way to communicate contracts to other members of your organization is through unit tests. A test can make a software contract more explicit be demonstrating the semantics that you expect.

```
[Test]
[ExpectedException(typeof(DivideByZeroException))]
public void DivideByZero()
{
    Calculator c = new Calculator();
    double d = c.Divide(1, 0);
}
```

This test makes it clear that the author of the `Divide` method expects an exception of type `DivideByZero Exception` to be thrown in the case of a zero divisor. This particular test is a bit tricky, because while it makes the author's intentions clearer, it also represents a codified violation of our implied contract. It implies that it is okay for `Divide` to throw an exception rather than return a result. We'll talk more about error handling in a separate chapter.

Unit tests can't communicate with customers, but for other developers in your organization, they can be a great learning tool and a good way for external users to understand all the semantics of your software contract. See Chapter 5, "Testing," for more information on expressing developer intent through unit tests.

At runtime, there are several ways of enforcing and communicating your contract to callers. One of those is the use of debug assertions. Assertions are often compiled out in production software, but in debug code, they provide a good way to enforce contracts in a way that will be helpful to anyone consuming your software.

```
public double DivideAndAssert(int divided, int divisor)
{
    Debug.Assert(divisor > 0, "divisor must be greater than zero");

    return divided / divisor;
}
```

This `Assert` will now make sure that the divisor is always greater than zero. If it isn't, the method will fail. In an automated unit test using `MbUnit`:

```
[Test]
public void DivideWithAssert()
{
    Calculator c = new Calculator();
    double d = c.DivideAndAssert(1, 0);
    Assert.Fail("Should have caused an Assert.");
}
```

The assertion produces the following result:

```
[failure] CalculatorTests.DivideWithAssert
TestCase 'CalculatorTests.DivideWithAssert' failed: divisor must be greater than zero
    MbUnit.Core.Exceptions.DebugFailException
    Message: divisor must be greater than zero
    Source: MbUnit.Framework
```

In the testing environment, `MbUnit` picks up on the assertion and turns it into a test failure. When code is running outside a debug environment, assertion failures often result in a modal dialog box, which the user must click on to proceed, that describes the nature of the assertion failure. Asserts communicate information about contracts at development time by causing obvious and traceable failures.

The assertion represents the first step toward making the implicit contract explicit. Asserts are really meant to express your intentions to consumers at design time, and no Asserts should be firing in production-ready code. That is why debug assertions are often compiled out of production code, as the assumption is that they are meant to catch model-level problems during development time. If you hit an assertion during development, this means that someone isn't clear enough on the (implicit or explicit) contract.

An even better solution for expressing and communicating your contract is to validate the input parameters explicitly:

```
public double DivideAndValidate(int divided, int divisor)
{
    if (divisor == 0)
        throw new ArgumentException("Divisor must be greater than zero",
"divisor");

    return divided / divisor;
}
```

This comes much closer to explicitly enforcing the contract. By validating input parameters and returning the appropriate exception class, the contract is enforced programmatically. If any caller passes a value of zero for the divisor, they will get concrete feedback that passing a zero breaks the contract. Such explicit parameter checking constitutes "defensive" programming. The method makes sure that all of its inputs are acceptable according to its understanding of the contract. If you are sure of your inputs before starting the real work, you won't be surprised by invalid values afterward. Throwing ArgumentException, or something similar, also advertises your intentions about the contract to callers in much the same way that debug assertions do.

This is a hotly debated topic. Many developers feel that it is overkill to always validate one's input parameters. They assert that it takes too long to write the code and that it represents a drain on system performance. Many argue that if you have proper unit testing, then there is never a reason to validate your input parameters. I disagree with all of those points. I don't think that it is overkill to properly communicate and establish your software's contract with callers. There are many tools available that will help you generate parameter-checking code, so it shouldn't be a drain on developer resources. As far as being a drain on performance, the reality of our business today is that processors are much cheaper than developers. If you can burn a few extra processor cycles to make sure that more bugs are found during development than after your product ships, the savings in developer time will far outweigh the processor time it takes to make sure that your parameters are valid. Finally, counting on unit tests to catch all possible contract violations works only if you are in total control of your software. In an organization that controls all access to its software, such as a company running a hosted web site, you might be able to write unit tests that represent all possible cases that are exercised by the real application. However, if any part of your software leaves your control, either through being sold to customers or by being used by another group in your organization, then you can't possibly write tests to cover all the cases that someone you've never met might throw at your code. Take the time to make your contract explicit by validating your arguments. It may seem like extra work now, but it will pay off.

Every method has requirements about the parameters passed to it, and checking input parameters is one of the best ways of establishing and communicating those requirements to callers.

In languages that support "programming by contract" (such as Eiffel), those requirements are known as preconditions. Our Divide method has a precondition that callers pass a non-zero divisor. Microsoft Research has produced a programming language called Spec#, which is a superset of C# that supports explicit programming by contract. In Spec#, our Divide method could be written as:

```
public static double Divide(int divided, int divisor)
    requires divisor > 0;
{
    return divided/divisor;
}
```

In Spec#, our precondition is expressed as a first-class language construct. By specifying preconditions as a part of the method signature, the contract is made much more explicit. It isn't necessary for the method body to check for a divisor greater than zero, because that precondition will be enforced by the runtime based on the requires statement. Not only do you not have to code defensively to make sure that the divisor is greater than zero, but the requirement is also made clear to the consumer of the method. The actual Microsoft Intermediate Language (MSIL) generated by the Spec# compiler looks like this:

```
[Requires("::>(i32,i32){$1,0}", Filename=@"C:↵
\ContractInSpec\ContractInSpec\Program.ssc", StartLine=0x20, ↵
```

```
    StartColumn=13, EndLine=0x20, EndColumn=0x18, SourceText="divisor > 0")]
    public static double Divide(int divided, int divisor)
    {
        try
        {
            if (divisor <= 0)
            {
                throw new RequiresException("Precondition 'divisor > 0' ↵
    violated from method 'Program.Divide(System.Int32,System.Int32)'");
            }
        }
        catch (ContractMarkerException)
        {
            throw;
        }
        double return value = divided / divisor;
        double SS$Display Return Local = return value;
        return return value;
    }
```

The [Requires] attribute is the .NET way of attaching additional metadata to an operation that can be used at runtime to influence behavior. In this case, it tells the Spec# runtime that the method has a precondition that the runtime must enforce. Just like with debug assertions or parameter validation, the exact nature of the Divide method's preconditions have been spelled out in code rather than in documentation.

Other "programming by contract" languages have similar constructs by which methods can announce their expectations (preconditions) and their deliverables (postconditions). With the pre- and postconditions spelled out in code rather than in documentation, it becomes very easy to write tests and to rely on parameter validation provided at the language level. There are "design by contract" extensions for many programming environments that provide services similar to those that Spec# adds to C#. There are extensions for Java, JavaScript, Ruby, Python, and a number of others that can bring programming by contract to your language of choice. If you are interested in enforcing contracts at the runtime level, it is worth the time it takes to investigate the available options. Contracts declared at design time mean more explicit contracts, fewer defects, and less time spent chasing problems during testing.

If you are not using a design by contract–capable language or extension, it is still possible to be more explicit about your contracts; you just have to do the work yourself rather than relying on declarative information processed at runtime. You can make use of good documentation, good naming conventions, and debug assertions and parameter checking to make sure that your contract is clear and understood by developers using your software.

Public Interfaces

One common way of codifying a contract that is used in many programming environments is the interface. There are many ways of defining an interface, depending on what language you are using, but the concept is common among many. An interface serves to group together a set of methods with specific signatures as a unit that can be implemented by different concrete pieces of code. For example:

```
public interface IHtmlFormatable
{
    void FormatAsHtml(HtmlTextWriter writer);
}
```

In this case, any object that implements the IHtmlFormatable interface must provide a FormatAsHtml method. The object agrees to abide by the contract that the interface establishes. The interface definition doesn't make any requirements for how the method is implemented as long as it fulfills the contract. The following code demonstrates a BankTransfer class that can implement IHtmlFormattable for display purposes:

```
public class BankTransfer : IHtmlFormatable
{
    private string toAccount;
    private string fromAccount;
    private decimal amount;

    public string ToAccount
    {
        get
        {
            return toAccount;
        }
        set
        {
            toAccount = value;
        }
    }

    public string FromAccount
    {
        ...
    }

    public decimal Amount
    {
        ...
    }

    #region IHtmlFormatable Members

    public void FormatAsHtml(HtmlTextWriter writer)
    {
        writer.RenderBeginTag("table");
        writer.RenderBeginTag("tr");
        writer.RenderBeginTag("td");
        writer.Write("Account to transfer from: {0}", fromAccount);
        writer.RenderEndTag();//td
        writer.RenderBeginTag("td");
        writer.Write("Account to transfer to: {0}", toAccount);
        writer.RenderEndTag();//td
        writer.RenderBeginTag("td");
```

```
            writer.Write("Amount of transfer: {0}", amount);
            writer.RenderEndTag();//td
            writer.RenderEndTag();//tr
            writer.RenderEndTag();//table
        }

    #endregion
    }
```

The BankTransfer class promises to be formatable as HTML. Such an interface could come in quite handy when building a web site, since any object could implement this interface, and the developers building the web site would be able to rely on each such object to format itself as HTML. Not only is the interface a promise to behave in a certain way, but in most languages that support interfaces as a first-class construct, the interface is also a marker that can be tested for. If the web site designer needed to work with an unfamiliar object, that object can be tested for the presence of the IHtmlFormatable interface. If it is present, then certain behavior is expected.

At the same time, this example points out one of the difficulties of relying on interfaces as the sole means of establishing a contract. Implementing an interface is like having a driver's license. If a person has a driver's license, it doesn't mean that they drive well; it doesn't imply anything about the way they drive. All the license represents is the contract between the individual and the licensing authority. The person holding the license agrees to follow the rules of the road, and in return the licensing authority grants them the right to operate a motor vehicle. As you know, there are plenty of examples on the road of people who have problems fulfilling that contract in the way you might expect.

In the example of the IHtmlFormatable interface, all the implementer is agreeing to is that they will format themselves as HTML. What does that really mean, though? There are a hundred different ways that the BankTransfer object could describe itself in HTML. In the example, I chose to use a table and some simple formatting so that it would come out like this:

```
<table>
    <tr>
            <td>Account to transfer from: 1234</td>
            <td>Account to transfer to: 5678</td>
             <td>Amount of transfer: 99.95</td>
    </tr>
</table>
```

Is that the HTML the caller would expect? Is it the HTML they want? In this case, the contract implied by the name of the interface and the method don't provide you with enough information to make sure that just by writing out "some" HTML you are meeting the expectations of the designer of the interface or the caller implementing the method.

An interface definition by itself is often not enough to express all the details that an implementer needs to know about the semantics of the interface. Some of the techniques previously described, such as parameter validation, won't help in this case either. As long as the writer object isn't null, there is nothing you can communicate to the client that can be expressed in code about what the HTML produced will look like. The only solution is to resort to out-of-band methods, such as documentation or training, to make sure that everyone is clear on the semantics. It might turn out that generating a formatted table is exactly what is expected of the FormatAsHtml method, in which case callers should expect a formatted table from every implementer of that interface. To be more explicit about the interface, you could add additional methods that get to the point better when describing what they will do.

```
public interface IHtmlFormatable
{
    void FormatWithTable(HtmlTextWriter writer);
    void FormatWithSpans(HtmlTextWriter writer);
    void FormatWithDivs(HtmlTextWriter writer);
}
```

That still doesn't tell us exactly what to expect, but it comes much closer. Given the vagaries of HTML, it is still not entirely clear what HTML you'll get back, but at least the consumer can get a better idea of what the author of the interface intended. The trick of designing good interfaces, then, has a lot to do with coming up with ways to express the semantics of the interface rather than just the inputs and outputs. Sometimes the only way to do that effectively is through documentation, but naming conventions and careful consideration about structure can go a long way toward ameliorating the problem.

One of the most important things to keep in mind about interfaces is that even if you are not using whatever formal construct your language has for interfaces you are still defining a contract that you agree to support. In short, every publicly accessible field, property, or method that you expose becomes a part of your interface. We'll look at this issue in more detail in Chapter 9, "Limiting Dependencies," but for now remember that everything you expose to the outside world is really a part of the contract that you are advertising. If you don't want those things to be included in the contract that you expose to consumers, then find a way of making them inaccessible to callers. As soon as they are available to callers once, you will have to support them as a part of your interface indefinitely.

Data Contracts

Contracts in software can define things besides the interface presented to outside callers. Using well-defined contracts can also make working with databases or other storage mediums much easier and more transparent for developers. Not every developer is familiar with SQL, and even if they are, they may not be familiar with formal database design principles. When developers with this type of skill set design databases, they may not define them in the most efficient manner from a database perspective. One way to solve that problem is with data contracts. Decide what it is that needs to be persisted from the application's perspective, and make that into a data contract.

In the same way that interface does not dictate implementation, the data that an application needs to store does not dictate a specific database layout. Application developers can define their data contracts, and database designers or DBAs can dictate how that data gets stored in a database. That leaves app developers free to worry about application design without worrying about database storage, and it leaves DBAs free to optimize database storage for maximum performance, reliability, or disaster recovery.

Consider a typical order entry or eCommerce system. The application needs to be able to store records of customer orders. In C#, that data might look like this:

```
namespace ContractsInCSharp
{
    public class CustomerOrder
    {
```

```
        public Customer Customer;
        public Address ShippingAddress;
        public Address BillingAddress;
        public int OrderNumber;
        public decimal OrderTotal;
        public OrderItem[] OrderDetails;
    }

    public class Customer
    {
        public string FirstName;
        public string LastName;
        public string MiddleInitial;
        public Gender Gender;
    }

    public enum Gender
    {
        Female,
        Male
    }

    public class Address
    {
        public string Line1;
        public string Line2;
        public string City;
        public string State;
        public string Zip;
    }

    public class OrderItem
    {
        public string SKU;
        public int Quantity;
    }
}
```

This is the way an application developer would want to think about the order. Everything is in one place, and the order can be created and saved to the database as a unit, which is the way it is conceptualized in the commerce application. That data structure can be coupled with an interface for storing and retrieving those order objects.

```
    public interface OrderStore
    {
        void Save(CustomerOrder order);
        CustomerOrder GetOrderById(int orderId);
        CustomerOrder[] GetOrdersForCustomer(Customer customer);
        CustomerOrder[] GetOrdersForItem(OrderItem item);
    }
```

There are a number of ways of storing this data in a database and a number of factors that influence which storage format you might choose. It could be very flat, like the simple database layout shown in Figure 8-2.

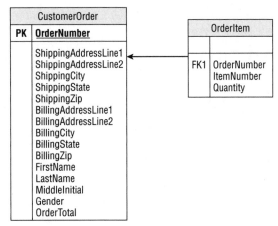

Figure 8-2

Such a structure might be perfectly appropriate in a simple, low-volume system with limited reporting needs. It is well optimized for reading orders, which might be the most common use of the system. On the other hand, it might be laid out in a more normalized fashion, as shown in Figure 8-3.

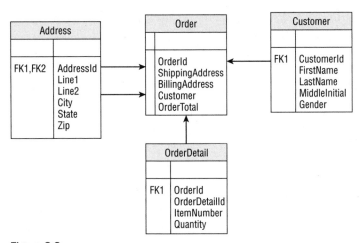

Figure 8-3

In the context of a broader system, it may be important to normalize the order data to work with the rest of the database with minimal repetition of data. If the data is normalized like this, the one thing you absolutely don't want is for the application developer to need to know about the normalization, or the relationships between tables. It is not uncommon for a database design such as the one above to lead to an interface that looks like this:

```
public interface NormalizedOrderStore
{
    int SaveCustomer(Customer customer);
    int SaveAddress(Address address);
```

```
        void SaveOrder(int customerId, int addressId, CustomerOrder order);
        int GetCustomerByName(string name);
        int[] GetOrdersForCustomer(int customerId);
        CustomerOrder GetOrder(int orderId);
    }
```

Such an interface essentially makes the caller responsible for properly maintaining the foreign key relationships in the database. That directly exposes the details of the database design to the application developer. Those details are interesting and important to a database designer or DBA, but they should not be in any way important to an application developer. What the application developer cares about is the data contract.

Application developers fundamentally deal with entities and should be able to do so without regard to how or in what format those entities are stored. The application doesn't care about the storage format, or at least it should not. Entities can be mapped to database objects in a variety of ways, freeing the DBA to modify how data is stored and freeing the app developer from having to understand the details of same.

There have been numerous attempts throughout the industry to make this process of mapping entities to databases easier, from object databases such as POET to entity mapping schemes like Java Entity Beans or the forthcoming Microsoft Entity Data Framework project to any number of object-relational mapping systems like Hibernate, to the Active Record pattern favored by Ruby on Rails. Any of those schemes represent data contracts in one form or another. How you choose to map data contracts to storage is up to you. It is a very complicated subject and has been the center of raging debate (Ted Neward famously described object-relational mapping as "our Vietnam") for years and will continue to be just as contentious for years to come.

What is important is establishing the contract. Whether you choose to use one of the aforementioned schemes or you write your data-storage classes by hand, the important part is establishing the contracts, and separating the theoretical notion of what data needs to be stored and how it needs to be saved and retrieved from what the underlying data store looks like.

Just as an outwardly facing software contract allows you to commit to interface without implementation, so, too, does a data contract allow you to commit to data types without storage layout.

Summary

By establishing firm software contracts before beginning development, you can commit to an interaction model and a set of features without regard to how those features are implemented. That leaves you, as the developer, free to change the underlying implementation as circumstances require without changing the interface presented to callers. If you are free to make those changes, it will be easier to develop your application, and easier to maintain it over time.

Spend time up front thinking about the interface you present to callers and the data-storage requirements of you application. Those interfaces become the contracts that you establish both with callers and with your data-storage mechanism.

9

Limiting Dependencies

The fewer dependencies the code you write has on other code, the easier it will be to change and the more resilient it will be when faced with changes elsewhere. If your code depends directly on code that you don't own, it is liable to be fragile and susceptible to breaking changes. That means that if you have a compile-time dependency on another package that you didn't write, you are in some respects at the mercy of whoever developed that package.

A compile-time dependency means a direct reference to a "foreign" library/package/assembly that makes it necessary for the compiler to have access to that foreign library. For example, to add some simple logging to a piece of .NET code, you might use the popular log4net library from the Apache Foundation. The following code shows a compile-time dependency on log4net.

```
public class Dependent
{
    private static readonly ILog log = LogManager.GetLogger(typeof(
Dependent));

    public int Add(int op1, int op2)
    {
        int result = op1 + op2;

        log.Debug(string.Format("Adding {0} + {1} = {2}", op1, op2, result));

        return result;
    }
}
```

This call to log4net's `ILog.Debug` method will log the message you compose to whatever log writers are configured currently. That might mean writing out the log message to the debug console, to a text file, or to a database. It is simple, easy to use, and provides a lot of functionality that you then don't have to write yourself.

However, you've now incurred a compile-time dependency on the log4net library. Why is that a problem? In this example, your exposure is obviously limited, but if you wrote similar logging code throughout a large application, it would represent a significant dependency. If anything changed in subsequent versions of log4net, or if it stopped working, or failed to provide some feature you discover you need later, you might have to make extensive changes to your code to fix or replace all of the calls to log4net's classes.

This is called compile-time dependency because the compiler has to have access to the log4net library to compile the code. It is different from a runtime dependency. A runtime dependency means that the code you are dependent on (log4net in this case) must be loaded into your process at runtime for your code to function correctly, even if it may not be required directly by the compiler.

What does this compile-time dependency mean for your code? It means that if anything changes with log4net's interface, your code will either break or require changes to be made to it. That makes your code more fragile and subject to outside influences, and thus harder to maintain. Plus, at some later time you might want to change logging libraries, or write your own if you can't find one with the right features. In the preceding example, you would have to change all of your code to use a new logging library.

As a general rule, your code should not have any compile-time dependencies on code that you don't own. That is a pretty tall order, but it is achievable. It is up to you to decide how far you want to take that axiom. You can at the very least substantially limit your exposure to external changes by using interfaces. You could, for instance, rewrite the previous example using an interface between your code and the code doing the logging:

```
public interface ILogger
{
    void Debug(string message);
}

public class MyLogger : ILogger
{
    private static readonly log4net.ILog log =
            log4net.LogManager.GetLogger("default");

    #region ILogger Members

    public void Debug(string message)
    {
        log.Debug(message);
    }

    #endregion
}
```

Then in your implementation class, you would call the interface as shown in the following example, not the log4net method(s) directly:

```
public class LessDependent
{
    public static readonly ILogger log = new MyLogger();

    public int Add(int op1, int op2)
    {
        int result = op1 + op2;
```

```
        log.Debug(string.Format("Adding {0} + {1} = {2}", op1, op2, result));

        return result;
    }

}
```

Now your code is less dependent on log4net. By creating a wrapper that uses the new ILogger inter-face, you are shielding your code from compile-time dependencies. Of course, the wrapper itself is still dependent on log4net, but that is a very limited exposure. If you decide to change to another logging implementation or a new version of log4net that has breaking changes, you only have to change the wrapper class and not the rest of your code.

Removing the logging code has a further advantage as well. If you want to use different logging mech-anisms in different parts of your application, you can create a second implementation of the ILogger interface that uses a different underlying logging system. Then you remove all knowledge of the actual logging implementation from the calling code by introducing configuration and dynamic loading. You'll see more about that technique, called dependency injection, later in this chapter.

A simple step you can take in that direction is to introduce a factory class, which is then the only class that needs to know about the actual implementation of the interface it returns. The clients of the factory only need to know that they will be provided with whatever implementation of the interface (ILogger in this case) they require. The following code shows a factory that creates ILogger instances.

```
public static class LoggerFactory
{
    public static ILogger Create()
    {
        return new MyLogger();
    }
}
```

With the introduction of the factory, it is also traditional to restrict access to the implementation class. The whole point of the factory is to encapsulate the creation of the class that implements the right interface. Therefore, if clients can construct their own implementation classes, they might unknowingly bypass necessary construction or configuration details.

In .NET, one of the easiest ways to disallow that is to make the constructor for the implementation class "internal," meaning that only other classes in the same assembly can construct one, as shown in the following example:

```
public class MyLogger : ILogger
{
    private static readonly log4net.ILog log =
        log4net.LogManager.GetLogger("default");

    internal MyLogger() { }

    #region ILogger Members

    public void Debug(string message)
```

```
    {
        log.Debug(message);
    }

    #endregion
}
```

There are a number of strategies for limiting access to implementation classes, and probably too many to go into in detail here. The strategies vary slightly, depending on what language you are working in, but not by very much. The underlying mechanisms are usually very simple.

The introduction of the factory class also provides a convenient way to deal with implementation classes that are singletons. If your implementation is a singleton, you want to make sure that at most one copy is created and the same instance is reused by multiple clients. This is typically done for objects that require a costly initialization. However, that is strictly an implementation detail and isn't important to the clients consuming your interface. Given that, the factory is the perfect place to deal with the construction of a singleton, because it hides the details of construction. There is some debate about the best way to construct a singleton in C#, but arguably the simplest is to use a static initializer. The following code shows a factory that returns a singleton MyLogger instance using such a static initializer.

```
public static class LoggerFactory
{
    private static readonly MyLogger logInstance = new MyLogger();

    public static ILogger Create()
    {
        return logInstance;
    }
}
```

If you put all of the interface definitions, along with their implementations and the factories that construct them, in the same assembly or library, you will greatly reduce the dependencies that clients must take on your implementation. Clients become dependent only on the interface definitions and factory classes, rather than on the implementation classes themselves and any other libraries that those implementations may be dependent upon.

Limiting Surface Area

Remember the "if you build it, they will come" baseball-field theory? The corollary in software development should be "if you make it public, they will take a dependency on it." A common problem associated with supporting software libraries has to do with customers using more of your code than you had intended. It is not unusual at all to look back on support problems with statements such as "I never thought anyone would do *that*."

The reality is that anything in your software libraries that you make public (in the programming language sense, that is, creatable by anyone) you will have to support forever. Even if you thought nobody would use a particular class, or if it were undocumented and you hoped nobody would notice it, you still have to support it indefinitely. Once a public interface is out in the wild, it becomes very difficult to change. This can be particularly troubling when it involves undocumented classes that you considered "internal." Most of the programming languages that are popular today involve bytecode of some kind, or interpreted script. Either way, anyone consuming your code basically has access to — or at least visibility into — your entire implementation. Those undocumented classes are still discoverable, and they may well end up getting used by customers.

Once those undocumented classes start being used by your customers, they become a full-fledged part of your public interface and have to be supported as such. It is very difficult (and unpopular) to have to go back to your customers with changes that break their software and tell them that you never expected them to use those classes that you just broke. That doesn't make their software any less broken.

What all this boils down to is that if you make something public, it had better be public. If you don't want customers to use "internal" classes or take dependencies on classes that they shouldn't, take the time to make sure that they cannot do those things. Then you won't have to explain those nasty breaking changes later.

There are, of course, limits to what you have to support. You don't have to support customers who use reflection to create nonpublic classes or call nonpublic methods. That represents "cheating," and everyone involved will understand it that way. Customers cannot expect you to support such behavior, and the consequences of such changes fall to the customer, not to you.

How you go about limiting your surface area will depend on what language you are working in. Most modern programming languages support some notion of accessibility. It is common practice to mark fields as private when you don't want other classes accessing them. The same is true of private methods that provide internal implementation. It takes a bit more planning to make sure that only classes that you want clients to use are publicly creatable. It takes even more planning to make sure that your classes cannot be inherited from, which can expose otherwise protected implementation details.

Some of this complexity comes from the fact that many modern languages express a certain openness that wasn't always the case. In the days of C++, you had to go out of your way to mark methods as virtual if you wanted anyone to be able to override them. In Java, on the other hand, methods are considered virtual by default unless marked otherwise. That turned the tables a bit, and meant that, where in the past you would have to take a concrete step to make your classes inheritable, now you have to take pains to prevent your classes being inherited from.

In C#, even if you don't explicitly mark methods as virtual, your classes can still be inherited from unless they are marked as sealed. The following class contains no virtual methods, but it does have a protected one:

```
public class Inheritable
{
    protected void implementation()
    {
        //something we don't want the outside world calling
    }

    public void Method1()
    {

    }

    public void Method2()
    {

    }
}
```

In this case, there is nothing to prevent a consumer from inheriting from the class and accessing the protected method as shown in the following example.

```
public class Sneaky : Inheritable
{
    public void CallingProtectedMethod()
    {
        implementation();
    }
}
```

There are two ways to prevent this. One would be to mark the implementation method `private` instead of `protected`. If you don't want anyone inheriting from your class, there is no reason to make methods `protected`. The other way would be to mark the class as `sealed`. The `sealed` keyword prevents anyone from inheriting from your class.

```
public sealed class Inheritable
{
    private void implementation()
    {
        //something we don't want the outside world calling
    }

    ...

}
```

It turns out that marking a class in C# as `sealed` has an additional benefit. Because the framework knows that no other class can inherit from one that is sealed, it can take some shortcuts when dealing with your sealed class that make it faster to construct. Thus, not only do you explicitly prevent consumers from inheriting from your class in ways you didn't expect, but you also get a minor performance improvement.

Most other object-oriented (OO) languages have similar concepts, allowing you to control who is using your interfaces to do what. One construct that is particular to .NET and that can be confusing is C#'s `new` keyword. While not strictly speaking related to accessibility, it can feel like it is, and is worth a moment here.

Even if a class has methods not marked as virtual, the `new` keyword allows you to "hide" inherited members with your own implementation, as shown in the following code.

```
public class Hiding : Inheritable
{
    public new void Method1()
    {
        //does something different from Inheritable::Method1
    }
}
```

Using the `new` keyword means that any clients that call `Hiding.Method1()` will get the derived class's implementation, with no reference to the parent class's implementation whatsoever. The base class's implementation is "hidden" by the derived class's implementation. This allows a limited form of "overriding" the behavior of the base class. The biggest thing to keep in mind about the `new` keyword is that it creates a completely new method that happens to have the same name as the base class method, but it is in no way related. In terms of the internal details, each method in a .NET class occupies a slot in a VTABLE (just like in C++ or Java) that forms the internal representation of all the methods on any given class. It is the VTABLE that allows polymorphism to work, because each derived class has a VTABLE that is laid out in the same way as its base class's VTABLE. Overridden methods occupy the same slot in the VTABLE as those in the base class, so when code calls classes in a polymorphic fashion, it calls the same slot in the VTABLE for each polymorphic class. The new keyword in C# creates a completely new slot in the VTABLE, which means that polymorphism will not work the way you might expect. The new method will not be called by code depending on polymorphism because the new method occupies the wrong place in the VTABLE, and it will be the base class's implementation that really gets called.

The issues that you face in hiding your nonpublic interface will vary a bit from language to language, but the overall goal remains the same. If your customers can't access something directly, it means you don't have to support it. You can make changes as required without causing anyone any trouble. If you don't take the time up front to think about what to expose, however, you will end up having to support a lot more of your code than you might want to.

Dependency Injection

One of the best ways to limit dependencies between libraries is by using "dependency injection," which, in short, means trading compile-time dependencies for runtime dependencies by using configuration.

If your code is already factored to use interfaces, dependency injection is as simple as loading libraries dynamically based on some form of configuration. The easiest way to do that (at least in C#) is to enhance the factory class you looked at earlier in the chapter. Instead of loading the real logging implementation class in compile-time code like this:

```
public static class LoggerFactory
{
    private static readonly MyLogger logInstance = new MyLogger();

    public static ILogger Create()
    {
        return logInstance;
    }
}
```

You can load it through dependency injection. First, you need some form of configuration:

```
<?xml version="1.0" encoding="utf-8" ?>
<configuration>
  <appSettings>
    <add key="LimitingDependencies.ILogger" value="LimitingDependencies.MyLogger"/>
  </appSettings>
</configuration>
```

This is about the simplest way to configure dependency injection in .NET. It maps the interface type to the concrete type that implements the interface. The factory class reads the configuration and uses it to create the concrete type as shown in the following example.

```
public class DependencyInjector
{
    public static object GetAnInterface(Type interfaceType)
    {
        string interfaceName = interfaceType.FullName;
        string typeName = ConfigurationManager.AppSettings[interfaceName];
        Type t = Type.GetType(typeName);
        object result =
t.InvokeMember("ctor", BindingFlags.CreateInstance,
null, null, null);
        return result;
    }
}
```

By creating the concrete type in this way, the calling code only has a dependency on the interface definition, and not on the implementation class. The compile-time dependency has become a runtime dependency. If the configuration is incorrect or the implementation type cannot be created dynamically, the problem will only be discovered at runtime. That is the biggest drawback of dependency injection. You can test the configuration, but the reality is that you won't really discover problems until you actually run your application.

The benefits far outweigh this minor drawback. With a dependency injection framework in place, it is trivial to replace the logger implementation with a different one. All that has to change is the configuration, and neither the calling code nor the factory knows any different. The calling code just has to ask for what it wants. The following code requests an ILogger interface:

```
[Test]
public void GetALogger()
{
    ILogger log = (ILogger)DependencyInjector.GetAnInterface(typeof(ILogger));
    log.Debug("blah");
}
```

This is a very simple implementation. Dependency injection can be much more complex, but the basic idea remains the same. By creating types dynamically based on configuration, you can remove compile-time dependencies on just about everything except interface definitions. To take the idea to its logical extreme, you can make the concrete implementation classes creatable only by the dependency injection framework. That prevents callers from creating the concrete types no matter how they find them.

Dependency injection is one of the best ways to limit your surface area, because you can make sure that callers only know about interfaces and not implementations. That means you don't have to support any single concrete implementation, as long as the one you do support implements the interface passed to clients properly.

As a side benefit, a dependency injection framework also enables you to support a pluggable add-in model. You define the interface and provide access to the configuration, and users can create their own implementations of your interfaces and run them as plug-ins.

Another advantage of dependency injection is that you can easily replace implementation classes with test versions. This allows you to limit the scope of your unit tests to only the code under test, and not the code it depends upon. If you are using a factory/configuration setup as described earlier, you can use a test configuration when running unit tests, and create test implementations of your interfaces rather than the actual implementations. If you are testing code that depends on logging, you can insert a test logger that either does nothing or writes its output to some location useful for your tests, such as a debug console.

Inversion of Control

Another way to deal with dependencies is to use what is known as inversion of control (IoC). Inversion of control means that rather than code creating its dependencies before calling them, those dependencies are created at the top and pushed down.

For example, rather than having code that requires a logger, create that logger, as in this example:

```
public class LessDependent
{
    public static readonly ILogger log = new MyLogger();

    public int Add(int op1, int op2)
    {
        int result = op1 + op2;

        log.Debug(string.Format("Adding {0} + {1} = {2}", op1, op2, result));

        return result;
    }

}
```

The logger is created someplace above the LessDependent class and pushed down into it via its constructor as shown here:

```
public class LessDependent
{
    private ILogger log;

    public LessDependent(ILogger log)
    {
        this.log = log;
    }

    public int Add(int op1, int op2)
    {
        int result = op1 + op2;

        log.Debug(string.Format("Adding {0} + {1} = {2}", op1, op2, result));

        return result;
    }
}
```

It is then incumbent on the code calling this class to create the right dependencies and pass them down, as in the DoAddition method here:

```
public class Top
{
    public void DoAddition()
    {
        ILogger log = new MyLogger();
        LessDependent less = new LessDependent(log);
        int result = less.Add(1, 2);
    }
}
```

Although this is a simple example, it demonstrates the principle. Just as with a factory class, the calling code has no idea how the dependencies were constructed or anything about the implementation classes themselves.

As with a factory, inversion of control lends itself well to dependency injection. Whoever creates the objects supporting the interfaces you require can just as easily create them from configuration as at compile time. IoC lends itself so well to dependency injection, in fact, that the two are often confused and comingled. It is certainly possible to have one without the other, but together they provide an even greater degree of dependency reduction.

Another major advantage of inversion of control is that the IoC pattern works well with mocking frameworks. If all of your code's dependencies are passed into it, it becomes even simpler to mock those interfaces, as shown in the following test code.

```
[Test]
public void MockingFramework()
{
    MockRepository mocks = new MockRepository();
    ILogger mockLog = mocks.CreateMock<ILogger>();
    using (mocks.Record())
    {
        mockLog.Debug("");
        LastCall.IgnoreArguments();
    }
    using (mocks.Playback())
    {
        LessDependent less = new LessDependent(mockLog);

        int result = less.Add(1, 2);
        Assert.AreEqual(3, result);
    }
}
```

This particular example demonstrates the Rhino.Mocks framework, a popular .NET mocking framework that is freely available and very easy to use. In this example, a MockRepository is created and used to create a "mock" implementation of the ILogger interface. Once the mock interface is created, you can record your expectations for how the mock interface will be called. In this case the code is asserting that the ILogger.Debug method will be called once, and that you don't care what arguments are passed to it. During playback, the mock version will respond in whatever way you have established in the recording section.

Mocking the interfaces used in an IoC pattern allows for targeted testing because all of the interfaces the code under test depends upon can be mocked and passed into the constructor of the object under test. Some mocking frameworks even allow you to mock interfaces you don't pass in directly, but that is a more difficult pattern to write, and those frameworks tend to be more invasive and harder to set up. The big advantage to Rhino.Mocks and others like it is that they are easy to use and require relatively low overhead.

In the case of the ILogger interface, the Debug method returns void, so it doesn't highlight how easy it is to mock results. The following example code is dependent upon a calculator interface:

```
public interface ICalculator
{
    double Add(double op1, double op2);
    double Subtract(double op1, double op2);
    double Multiply(double op1, double op2);
    double Divide(double op1, double op2);
}

public class UsesCalculator
{
    private ICalculator calc;

    public UsesCalculator(ICalculator calc)
    {
        this.calc = calc;
    }

    public string StringAdd(string operand1, string operand2)
    {
        double op1 = double.Parse(operand1);
        double op2 = double.Parse(operand2);

        double result = calc.Add(op1, op2);

        return result.ToString();
    }
}
```

In test code that exercises the UsesCalculator class, you can only test its code, and not that of the ICalculator implementation, which is hopefully tested elsewhere. Rather than create a test version of ICalculator, you can mock it, like this:

```
[Test]
public void StringAdd()
{
    MockRepository mocks = new MockRepository();
    ICalculator calc = mocks.CreateMock<ICalculator>();

    using (mocks.Record())
    {
        Expect.Call(calc.Add(1.0, 2.0)).Return(3.0);
    }
```

```
using (mocks.Playback())
{
    UsesCalculator uses = new UsesCalculator(calc);
    string result = uses.StringAdd("1", "2");
    Assert.AreEqual("3", result);
}
    }
```

Now the test is only testing the functionality of the `UsesCalculator.StringAdd()` method, without testing the `ICalculator` implementation it depends upon. Using a mocking framework, you assert your expectations about how that dependency will behave and how it will be used. The mocking framework will exhibit the behavior you specify, and verify that it has been called correctly.

Without using inversion of control, you might have to mock the factory class as well, which can be tedious and time-consuming. It is much simpler to deal with mock interfaces when using the IoC pattern.

Once you start using the IoC pattern described in this section, it can rapidly lead to more and more constructors that take more and more interface references, until it seems all of your constructors start taking four, five, even ten or more interface references. That means an awful lot of time spent managing interface references, and passing them around from place to place. The solution is to use what is known as an inversion of control container. At its best, an IoC container combines the functionality of IoC, dependency injection, and factory classes.

You configure the container to know about your interface types and the concrete classes that implement those interfaces. The container itself provides a factory-like interface through which you can request an instance of a particular class. The container examines the constructor of that class looking for interface types and creates concrete implementations of those interfaces, and then passes them to the constructor. The container keeps track of who needs what (by looking at the constructors) and creates those dependencies based on configuration. This takes much of the burden off the code requesting the objects, and nobody (except whoever configures the system) has to worry about where the dependencies come from or how they are created. This type of container has become increasingly popular, and there are implementations for many different platforms. One prevalent .NET IoC container is Castle Windsor, part of the Castle Open Source project. Windsor provides a full-featured, relatively easy-to-use IoC container for use with .NET applications.

Using an IoC container such as Windsor represents a significant investment. It requires understanding the IoC pattern and how it is implemented, how to configure the factory, and how to use the container properly. It also requires you to design your objects around the IoC pattern. All of your interfaces must be properly factored out, and your objects must be ready to accept interfaces passed to their constructors. Getting everything running the first time takes serious effort and requires everyone on the team to be trained to use the container and to write their objects to take advantage of it. If you are willing to make such an investment, you will greatly reduce compile-time dependencies between your libraries, which makes code easier to maintain and to modify, if slightly more complex to design and implement. If you have a large and/or complex system, the additional work necessary to introduce an IoC container may save you quite a bit of effort later on when it comes to making changes to or maintaining your application.

Summary

Dependencies between libraries can be a real problem. The more interdependent your code is, the harder it is to make changes to. The harder it is to make changes to, the harder it is to fix bugs and add new features once the software is initially developed, and that means additional time and money.

There are several strategies available to reduce those interdependencies and to make your application easier to modify and maintain. The first step is to introduce interfaces, so that clients of your code can be dependent on only those interface definitions and not on concrete implementations, leaving you free to modify those implementations more easily. Once you have interfaces, you can introduce factory classes, further reducing the need for client knowledge of (and thereby dependence on) concrete implementation classes.

Dependency injection is the process of introducing configuration into those factories so that even more dependency issues are removed. Dependency injection removes compile-time dependencies and replaces them with runtime dependencies that can be changed without needing to recompile any client code.

By making sure that only those portions of your application that you really intend clients to use are exposed, you can keep clients from taking dependencies on internal objects that you may want to change later. That reduces the cost of change, and makes it easier to modify and maintain your application.

Last, you can combine all of those patterns by using an inversion of control container to manage your dependencies, create them for you, and make sure that they are introduced to the classes that require them for the ultimate flexibility in managing dependencies among your libraries.

10

The Model-View-Presenter (MVP) Model

One of the biggest challenges in adopting Test-Driven Development and, ultimately, Continuous Integration is figuring out how to test the user interface (UI) portion of your application (if it has one). TestRunner applications that simulate user mouse and keyboard events are costly, difficult to set up, and often require learning a proprietary scripting language. Additionally, it is hard to integrate such tools into a Continuous Integration process because they are often not designed for XML reporting. In the chapter on testing, you learned about functional testing platforms such as Watir, but those only work with web-based applications (rather than with desktop applications).

There are strategies that you can pursue, however, which make it easier to test your user interface without relying on simulating user interactions. One such strategy has come to be called the Model-View-Presenter (MVP) model. MVP is a design pattern for UI-based applications that makes it much easier to automate testing of almost the entire application.

The fundamental strategy employed by MVP is to separate the bulk of the application from the very thinnest layer of the user interface. Everything but that very thin layer can then be tested using the same unit testing frameworks discussed in Chapter 5 ("Testing"), such as NUnit. The remaining thin slice of user interface code can then be quickly inspected visually by human testers with relatively little effort.

Why MVP?

There have been various attempts to make UI applications easier to test. Some involve making it easier to simulate user actions by adding hooks that can be called programmatically. Some host UI components in a test framework so that they can be interacted with via code. All of these efforts have their pros and cons. The biggest drawback to all of them is that they rely on instantiating the UI elements of the applications on a desktop or other such drawing surface. This makes it harder to automate and test in a server environment such as a Continuous Integration build server.

The advantage to MVP is that it removes the UI elements from the equation. By removing that very thinnest layer, which actually draws to the screen, it becomes much easier to automate testing and, therefore, much easier to integrate into a TDD process. The level of automated testing that can thus be achieved is typically much higher than if the UI is tested at the user layer. That leaves only the thinnest veneer to be validated by testers, who only need to verify that the user interface components look right and that the user input methods function as desired.

What Is MVP?

Many developers are familiar with the Model-View-Controller (MVC) model, which has long been popular for building UI-based applications. In the MVC model, pains are taken to separate the application into three distinct layers.

❑ **Model** — The lowest layer of the application that represents the domain model and what is traditionally regarded as "business logic"

❑ **View** — the UI portion, containing input fields, buttons, and other user interface elements, but no business logic

❑ **Controller** — The controller's job is to take information from the model and push it into the view, and to take input supplied by the user from the view and pass it to the model for processing.

In practice, the controller can't do everything, and in some cases, there is direct interaction between the model and the view, as well as interactions mediated by the controller. The controller is concerned primarily with data exchange, pushing user input down, but the view often directly accesses the model for display purposes. The components form a triangular relationship, as shown in Figure 10-1.

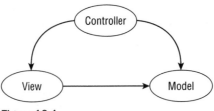

Figure 10-1

In a .NET desktop application, for example, the Windows Form–derived class that represents a single form is playing the part of both View and Controller because the form typically contains not only the user interface elements, but also event-handling methods that receive events from the UI and call the Model, thus playing the part of the Controller. This unification makes it difficult to automatically test Windows Forms applications directly because the view and controller are difficult to tease apart. To test the Controller portion, you would have to simulate .NET events coming from UI elements to trigger the Controller behavior.

There are examples of MVC applications written for Windows Forms, and frameworks designed to make that model easier to implement in Windows Forms, but it is not the default model.

That's where the MVP pattern (see Figure 10-2) comes in. In an MVP application, there is a strict isolation of the Model from the View. The View is not allowed to interact directly with the Model, but it can interact with the Presenter. The Presenter is responsible for receiving events from the View, representing user actions, as well as passing user data down to the Model and pushing data from the Model up to the View for display. The MVP model is broken into three layers:

❏ **Model** — Essentially, as in the MVC model, the Model contains domain objects and business logic.

❏ **View** — A very thin user interface layer containing no logic except that required to respond to user events and to display data. In most implementations, the View is represented by a specific interface.

❏ **Presenter** — The Presenter receives user input from the View and pushes data into the view for display to the user.

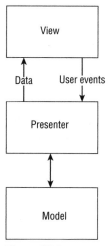

Figure 10-2

The View only knows how to take input from the user and display data from the Presenter in ways that make sense to the user. Those are both tasks that are highly specific to the user interface framework being used. For example, the View in a .NET application might know how to receive events from a button control and to populate a tree control with information pushed to it by the Presenter.

Such a thin layer, which is only concerned with the details of the user interface, can easily be simulated by nonuser interface code. If the View can be simulated, testing of the application can be done without resorting to simulating user actions such as mouse movements. Instead, it can be done through a test view.

That leaves only the code dealing directly with user interface elements to be validated by human testers. Those pieces are easy to validate, and this can generally be done visually in a short time. The rest of the application, including the logic that builds the display, can be tested automatically using a unit testing framework.

An added advantage of the MVP pattern is that it is very easy to build alternate Views that use the same Presenter and Model. For example, if constructed correctly, a Presenter built for a Windows application could be reused as part of a web application. Only the View would have to be rewritten, without having to duplicate the user interface display logic that is part of the Presenter. The details of how Windows applications or web applications draw controls, or accept input from users, remain isolated in the View code where they belong.

The MVP model is still relatively new, and there remains debate about how best to go about implementing the pattern. There are certainly some challenges to be faced in implementing such a pattern. There are different ways of handling the communication between View and Presenter (more detail in a moment), and those strategies can be harder or easier to implement, depending on what language or application platform you are using. The differences between web and desktop applications suggest different approaches, and if you plan to implement web and desktop Views for the same application, then the design bears some thinking about.

Another part of the design that takes some careful consideration is the data types passed between the View and the Presenter. Those data types need to be agnostic of the display technology used by the View. As an example, if your View renders a tree structure such as a file system, you must pass a display-agnostic structure such as a hierarchical dictionary, rather than a collection of tree nodes. The use of tree nodes is specific to the implementation of the View and, therefore, should be unknown to the Presenter. The View is responsible for turning the display-agnostic hierarchy into tree nodes if they are required to display them to the user. Similarly, if the View needs to report on user activity to the Presenter, it should use some method unrelated to the controls the user interacts with. Don't expose a button click event to the presenter, for instance, because that is tied to the nature of a button. Instead, you could use a separate event type known to the Presenter. This interaction is illustrated in Figure 10-3.

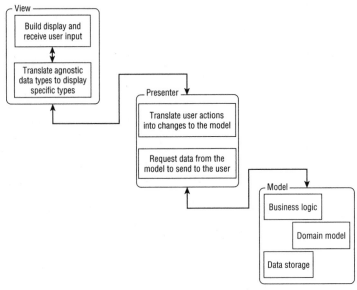

Figure 10-3

If the pieces are factored correctly, almost the entire application can be tested automatically, using the same tools employed for the rest of unit testing.

Constructing the MVP Application

Constructing the Model portion of the application is no different from the MVC model. The Model encompasses the domain model as well as the business logic and data access layer, if there is one. We won't go into detail about constructing the Model. Not only should it be fairly familiar, but there are many different strategies and patterns for constructing your Model that are independent of participation in an MVP application. You might choose a traditional OOD (Object Oriented Design) method, a Domain-Driven Design method, or possibly even a message-passing or SOA (Service Oriented Architecture) method. Any of these could be used successfully for building a user-centric application's Model.

The trickiest part of the MVP design process is the View. It must represent all of the interaction you will have with your user, using display-agnostic data types. The View, in essence, forms your application's contract with what is "on the glass" or visible to the user on their monitor. If you are following a TDD development process, your View is likely to change and evolve during the course of development, as requirements become more apparent. That should be easy to do if the proper separation between View and Presenter is maintained, although a little refactoring along the way never hurt anyone.

In most languages, it is easiest to represent your View as an interface. The concrete class directly responsible for display will implement the View interface. When you write your test code, you can create another implementation of the View interface for testing purposes that has no actual user interface elements associated with it.

There is one major decision to make before starting work on your View interface. Will your View expose events directly? Or will it call the Presenter to report user activity? This is often debated when starting an MVP project, and there are adherents in both camps. To put the cards on the table up front, I personally favor the former from an architectural perspective. It offers the cleanest separation between View and Presenter because the View need know nothing at all about the Presenter. It only receives data pushed to it and fires events that represent user actions. From a practical standpoint, however, there are cons. Using events may be difficult in some implementation environments. Specifically in a web application, it may be difficult for your server "page" to fire events, and just as difficult for your Presenter to subscribe to them. It can be much easier in such an application to provide the View with direct access to the Presenter so that user events can be reported directly as method calls. That potentially makes it easier to deal with the issue of display-agnostic data types as well. If your View's user interface element (a button, say) fires events, and the View has to catch those events, translate from display data types to neutral data types, and then fire a second event, the code could become quite cumbersome.

Let's look at how the code would work. The first example takes the second approach, where the View directly communicates with the Presenter. The example is that of a simple survey application, with a list of users and a set of questions (see Figure 10-4). The user of the application can select each user in turn from the list and then answer the questions. When the application loads, the View (in this case the `WindowsForm` class that represents the main form) gets a reference to the Presenter, and passes the Presenter a reference to itself. This forms a two-way link between View and Presenter so that they can communicate back and forth.

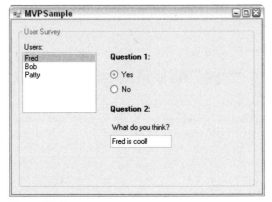

Figure 10-4

The View interface contains properties that represent each of the UI elements in the view.

```
public interface ISurveyView
{
    List<string> Users { get; set; }
    bool Question1 { get; set; }
    string Question2 { get; set; }
}
```

Notice that the data types are not those used by the user interface. The Users property is a generic list of strings, not a list of ListBoxItems, which is how the UI represents the list. It will be the job of the View to convert between the different data types.

The Presenter is responsible for receiving events from the View, and getting data from the Model.

```
public class SurveyPresenter
{
    private static Dictionary<ISurveyView, SurveyPresenter> _presenters =
new Dictionary<ISurveyView, SurveyPresenter>();
    private static readonly object lockObject = new object();

    public static SurveyPresenter Instance(ISurveyView view)
    {
        lock (lockObject)
        {
            if (!_presenters.ContainsKey(view))
                _presenters[view] = new SurveyPresenter(view);
            return _presenters[view];
        }
    }

    ISurveyView _view;

    private SurveyPresenter(ISurveyView view)
    {
```

```csharp
            _view = view;
        }

        public void OnLoad()
        {
            //this is where you would go to the
            //model for data, but we'll cheat
            List<string> users = new List<string>(new string[] ↵
{ "Fred", "Bob", "Patty" });

            _view.Users = users;
        }

        public void SelectedIndexChanged(int index)
        {
            //go to the model and get answers for questions
            //we'll make it up

            //this is also where the answers to the previous
            //questions would be saved back to the model

            _view.Question1 = true;
            _view.Question2 = string.Format("{0} is cool!", _view.Users[index]);
        }
    }
```

To facilitate the two-way relationship between View and Presenter, the Presenter is a singleton. The View can use the static `Instance()` method to get a reference to the Presenter, and because it passes a reference to itself, the Presenter will have a handle back to the View.

```csharp
    public partial class MvpMain : Form, ISurveyView
    {
        public MvpMain()
        {
            InitializeComponent();
        }

        private SurveyPresenter _presenter;

        #region ISurveyView Members

        public List<string> Users
        {
            get
            {
                List<string> users = new List<string>();
                foreach (object item in userList.Items)
                {
                    users.Add((string)item);
                }
                return users;
            }
            set
            {
```

```
                userList.Items.Clear();
                foreach (string user in value)
                {
                    userList.Items.Add(user);
                }
            }
        }

        public bool Question1
        {
            get
            {
                if (yesButton.Checked)
                    return true;
                else
                    return false;
            }
            set
            {
                if (value)
                {
                    yesButton.Checked = true;
                    noButton.Checked = false;
                }
                else
                {
                    yesButton.Checked = false;
                    noButton.Checked = true;
                }
            }
        }

        public string Question2
        {
            get
            {
                return question2Box.Text;
            }
            set
            {
                question2Box.Text = value;
            }
        }

        #endregion

        private void MvpMain_Load(object sender, EventArgs e)
        {
            _presenter = SurveyPresenter.Instance(this);
            _presenter.OnLoad();
        }

        private void userList_SelectedIndexChanged(object sender, EventArgs e)
        {
```

```
        _presenter.SelectedIndexChanged(userList.SelectedIndex);
    }
}
```

When events happen in the user interface, such as the loading of the form, or the changing of the selected index in the list box, the View calls methods on the Presenter to inform it of these actions. When those events are reported to the Presenter, the Presenter then updates the UI by setting properties in the View.

In the second case, the application functions in exactly the same way, but the View interface includes events instead.

```
public interface ISurveyView
{
    List<string> Users { get; set; }
    bool Question1 { get; set; }
    string Question2 { get; set; }
    event SelectionChangedDelegate SelectionChanged;
    event OnLoadDelegate OnLoad;
}

public delegate void SelectionChangedDelegate(int index);
public delegate void OnLoadDelegate();
```

The View can fire events instead of calling methods on the Presenter to report user actions. The View need know nothing at all about the Presenter; it just needs to pass a reference to itself to the Presenter's constructor.

```
public class SurveyPresenter
{

    ISurveyView _view;

    public SurveyPresenter(ISurveyView view)
    }
        _view = view;
        _view.OnLoad += new OnLoadDelegate(OnLoad);
        _view.SelectionChanged += new ↵
SelectionChangedDelegate(SelectedIndexChanged);
    }

    public void OnLoad()
    {
        //this is where you would go to the
        //model for data, but we'll cheat
        List<string> users = new List<string>(new string[] ↵
{ "Fred", "Bob", "Patty" });

        _view.Users = users;
    }

    public void SelectedIndexChanged(int index)
    {
```

```
            //go to the model and get answers for questions
            //we'll make it up

            //This is also where the answers to the previous
            //questions would be saved back to the model.

            _view.Question1 = true;
            _view.Question2 = string.Format("{0} is cool!", _view.Users[index]);
        }
    }
```

The Presenter hooks up the events from the View in the constructor, so that when the View fires events, the Presenter can respond. Nothing in the Presenter has changed at all in this case, except that the events are hooked up.

In the View, a few things have changed. The View now supports the additional events, and it fires those events instead of calling methods on the Presenter. The View still has to create an instance of the Presenter, but all it needs to know about the Presenter is the constructor. The changed (highlighted) code makes no reference to the Presenter, so the View is isolated from the implementation of the Presenter.

```
        public partial class MvpMain : Form, ISurveyView
        {
            public MvpMain()
            {
                InitializeComponent();
                _presenter = new SurveyPresenter(this);
            }

            private SurveyPresenter _presenter;

            #region ISurveyView Members

            public List<string> Users
            {
                get
                {
                    List<string> users = new List<string>();
                    foreach (object item in userList.Items)
                    {
                        users.Add((string)item);
                    }
                    return users;
                }
                set
                {
                    userList.Items.Clear();
                    foreach (string user in value)
                    {
                        userList.Items.Add(user);
                    }
                }
            }
```

```csharp
public bool Question1
{
    get
    {
        if (yesButton.Checked)
            return true;
        else
            return false;
    }
    set
    {
        if (value)
        {
            yesButton.Checked = true;
            noButton.Checked = false;
        }
        else
        {
            yesButton.Checked = false;
            noButton.Checked = true;
        }
    }
}

public string Question2
{
    get
    {
        return question2Box.Text;
    }
    set
    {
        question2Box.Text = value;
    }
}

public event OnLoadDelegate OnLoad;
public event SelectionChangedDelegate SelectionChanged;

#endregion

private void MvpMain_Load(object sender, EventArgs e)
{
    if(OnLoad != null)
        OnLoad();
}

private void userList_SelectedIndexChanged(object sender, EventArgs e)
{
    if(SelectionChanged != null)
        SelectionChanged(userList.SelectedIndex);
}
}
```

The rest of the View remains the same. The View responds to user events and populates its controls in the same way as before; all that has changed is its interaction with the Presenter.

In either case, the Presenter remains insolated from the details of the View, which makes the Presenter easy to test. The code remaining in the View itself is concerned only with populating controls and firing events, and it is thus very easy to validate using human testers.

Testing MVP Applications

The main advantage to following the MVP pattern is that it makes your application easy to test. To test an MVP application, you create a simulated or test version of your View interface. The Presenter then interacts with the simulated View rather than the actual View implementation. You can add additional infrastructure code to the simulated View that allows you to simulate user interactions from your test code.

To test the sample application, you would write a simulated View such as the following. Note that this is the first example View that calls the Presenter directly.

```
class TestSurveyView : ISurveyView
{
    List<string> users;
    bool question1;
    string question2;

    //get the back reference to the
    //presenter to events can be reported
    public TestSurveyView()
    {
        presenter = SurveyPresenter.Instance(this);
    }

    //the presenter reference
    SurveyPresenter presenter;

    //to be called by test code
    public void DoOnLoad()
    {
        presenter.OnLoad();
    }

    //to be called by test code
    public void ChangeSelection(int selectedIndex)
    {
        presenter.SelectedIndexChanged(selectedIndex);
    }

    #region ISurveyView Members

    public List<string> Users
    {
        get
        {
```

```
            return users;
        }
        set
        {
            users = value;
        }
    }

    public bool Question1
    {
        get
        {
            return question1;
        }
        set
        {
            question1 = value;
        }
    }

    public string Question2
    {
        get
        {
            return question2;
        }
        set
        {
            question2 = value;
        }
    }

    #endregion
}
```

The extra methods DoOnLoad() and ChangeSelection() allow the test code to fire events that simulate user interaction. No user interface is required, and all of the functionality of the Presenter (and ultimately of the Model, although it should be tested separately) can be tested.

To use the simulated View in the preceding example from NUnit test code, you can write tests that create the simulated View, use its extra methods to fire user events, and then validate the results pushed back to the View by the underlying Presenter:

```
[TestFixture]
public class MainFormTests
{
    [Test]
    public void TestViewLoading()
    {
        List<string> expected =
new List<string>(new string[] { "Fred", "Bob", "Patty" });

        TestSurveyView view = new TestSurveyView();
```

```
        //simulate loading of the view
        view.DoOnLoad();

        //the presenter should have populated the list
        List<string> actual = view.Users;

        Assert.AreEqual(expected, actual);
    }

    [Test]
    public void TestUserSelectionQuestion1()
    {
        TestSurveyView view = new TestSurveyView();

        //load the user list so selection can be changed
        view.DoOnLoad();

        //change the selection, simulating user action
        view.ChangeSelection(1);

        Assert.AreEqual(true, view.Question1);
    }

    [Test]
    public void TestUserSelectionQuestion2()
    {
        TestSurveyView view = new TestSurveyView();

        //load the user list so selection can be changed
        view.DoOnLoad();

        //change the selection, simulating user action
        view.ChangeSelection(2);

        Assert.AreEqual("Patty is cool!", view.Question2);

        view.ChangeSelection(0);

        Assert.AreEqual("Fred is cool!", view.Question2);
    }
}
```

It is important to note that in this example, you are using a "fake" Presenter that returns fixed data rather than going to a real Model for it. In a real application, the best strategy for testing the Presenter would involve not only writing the simulated View described previously, but also using something like a mocking framework to simulate the Model. This way the testing of the Presenter can be separated from testing the Model.

In a more complex example, the simulated View will need additional code to be able to simulate potentially complex user action. This may seem like a lot of extra work, but it will prove itself worthwhile given the improvements it will make in the reach of your tests. When you can automatically test the majority of your application without relying on human testers, you will improve your code coverage, find more defects early on, and have a comprehensive set of regression tests that will help you find more defects later in development as well.

Summary

One of the most difficult things about adopting Test-Driven Development can be testing the user interface portion of an application. Functional testing using TestRunner tools can be difficult to integrate with the rest of a comprehensive testing process. One of the best ways to solve this problem is by building your user interface–based application using the Model-View-Presenter pattern. This pattern separates the thin user interface layer of your application from the code responsible for populating and responding to that user layer.

Following the MVP pattern allows you to write simulated View code so that your Presenter can be driven automatically by unit tests. This reduces the amount of testing that requires human interaction with your application and helps you integrate your functional testing into a comprehensive test suite.

## 11

Tracing

What is tracing? Ask any two developers, and you are likely to get different answers. I'm talking about tracing that means, in a nutshell, reporting what happens inside an application while it is running, whether what happened was good or bad, happy or sad. That definition covers a lot of ground. It includes tracing (sometimes referred to as logging) meant for other developers, tracing meant for support personnel, and even error reporting meant for end users. These all involve reporting in some fashion about something that happened inside the application that you want one of those constituencies to know about. You may want them to know about it right away, or you may want to squirrel away the information for later reference. Tracing can be used to inform support personnel about steps they need to take right away, or it might be done for archival and research purposes to track the long-term behavior of a given application.

Because tracing can cover so many different situations, it's important to come up with a comprehensive way to deal with tracing as a whole so that all of the pieces are well integrated. If you use three different tracing systems to reach three different sets of users, it can become very difficult to keep track of what goes where and which system should be used when. And then it becomes hard to switch from one tracing mechanism to another or to report the same problems to different people.

Different Kinds of Messages

At the highest level, tracing can be divided into simple quadrants (see Figure 11-1), based on whom the information is intended for and whether the information is about the code or the functioning of the application.

Information intended for developers is usually either about a specific defect in the code, such as an unexpected exception, or about a specific detail relating to the functioning of the application, such as why a user could not log in. That information is intended to be used for defect resolution and problem solving, and thus needs to be detailed and very specific. Tracing messages meant for developers need to explain exactly where the issue occurred, what exactly happened, and preferably what values were in play at the time of the issue.

	Developers	Users
Information about code	"ArgumentNullException" on line 36 of foo.cs	"An error occured in the application"
Information about the application	User X could not be found in the LDS directory	User X failed to log in correctly

Figure 11-1

Similarly, information intended for users can be either about the code (informing the user that a defect occurred, without the need to be specific) or about something that applies to the logic of the application (such as the fact that a given user failed to log in correctly four times in a row). Messages for users need to be simple and nontechnical, and tell them how to fix the problem. A user doesn't need to know that the person trying to log in couldn't be found in the LDAP directory at ldap://ou=Users,ou=MyCompany,o=Com. They do need to know that they presented incorrect credentials, or that the user directory could not be contacted at the configured address.

Log Sources and Log Sinks

One way to make sure that tracing messages get to the right audience is to use some form of log sources and log sinks. Many of the popular tracing (logging) frameworks available use this concept of sources and sinks. Log4j (Java), log4net, and the .NET 3.0 Tracing subsystem all split the notion of where messages are created in the code from where they are ultimately recorded.

In log4j and log4net parlance, log sources are called "loggers" and log sinks "appenders." Loggers can be identified by unique names or they can be associated with specific types or namespaces. Code that writes tracing messages only needs to know which logger to ask for. In the following code, the Calculator class only has to ask for a logger based on its type.

```
public class Calculator
{
    private static readonly ILog log =
            LogManager.GetLogger(typeof(Calculator));

    public int Divide(int op1, int op2)
    {
        try
        {
            return op1 / op2;
        }
```

```
            catch (DivideByZeroException dbze)
            {
                log.Error("Divide by zero exception.", dbze);
                throw;
            }
        }
    }
```

All the `Calculator` class needs to do is ask for the logger associated with its class. When the `Divide` method needs to log an error, it uses that logger to write its message. It knows nothing about how that message will look, or where it will be recorded. All that the caller needs to decide is how to categorize messages by severity or error level. In this case, the caller is logging at the "Error" level, which represents nothing more than a categorization of the message.

Log sources (loggers) are associated with log sinks (appenders) via configuration. There are a number of ways to configure log4net, but one of the most common is through the `.config` file:

```xml
<?xml version="1.0" encoding="utf-8" ?>
<configuration>
  <configSections>
    <section name="log4net"
type="log4net.Config.Log4NetConfigurationSectionHandler, log4net" />
  </configSections>
  <log4net>
    <appender name="DebugAppender" type="log4net.Appender.DebugAppender" >
      <layout type="log4net.Layout.PatternLayout">
        <conversionPattern value="%date [%thread] %-5level %logger [%ndc] -
%message%newline" />
      </layout>
    </appender>
    <root>
      <level value="INFO" />
      <appender-ref ref="DebugAppender" />
    </root>
  </log4net>
</configuration>
```

This config file defines an appender that writes a message to the debug output stream using the Win32 `OutputDebugString()` method. If also defines a layout for that message. The caller doesn't define what the message will ultimately look like; the configuration does. Once the appender is defined, it needs to be associated with one or more loggers so that it can be applied at runtime. This configuration defines one logger called `root` that represents the one logger defined. No matter what logger the caller asks for, it gets the root logger. If the calculator code throws a `DivideByZeroException`, the resulting log message (given the preceding configuration) will look like this:

```
Tracing.Calculator: 2007-12-19 21:27:54,125 [4276] ERROR Tracing.Calculator [] -
Divide by zero exception.
Exception: System.DivideByZeroException
Message: Attempted to divide by zero.
Source: Tracing
    at Tracing.Calculator.Divide(Int32 op1, Int32 op2) in C:\Visual Studio
2005\Projects\Tracing\Tracing\Class1.cs:line 16
```

The logging configuration defines how the message looks and where it will be recorded. Other loggers can be configured to write to other locations, more than one location, or only if they are categorized at a certain level. Log4net has specific knowledge of namespaces, so you can define loggers for each level of a namespace hierarchy or only for the top level. For example, if you define a `root` logger, and one called `MyNamespace.Math`, the calling code in the class `MyNamespace.Math.Calculator` will match the `MyNamespace.Math` logger rather than `root`.

By formatting messages differently for different log sinks, you can create logs for various purposes. For example, you might format debug messages as formatted text (as shown earlier), but you might format files written to disk as XML, using a different formatter and the XML appender. One is intended for human consumption and the other for use by other applications.

By separating logging sources from logging sinks, you remove the need for the caller to know where things need to be logged. The caller can focus on what information needs to be logged and how it is categorized. How those messages get formatted and where they are written can be decided later or can be changed at any time based on configuration. As requirements change or new logging sinks are added, all that needs to change is configuration, not the code that calls the tracing API.

Activities and Correlation IDs

Another feature that will greatly improve the value of your tracing is some notion of correlation or activities. You can create additional structure that has meaning in the context of your application by grouping tracing messages by activity. For example, a user might want to transfer money from one bank account to another. That could involve multiple logical activities such as retrieving current balances, debiting from one account, crediting to another account, and updating the account balances. If each of these is defined in the code as a separate tracing activity, tracing messages can be correlated back to those activities. That makes it much easier to debug problems after the fact by giving developers a better idea of where in the process an error may have occurred. Rather than seeing just a stream of unrelated trace messages, a developer reading the logs can see a picture showing which tracing messages are associated with a single user's activity.

The easiest way to associate tracing messages with an activity is to use some form of correlation ID. Each tracing statement in the activity uses the same correlation ID. When those trace messages are written to a log sink, the sink records the correlation ID along with the message. When the trace logs are read later, either by a human or by an application designed for the purpose, those messages can be sorted by correlation ID and thereby grouped into activities. The hard part can be figuring out how to propagate those correlation IDs across method, thread, or possibly even application boundaries in a complex application.

Some tracing systems have already solved that problem. The Tracing subsystem that shipped with .NET 3.0 provides a facility for activity tracking and can propagate activity IDs across some boundaries automatically, including across in- or out-of-process calls using the Windows Communication Foundation (WCF). WCF makes very good use of activities in tracing, and the Service Trace Viewer application, which is part of the Windows Vista SDK, can display trace messages by activity in a Gantt chart–like format that is very easy to read.

If you have to create your own correlation system, spend some time thinking about how best to propagate and record those activity IDs so that they can be used to reassemble sets of messages when it comes time to view your logs.

Defining a Policy

As part of any software project, you should define and disseminate a tracing policy. It is important that every member of your team has a common understanding of this policy and how to apply it. Your tracing policy should include such elements as which tracing system to use (you don't want half the team using .NET tracing and half using log4net, for instance), where tracing should be done in the code, and how each message should be composed and formatted.

Keep your policy short. Most developers won't read more than a page or two of text, so keep it concise and to the point. Make sure that everyone reads the policy, and follow up with periodic reviews and inspections to make sure that the policy is being implemented properly.

Because many of the details around tracing may be defined at configuration rather than compile time, the critical things for developers to be aware of are how to categorize their traces' messages by trace level and what information needs to be included. How these messages are distributed, saved, and formatted can be defined as part of your applications configuration, and may not be within the purview of the developers at all, but rather handled by an operations or IT department.

A sample tracing policy might look something like this:

❑ More information is better than less as long as trace messages are characterized properly. It is harder to add tracing statements later than it is to turn off tracing if you don't need it. Make sure that you are capturing the information you need to properly format the trace messages later on.

❑ Always use the same mechanism for tracing. Do not mix methods. If you write some messages to the console, some to System.Debug (or stderr and so on), and some to your tracing system, it is much more difficult to correlate those messages later, and it is important that there be only one place to look for tracing information. For the purposes of this project, all tracing should be done using the System.Diagnostics.Trace class.

❑ Setting the correct trace level should be done based on the following criteria:

❑ Messages written for the purpose of debugging — "got here" style debugging messages, for example, or messages about details specific to the code or its workings — should use the lowest level. (In many systems, including log4net, that lowest level is Debug, although others use Verbose, etc.) These are messages that will usually not be recorded unless code is actively being debugged. Nothing specific to the working of the application logic should be recorded at this level.

❑ Messages that provide information about the normal functioning of the application should use the next highest level (called Info in log4net). These messages should be much fewer in number than those at the Debug level so as not to overwhelm the tracing system. Assume that these messages will typically not be recorded unless support personnel are involved.

❑ If a problem occurs that does not cause any software contract to be violated (see Chapter 12, "Error Handling," for more information), use the next higher level, usually called Warning. Warning-level messages should be about unexpected or problematic issues related to the functioning of the application that have been recovered from or in some other way mitigated so that the application still functions properly. A good example would be a message-passing application that fails to send a message but succeeds on a retry. You want anyone reading the trace logs later to know that the initial send failed because the presence of many such messages may indicate a real problem. Because the message was sent in the end, however, the overall operation of the application was not affected. Assume that Warning messages may not be reported immediately but are likely to be reviewed at a later date.

❑ Messages that indicate serious errors requiring attention should be logged at the Error level. These are messages about problems that should be looked at immediately and indicate that the application is not functioning correctly in some way. Any part of the software that cannot properly fulfill its contract should log at this level. Assume that Error-level messages are immediately brought to the attention of support personnel in an operations center. That makes it imperative to only write Error-level messages for pressing issues. Writing unimportant or non-error Error messages only encourages support personnel to ignore messages or turn off logging at this level, potentially masking real problems. Because Error-level messages need to be seen right away and stand out, they should be written infrequently, only when there are real problems.

❑ The highest level messages (called Fatal in log4net) should be reserved for cases where the application is actually going to exit after writing such a message. If the outermost level of the application receives an unhandled exception, for example, the exception should be logged at the Fatal level so that it is seen as quickly as possible. If any problem occurs that causes the application to shut down, it should log at this level, even if the error does not indicate data loss or if the application is restarted automatically. A Fatal error may mean that the intervention of support personnel is required ASAP. Assume that Fatal messages cause someone to be paged at 2 a.m.

❑ Keep in mind the audience associated with each of these levels. The lowest levels (that is, Debug and Info) should never be seen by an end user. Consider them for the eyes of developers or support personnel only. Mid-level (Warning and Error) messages are for end users or support personnel in an operations-center context. Such messages may end up in the Windows Event Log (or other similar system accessible across a network) and trigger alerts in an op center. These messages should be written for the consumption of the end user or support person and should not contain technical details about the code. They should include enough information to make them actionable (more on that later). Fatal messages should be kept brief and to the point (remember the pager at 2 a.m.) and *must* contain information about the nature of the problem that can be understood by a non-developer.

❑ Every trace message must be composed using `String.Format` and rely on string resources for the sake of localization. Remember that every message may someday be localized, which includes changes in word order as well as character set. The exception to this rule is Debug-level messages that are not intended for end users and are specific to the code. The following example shows resources being used for error text with the `ResourceManager` class.

```
public int Divide(int op1, int op2)
{
    try
    {
        return op1 / op2;
    }
    catch (DivideByZeroException dbze)
    {
        ResourceManager resMan = new
        ResourceManager("Tracing.TraceMessages",
                Assembly.GetExecutingAssembly());
        string error =
resMan.GetString("DIVIDE_BY_ZERO_EXCEPTION");
```

```
                    Trace.TraceError(string.Format(error, op1), dbze);
                    throw;
                }
        }
```

Once you have established your tracing policy for developers, you may also need to write (or at least consult on the writing of) a similar policy for use by IT or operations staff. Such a policy should define which trace messages are recorded where, how long those stores are persisted, which levels are routed to which log sinks, and so forth. For example, you might define a policy that all Debug-level messages are written to log files on each of your servers, but Warning messages and up are recorded in a database, and Error-level messages go both to the database and to the Windows Event Log. Make sure that the operations people know about your logging policy so that they can judge which log levels (e.g., Debug, Info, or Error) they want to record and how often. It should be as easy as changing a configuration file — or better yet, a central configuration source — to change the level of messages that are recorded and where they are recorded (log file, event log, and so on), without restarting the application.

Make this easy for operations, not for developers. If you are writing a small application, this may not be an issue, but if you are writing a distributed application that is hosted on a number of servers, it isn't practical for operations personnel to change three configuration files on each of 10 servers just to increase the logging level when there is a problem they need to diagnose. Consider putting tracing configuration information in a central repository such as a database or network service. Ideally, there should only be one place where changes need to be made to log more or fewer messages or to send those messages to different repositories. Log4net, for example, can be configured from any source of XML. That XML could easily be retrieved from a database or from a web service rather than from a file.

If possible, make it easy to configure logging levels without relying on direct editing of configuration files. The configuration editor for WCF, which ships with the Windows Vista SDK, allows for configuration of tracing information as well. It provides a graphical user interface that saves the end user from having to deal with XML configuration. Figure 11-2 shows the main tracing configuration screen in the Service Configuration Editor.

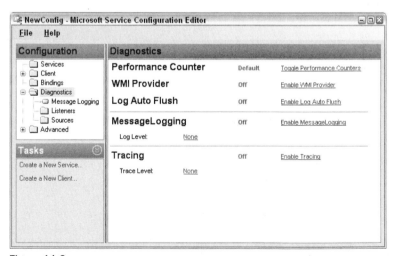

Figure 11-2

Figure 11-3 shows the dialog used for changing log levels in the Service Configuration Editor.

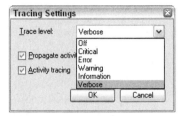

Figure 11-3

The tracing configuration screen, with tracing enabled, shows what will be logged and where (see Figure 11-4). It is shown when the user selects the Diagnostics folder in the tree at left.

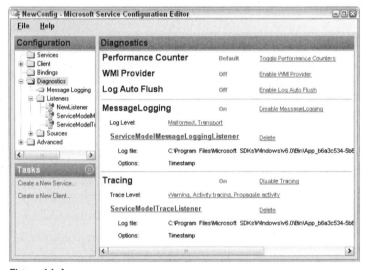

Figure 11-4

The Service Configuration Editor provides a very good example of how logging can be configured in a way that is accessible to non-developers. When tracing is turned on, the display shows what will be logged, what logging options are turned on, and exactly where each set of trace messages will be written to disk. Any changes made in the application take effect as soon as the configuration is saved, without any need to restart the application. This makes tracing much easier to use and more useful and useable to operations staff, which is ultimately the goal of a good tracing system.

Making Messages Actionable

After making tracing easy to configure, the second most important thing that you can do to make logging more useful to support personnel is to make sure that all of your trace messages (or at least those intended for non-developers) are *actionable*. In most cases, if a developer writes code to generate a trace message, he knows why that message needs to be written. Something caused the event that generated the message, and most of the time the developer doing the writing has a pretty good idea of not only what that event is, but *why* it occurred.

It is vitally important to make sure that any error message you report to the end user, or especially to support personnel, contains information on *what* happened, *why*, and *what to do* about it. There is no use reporting an error to operations if they can't tell what actually went wrong. If they have to look up what to do about it in a manual somewhere, they're wasting valuable time and energy that could be better spent on fixing the problem.

The worst case is showing a customer an error that only makes sense to a developer:

```
TcpException in MyApp.Network.dll, MessageSender.cs line 42.
```

This does not help the operations center at all. This kind of message results in the customers calling your support center, which makes them unhappy and costs you money. It is slightly better to keep the technical details out of it:

```
Failed to send message to banking server.
```

While this spares the operations folk the technical details, it isn't much more helpful. It at least suggests that there is some problem with the network, but there is no indication of what sort of problem that might be. It could be that the server is down or that the address of the server is incorrectly configured or that the network card in the client machine has failed. Anyone receiving such a message will have to spend time trying to figure out what the real problem is before he or she can do anything about it.

This is a perfect example of how good error handling combined with good tracing can reduce your customer's support costs. If the code that sends this trace message uses well-thought-out exception handling (see Chapter 12), the real cause of the network failure will be known. If specific exceptions are caught in the message sending code, then specific tracing messages can be written to describe the real problem.

Here are some examples of error messages that are actionable:

```
While attempting to send a message to the banking server, the network socket could
not be opened on the client machine. This could indicate a faulty or incorrectly
configured network card on the client machine at address 10.0.1.1.

While attempting to send a message to the banking server, a connection to the
server was refused. This could indicate an improperly configured address for the
banking server. Please check the server name or IP address configured for the
banking server in the <bankingServer> section of the config file at c:\program
files\myapp\bankingclient.config. The currently configured value is 10.0.12.118.

While attempting to send a message to the banking server, the request timed out
after the server was contacted. This could be caused by network congestion, or a
problem with the banking server. Please check the logs for the banking server for
indications of an error. The banking server may need to be restarted.
```

People working in an operations center don't care what line of code threw an exception. They need to know what happened, what caused the problem, and potentially what can be done about it. The suggestion for how to fix the problem need not be definitive, but it should provide a clear hint about where to look. In each of these examples, the real cause of the failure can be known to the calling code, so why not make that reason known to the customer? Actionable messages make it more likely that the customer will be able to fix his or her own problems rather than having to involve your call center or (even more expensive) your developers.

It takes time, training, and experience to make this work. If you are working on an existing product, look for places where you might make errors more actionable. Ask your customers which error messages they get most often that they do not understand, and tackle those first. Making error messages more meaningful may require you to change your error handling as well. You need to be able to narrow down the real cause of any error before you can write a good error message describing how to fix it.

If you are working on a new project, make actionable error messages part of your tracing policy, and make sure that such a policy is coupled with a good error-handling policy. See the next chapter for an example of such a policy. By making your customer-facing error messages clearer and more actionable, you will reduce the total cost of ownership of your software for both your customers and yourself.

Summary

Coming up with a definitive tracing policy has a number of solid advantages. If your entire product uses the same tracing system in a consistent way, it makes your product easier to use, easier to debug, and easier to configure, and reduces the cost of ownership for your customers and the cost of support for your organization.

12

Error Handling

Dealing with errors is a vital part of any software development project, and like most aspects of development, it can be done very well, very poorly, or somewhere in between. Error handling sometimes gets short shrift because, of course, developers never make mistakes. Of course, you also know that isn't true, never was, and never will be. As software has become more complex, it has also become increasingly important to handle errors carefully and consistently.

Good error handling is key to lowering the cost of ownership of software for your customers. The purchase price paid for software pales in comparison to the cost of supporting that same software. The better your error handling, the lower that cost of support.

Error handling can really be divided into two main categories: how errors are handled internally, and how errors are presented to the user. The way that errors are handled internally mainly affects developers. Good internal error handling makes finding and fixing defects easier, and makes code easier to read and to understand.

The way errors are handed off to the user makes the difference between easily supported software, and costly and difficult-to-support software. Errors should only be handed off to the user if there is something that the user can do to correct the problem, and that needs to be clearly communicated. As discussed in the last chapter, it is vitally important to make your error messages to the user actionable. If an error message doesn't tell the user how to correct the problem, then there is no point in showing the user an error message.

Given the importance of error handling, it is not surprising that many developers have strong opinions about the subject. How errors should be handled programmatically and how they should be presented to the user can be quite contentious, and it is almost certain that 10 software developers in the same room will have at least 12 different opinions on how to go about it. Arguably the largest divide is between the "result code readers" and the "exception throwers."

Result Code Reading

Before there was such a thing as an exception, common practice was for all functions to return some sort of indication of success or failure. Anyone who has ever programmed against Microsoft's Component Object Model (COM) architecture will be familiar with this pattern. Some developers ("result code readers") still favor this style. The following code examples demonstrate the result-code-reading pattern:

```
public class ReturnCodes
{
    public const int S_OK = 0;
    public const int E_FAIL = -1;
    public const int E_NULL_REFERENCE = -2;
    public const int E_NETWORK_FAILURE = -3;

    public int ReadFileFromNetwork(string fileName, out Stream file)
    {
        //attempt to read file fileName

        //success case
        return S_OK;

        //else

        //network failed
        return E_NETWORK_FAILURE;

        //etc...

    }
}
```

The caller of such code would call each method and then check for success or failure:

```
public int ReadFile(string fileName, out Stream file)
{
    //check fileType

    //if network file
    if (ReadFileFromNetwork(fileName, out file) != S_OK)
    {
        //handle error and return
        return E_FAIL;
    }

    //continue with success case
}
```

Or alternatively, check for success each time rather than failure:

```
public int ReadFileTwo(string fileName, out Stream file)
{
    //check file type
```

```
            //if network file
            if (ReadFileFromNetwork(fileName, out file) == S_OK)
            {
                //proceed with success case
                if (DoNextThingWithFile(file) == S_OK)
                {
                    //proceed with success
                }
                else
                    return E_FAIL;
            }
            else
                return E_FAIL;
        }
```

In a longer method, this leads to deeper and deeper nesting of `if` statements, clouding legibility. The other big drawback to this method is that, because all functions have to return result codes, all outputs have to be passed as `out` parameters, which can be awkward.

Exception Throwing

The other major camp is that of the exception throwers. Many modern languages have some notion of exceptions, which can be thrown and caught. In an exception-aware model, every method can be assumed to succeed unless it throws an exception, so it isn't necessary to check for the success case. Even among exception throwers there is dissent, however. Not everyone accepts this vision of how exceptions should be used. Some feel that exceptions should only be thrown in an "exceptional" situation. I disagree. As mentioned previously, I favor the use of noun-verb naming conventions, wherein domain objects are nouns, and methods that act upon those objects are verbs. Those verb-oriented method names represent a contract, and any violation of that contract should cause an exception. To once again use a banking example, a method called `TransferFunds` should in fact transfer funds from one place to another. If it cannot fulfill that contract — for any reason — it should throw an exception indicating its failure to do so.

There is no reason why exceptions should be reserved for "exceptional" cases. Determining which cases are truly exceptional is far too subjective to be used as policy. It is much easier to simply think about contracts and the fulfillment of those contracts. You can assume that the advertised contract will be fulfilled, and then deal with exceptions if they should happen to come up. This makes for a much simpler programming model. The following code demonstrates the exception-throwing pattern:

```
    public class ExceptionHandling
    {
        public Stream ReadFileFromNetwork(string fileName)
        {
            //attempt to read file fileName

            try
            {
                Stream file = ReadFile(fileName);
            }
```

```
        catch (FileIOException fio)
        {
            throw new CannotReadFileException("failed to read file due to IO
problem", fio );
        }

        //success case
        return file;

    }
}
```

A client of such a method would follow a similar pattern of exception handling:

```
    public string GetFileContents(string fileName)
    {
        try
        {
            StreamReader sr = new StreamReader(ReadFileFromNetwork(fileName));
            return sr.ReadToEnd();
        }
        catch (CannotReadFileException crfe)
        {
            return null;
        }
    }
```

Arguably, the GetFileContents method should also throw an exception rather than returning null, but that will depend on the nature of its contract with *its* callers. The most important aspects of this exception-handling pattern are:

❑   Throwing an exception if your contract cannot be fulfilled

❑   Catching only those exceptions that you are prepared for

Catching exceptions that you aren't prepared to handle leads to unexpected errors being swallowed. Code such as the following is just asking for trouble:

```
    public string GetFileContents(string fileName)
    {
        try
        {
            StreamReader sr = new StreamReader(ReadFileFromNetwork(fileName));
            return sr.ReadToEnd();
        }

        catch (Exception e)

        {
            return null;
        }
    }
```

This code returns no information about what the problem was. Suppose that instead of an error reading the file from a network source, the `fileName` parameter passed in was null. This code would swallow the `NullReferenceException` thrown somewhere farther down the call stack. That leaves the caller with no hint that he has passed a bad file name. The caller may simply assume that there was an error reading the file that he requested, when in fact his calling code was flawed and passed a bad file name. The first version you saw caught only a specific exception (`CannotReadFileException`) that left no doubt about what the underlying problem was.

The other big advantage to throwing `CannotReadFileException` is that the specific exception type speaks to the nature of the problem rather than its implementation. If you are using interfaces, you might have two different file readers, one that reads from a network and one that reads from disk. The caller isn't supposed to care about how those different implementations work. If the first threw a network exception and the second a file-not-found exception, the caller would have to understand something about the implementation of each version. If, instead, each implementation of the interface catches exceptions specific to its implementation and wraps them in a `CannotReadFileException`, then the caller only needs to know that the file could not be read, not why. Proper tracing should ensure that a human trying to diagnose the problem would see some record of the original exception for debugging purposes, but for the sake of clean code, the calling code should be ignorant of those details.

By throwing some exceptions and wrapping others in specific exception types, you can significantly reduce the amount of error-handling code you need to write. Rather than having to check each method call to make sure that it returns successfully, you can assume that every method succeeds, and only worry about handling failure cases that you know what to do about.

Because exceptions can be very rich data structures, they can also convey much more information about the nature of an error than return codes can. With return codes, the caller is limited to looking up each code in some mapping table to determine the nature of the error or, alternatively, relying on some external method of retrieving error information such as the dreaded Win32 method, `GetLastError`, which returns a string containing an error message stored by whatever method last returned a failure result code. Checking to see if return codes indicate success and dereferencing information about the nature of the error make for a very cumbersome programming model that involves a great volume of error-handling code.

Importance of a Policy

As an architect or team leader, it is vitally important that you establish an error-handling policy, and make it clear to every member of your team or organization. Proper error handling only helps to reduce total cost of ownership for your customers if it is done consistently and with a clear vision of how it helps support both developers and eventual end users. Without a solid policy and a consistent implementation, even the most well-executed error handling only increases support costs.

When writing such a policy, it is important to keep the goal in mind: reducing cost. If other developers are calling your code, you must reduce the cost to them in terms of debugging time. Remember that adding additional error-handling code (even if it costs processor cycles at runtime) is cheaper than having developers debug problems with less-than-complete error information. If end users are running your code, you must reduce the cost to them in terms of technical support, installation, and configuration. Any problems with your application should be easy for your customer to diagnose, understand,

and resolve. By coming up with a consistent error-handling strategy that reports any errors to the customer in a way that is accessible to them (see Chapter 11, "Tracing"), you will reduce the amount of time it takes your customers to diagnose and resolve problems. If you can achieve that goal, your customers will save money, and in turn they will give more of their money to you in the form of additional purchases.

While working directly with customers on a large project, I was very surprised to get the feedback that what they wanted was not more features from the application I was working on, but better error handling so that they could lower their internal support costs. As a developer, it's pretty hard to think of great error handling as sexy, but if it saves your customers money, then sexy it must be. That fact supports the earlier assertions that the job of developers is not to write code but to solve problems for their customers using software. If that is really the goal, then a good error-handling policy should be just as exciting (maybe more so) than the next great set of features.

Defining a Policy

So what does an exception-handling policy look like? It should be short (developers don't read documents that are longer than 1–2 pages) and to the point. It should lay out how errors are to be returned in the case of a failure, and how errors should be reported to callers. It should also define how and where errors should be documented. A complete error-handling policy for code written in C# might look something like this:

- ❑ No method shall return a code to indicate success or failure. All methods must return a result, or void if none is required. In the event of an error (meaning the method's contract cannot be fulfilled), throw an exception.

- ❑ Any exception thrown should be specific to the problem being reported and contain as complete a set of information about the problem as possible. For example, do not throw an `Invalid OperationException` when something more specific and descriptive is available. If a more specific exception does not exist, create one.

- ❑ All new exception types should derive from `OurCompany.ActionableException` or one of its descendents. Every derived class must implement a constructor that takes a source and a resolution. Every time an exception is created at runtime, a source and resolution must be provided. The source should describe to an end user what caused the problem. The resolution should describe to an end user how to resolve the problem.

- ❑ Every method that is a part of the public interface must validate its input parameters. If any input parameter fails validation, the method must throw an `ArgumentException`, `Argument NullException`, or `ArgumentOutOfRange` exception. The message associated with each exception must specify (for a developer) in what way the parameter was invalid.

- ❑ Throwing exceptions of framework types should be avoided. Whenever feasible, framework exceptions should either be handled or wrapped with application-specific types. `Exception` and `ApplicationException` may never be thrown explicitly by application code. Throw a specific subclass of `ActionableException` instead.

- ❑ When catching and wrapping a framework or other exception, log the details of the original exception, and then include the original exception as the inner exception of the one being thrown, as shown in the following code. This preserves the original callstack and is vital for debugging.

```
        try
        {
            Stream file = ReadFile(fileName);
        }
        catch (FileIOException fio)
        {
            //logging original exception for diagnostic purposes
            log.Warning(fio.ToString());

            ,   throw new CannotReadFileException(
    "failed to read file due to IO problem", fio);
        }
```

❑ Exceptions may only be caught if:

❑ They are of a specific type.

❑ They are handled in a way that fulfills the containing method's contract **or** are rethrown using a more specific type.

❑ Any original exception is properly logged and included as the inner exception of a more specific type.

❑ Any exception explicity thrown by each method must be documented in that method's XML documentation comments. The following code shows properly formatted XML documentation comments that specify the exceptions that may be thrown.

```
/// <summary>
/// Reads a file from a newtork souce and retuns that file as a Stream.
/// </summary>
/// <param name="fileName">The file to read from the network source.
/// Must be properly formatted as a URI.</param>
/// <returns>The file to be read as a Stream object.</returns>
/// <exception cref="ArgumentException"><i>fileName</i> is not a well formed,
/// absolute URI</exception>
/// <exception cref="CannotReadFileException"><i>fileName</i> could not
/// be read from the underlying network source</exception>
public Stream ReadFileFromNetwork(string fileName)
{
    if (!Uri.IsWellFormedUriString(fileName, UriKind.Absolute))
        throw new ArgumentException(
            "The file name must be in the form of a well formed, absolute URI.",
            "fileName");
    try
    {
        Stream file = ReadFile(fileName);
    }
    catch (FileIOException fio)
    {
        //logging original exception for diagnostic purposes
        log.Warning(fio.ToString());
        throw new CannotReadFileException("failed to read file due to IO
problem",
```

```
fio);
    }
  return file;
}
```

Figure 12-1 shows how these comments look as formatted documentation. Each exception is clearly documented for the caller.

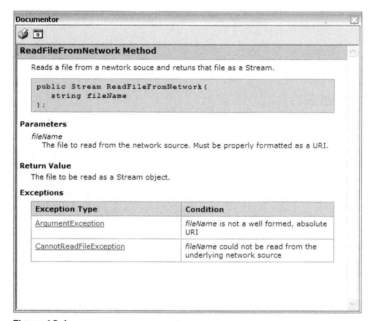

Figure 12-1

❑ Any exception that is not caught at the outermost level of the application will be considered unexpected and therefore fatal. The process must exit rather than handling the exception, after logging it as appropriate (see the section entitled "Defining a Policy" in Chapter 11).

Once you have such a policy in place, there are a couple of things to remember about it. You must make sure that every member of the team understands the policy. They do not have to agree with it. Error handling is a contentious issue, and I can almost guarantee that in a team of more than two people, you will not be able to arrive at a complete consensus without significantly watering down your policy. A solid error-handling policy is a great example of how a team lead/architect must rule by fiat. You also need to remember that the policy is only as good as its implementation, and that implementation must be overseen. The fact that developers tend to be rewarded for features rather than good code, coupled with the fact that not all of the developers on the team will agree with your policy, means that you must make sure that the policy is being followed by doing code reviews, spot checks, or whatever works for your team, to keep people compliant. If you can get people to be consistent and conscientious about error handling, eventually your customers will notice how much easier your software is to support, and they will reward you for it. If your software is too expensive for your customers to support, they will eventually start buying from someone with better error handling (or less buggy code) to lower their costs.

It is important not to ignore the documentation aspect of your policy. In a language such as C#, there is no way for the compiler to tell a caller which types of exceptions might be thrown. The only way for a caller to know which exceptions they need to catch when calling a method in C# is to read the documentation, assuming that the caller does not have access to your source. If callers know which exceptions can be thrown, then they can proactively prepare themselves to catch and handle those exceptions.

While it may seem like extra work up front, following a good error-handling policy such as the one described above (or one tailored to fit the specifics of your coding environment) will lead to less error-handling code overall, easier-to-read and more consistent code, and better error handling for both developers and end users.

Where to Handle Errors

Part of establishing a consistent error-handling policy is deciding where each error should be handled. One of the (many) beauties of exception handling is that exceptions will continue to bubble up a callstack until they either are handled or reach the top of the callstack and cause the application to fail. That means that each method only has to handle a specific set of exceptions and can leave the rest to be dealt with at a higher level. Each method in the callstack handles errors if it can, and leaves them to the next level up if it cannot. In the event that an exception isn't dealt with, it will cause the application to exit, which is much better for everyone than to have the system continue running in an inconsistent and/or unknown state.

One of the foremost reasons for not catching base-class exceptions is that if you don't know what kind of exception you are handling, you also don't know in what state you are leaving the application to continue. Far better to exit gracefully (or even catastrophically) than to continue in a state that might lead to incorrect results or data loss.

For example, take another look at the following file-reading code. The method that actually reads from the network source can't do very much to recover if the network source cannot be read.

```csharp
public Stream ReadFileFromNetwork(string fileName)
{
    if (!Uri.IsWellFormedUriString(fileName, UriKind.Absolute))
        throw new ArgumentException(
            "The file name must be in the form of a well formed, absolute URI.",
            "fileName");
    try
    {
        Stream file = ReadFile(fileName);
        return file;
    }
    catch (FileIOException fio)
    {
        //logging original exception for diagnostic purposes
        log.Warning(fio.ToString());
        throw new CannotReadFileException("failed to read file due to IO problem",
fio);
    }
}
```

Because the ReadFileFromNetwork method cannot return a Stream as its contract specifies, the best it can do is throw a more application-specific exception. The advantage to wrapping the FileIOException in this way is that if you have another method that reads files from disk instead, as shown in the following example:

```
public Stream ReadFileFromDisk(string fileName)
{
    if (!Uri.IsWellFormedUriString(fileName, UriKind.Absolute))
        throw new ArgumentException(
            "The file name must be in the form of a well formed, absolute URI.",
            "fileName");
    try
    {
        Stream file = ReadFileFromFileSystem(fileName);
    }
    catch (FileNotFoundException fnf)
    {
        //logging original exception for diagnostic purposes
        log.Warning(fnf.ToString());
        throw new CannotReadFileException(
            string.Format("no such file exists: {0}", fileName), fnf);
    }
    return file;
}
```

It internally handles a different failure, but returns a similar exception to the caller. The caller who wants to read the file doesn't care about the underlying failures, only that the file could not be read. The following client code only has to worry about the CannotReadFileException.

```
public string GetFileContents(string fileName)
{
    try
    {
        StreamReader sr = new StreamReader(ReadFileFromNetwork(fileName));
        return sr.ReadToEnd();
    }
    catch (CannotReadFileException e)
    {
        return null;
    }
}
```

The caller in this case chooses to return null instead of propagating the exception any further. In another context, the caller might choose to put up an alert dialog explaining the error, or in some other way report the error to the user without further propagating the exception. Where to catch exceptions depends on where the error needs to be dealt with. In the simple file-reading methods, the exception can be dealt with by whatever code is trying to read the file. There is no need to propagate the exception further up the callstack because it is the responsibility of the file-handling code to report the problem to the user and allow the user to choose a different file if appropriate. Failure to open the file is a recoverable problem, so it makes sense to catch the exception at that point. If, however, the file-reading code threw an OutOfMemoryException, it should not be caught because there is nothing the file-handling code can do about the application being out of memory. In that case, it makes more sense for the application to exit rather than continue in a state that could lead to data loss.

At some point, usually at the top of the callstack in the application's main processing loop, all that can be done about any exception is to log it properly for debugging purposes and then exit, as shown in the following example:

```
static class Program
{
    /// <summary>
    /// The main entry point for the application.
    /// </summary>
    [STAThread]
    static void Main()
    {
        try
        {
            Application.Run(new Form1());
        }
        catch (Exception e)
        {
            log.Fatal(e.ToString());
            throw;
        }
    }
}
```

If an unexpected exception has reached the outermost level of the application, there is really nothing more to be done. Because the error is unexpected, it is, by definition, also unrecoverable. All that can be done is to log the failure so that it can be diagnosed later and then exit the application to avoid proceeding in an unknown state. The whole mechanism behind throwing exceptions rather than returning error codes is designed to ensure that an application exits rather than remaining in an uncertain state. So wherever you decide to handle exceptions, make sure that you can actually recover from any exceptions you do catch. If you can't recover from the exception, don't catch it unless it is to log the problem and rethrow it.

If you are going to catch exceptions, make sure that you catch specific exception types that you know about and can do something about, and try to catch them as close as possible to where they are likely to be thrown. In the preceding file-handling examples, the catch block that handles FileNotFoundException is directly after the call that is likely to produce such an exception. You wouldn't want code several levels up the callstack to catch a FileNotFoundException, because the virtual "distance" between where the exception was thrown and where you are trying to catch it is too great. By the time you catch it there, it is too late for any reasonable form of recovery to be done that relates to the file not being found. The code that catches such an exception farther up the callstack may not even know how to read a file, so there is nothing that can be gained from catching file exceptions. If you need to propagate the file exception to a higher level in the stack, wrap it with something application specific such as the CannotReadFileException in the earlier examples. That way the catching code knows exactly what it is catching without having to relate it to the underlying implementation.

It is certainly convenient that exceptions propagate up the callstack automatically, but the reason they do that is to prevent the application from entering an unknown state, even if the calling code isn't properly checking for errors. Because that is really the underlying goal; catching exceptions that you can't handle or "swallowing" them by not handling or rethrowing them is counterproductive. Catching exceptions you don't know how to handle may leave the application in an incomplete or incorrect state that can lead to real problems, including data loss.

Summary

One of the most important things that you as a developer can do to reduce the cost of owning your software for your customers is to improve your error-handling code. If your application encounters errors, either those errors need to be handled correctly or the application needs to fail rather than enter an inconsistent state.

Rather than writing pervasive error-handling code that checks return values, use exceptions if your coding environment or language supports them. Using exceptions properly can greatly reduce the amount of error-handling code you need to write, as well as ensure that errors are reported to the caller and that the application exits rather than proceeding in a bad state.

To make best use of error handling in your code, establish a clear and simple policy for handling errors, and make sure that every member of your team is familiar with that policy. Keep it short and easy to read, and make sure that you follow up by reviewing the code your team produces to ensure that the policy is understood properly and is being followed consistently. Following a well-crafted policy consistently will make your software easier for both developers and customers to use and support.

Handle errors as close to the code that causes those errors as possible to avoid getting into a bad state, but make sure that you are handling only those errors that you can recover from.

Combined with a good tracing/error-reporting policy, good error handling will make it easier for users to discover the cause of errors and will, ultimately, make it less likely that errors will occur in the first place.

Part IV
Putting It All Together

13

Calculator Project: A Case Study

Bob the developer comes to work in the morning, catches up on his email, and then sets to work on his project. Bob is working on the Calculator project, which has just recently started up. The Calculator team has just begun their first development iteration, and Bob is anxious to start writing code and adding value to the project.

The first thing that Bob does is decide which task to work on. He goes to his project-management system and picks the highest-priority task that is currently unassigned.

> *For the sake of this narrative, Bob's team is using SCRUM to manage tasks and how they are assigned, but any development methodology would fit in here. The important point is that Bob chooses a task that has some form of task number associated with it.*

Bob's task for the day is **Task 5: Add subtraction to the calculator**. Bob has a pretty clear idea of what that task entails and how it fits in with the rest of the project, so he doesn't think that he needs to validate anything with the customer.

Bob knows that because his project is following the Model-View-Presenter model, he will have to make changes to a number of different files in several projects to complete his task. To make sure that all of the changes he makes can be correlated to the task, Bob creates a new task branch in his source control system (see Figure 13-1), after checking the build server to make sure that the current build has succeeded. Bob wouldn't want to create a task branch based on unstable code.

Once the new task branch is created, Bob checks out a new copy of the code from that location in source control to make sure that he is working with the latest source.

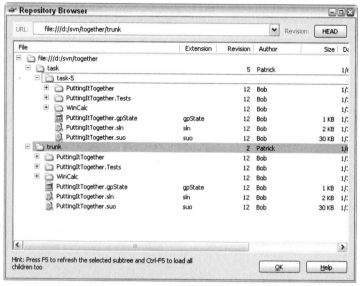

Figure 13-1

Bob takes a look at the existing tests for the core Calculator library and sees that there is only one test so far for the existing Add method:

```
[TestFixture]
public class CalculatorTest
{
    [Test]
    public void Add()
    {
        double op1 = 1.0;
        double op2 = 2.0;

        Calculator calc = new Calculator();

        double actual = calc.Add(op1, op2);
        double expected = 3.0;

        Assert.AreEqual(expected, actual);
    }
}
```

Before touching anything else, Bob starts writing some new tests to cover the new Subtract functionality:

```
[Test]
public void SubtractWithPositiveResult()
{
    double op1 = 2.0;
    double op2 = 1.0;

    Calculator calc = new Calculator();
```

```
        double actual = calc.Subtract(op1, op2);
        double expected = 1.0;

        Assert.AreEqual(expected, actual);
    }

    [Test]
    public void SubtractWithNegativeResult()
    {
        double op1 = 1.0;
        double op2 = 2.0;

        Calculator calc = new Calculator();

        double actual = calc.Subtract(op1, op2);
        double expected = -1.0;

        Assert.AreEqual(expected, actual);
    }
```

Bob is satisfied that these tests express his understanding of what the Subtract method is supposed to do. He might have to go back later and add some edge condition tests to make sure the contract is being properly enforced. Of course, this code doesn't compile yet, so Bob writes the code needed in the Calculator class to make the tests he has written pass:

```
public class Calculator
{
    public double Add(double op1, double op2)
    {
        return op1 + op2;
    }

    public double Subtract(double op1, double op2)
    {
        return op1 - op2;
    }
}
```

This is obviously a trivial example, but it is the process rather than the code that is important here.

Now that the tests pass, Bob turns to the next step in his task, which is to add the new functionality to the MVP-style application so that it will be available to users. Again, he starts with the tests, in this case the tests for the Presenter class. The following code shows the test for the new subtract functionality in the Presenter.

```
[TestFixture]
public class CalculatorPresenterTest
{
    [Test]
    public void Add()
    {
        TestCalculatorView view = new TestCalculatorView();
```

```
            view.Operand1 = 2.0;
            view.Operand2 = 2.0;

            CalculatorPresenter presenter = new CalculatorPresenter(view);

            presenter.Add();

            Assert.AreEqual(4.0, view.Result);
        }

        [Test]
        public void Subtract()
        {
            TestCalculatorView view = new TestCalculatorView();
            view.Operand1 = 2.0;
            view.Operand2 = 1.0;

            CalculatorPresenter presenter = new CalculatorPresenter(view);

            presenter.Subtract();

            Assert.AreEqual(1.0, view.Result);
        }
    }
```

To make the test pass, Bob adds code to the presenter:

```
    public class CalculatorPresenter
    {
        ICalculatorView _view;
        Calculator _calc;

        public CalculatorPresenter(ICalculatorView view)
        {
            _view = view;
            _calc = new Calculator();
        }

        public void Add()
        {
            double op1 = _view.Operand1;
            double op2 = _view.Operand2;
            double result = _calc.Add(op1, op2);
            _view.Result = result;
        }

        public void Subtract()
        {
            double op1 = _view.Operand1;
            double op2 = _view.Operand2;
            double result = _calc.Subtract(op1, op2);
            _view.Result = result;
        }
    }
```

Now the tests are in place for the core library and the presenter, and those tests pass, so the only thing left to do is add the Subtract functionality to the user interface. The highlighted code below hooks the presenter up to the user interface.

```csharp
public partial class CalculatorMain : Form, ICalculatorView
{
    CalculatorPresenter _presenter;

    public CalculatorMain()
    {
        InitializeComponent();

        _presenter = new CalculatorPresenter(this);

    }

    #region ICalculatorView Members

    public double Operand1
    {
        get
        {
            double op1;
            if (double.TryParse(op1Text.Text, out op1))
            {
                return op1;
            }
            else
                return double.NaN;

        }
    }

    public double Operand2
    {
        get
        {
            double op2;
            if (double.TryParse(op2Text.Text, out op2))
            {
                return op2;
            }
            else
                return double.NaN;

        }
    }

    public double Result
    {
        set { resultText.Text = value.ToString(); }
    }
```

```
#endregion

private void addButton_Click(object sender, EventArgs e)
{
    _presenter.Add();
}


private void subtractButton_Click(object sender, EventArgs e)
{
    _presenter.Subtract();
}

}
```

Figure 13-2 shows the Calculator application with the Subtract button added (Bob's team doesn't have a UI designer on board yet).

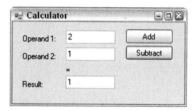

Figure 13-2

The new Subtract functionality works great, and Bob's pleased with how quickly that worked out. The MVP pattern made it easy to test everything that he needed to test, except whether the Subtract button really caused a subtraction, and that part, Bob knows, will be handled by the testers when they validate the application.

Bob knows that he's not quite ready to commit his code, though. He's got some work to do before the task is really "done." First, he checks to make sure that any tracing and error handling that might be necessary are in place:

```
public class Calculator
{
    public double Add(double op1, double op2)
    {
        if (op1 == double.NaN)
        {
            Trace.TraceError("double.NaN passed to Add method.  Inputs should
be validated.");
            throw new ArgumentException("Both operands must be valid (and real)
double values.", "op1");
        }
        if (op2 == double.NaN)
        {
            Trace.TraceError("double.NaN passed to Add method.  Inputs should
be validated.");
```

```
                        throw new ArgumentException("Both operands must be valid (and real)
    double values.", "op1");
                }

                return op1 + op2;
        }

        public double Subtract(double op1, double op2)
        {
                if (op1 == double.NaN)
                {
                        Trace.TraceError("double.NaN passed to Subtract method.  Inputs
    should be validated.");
                        throw new ArgumentException("Both operands must be valid (and real)
    double values.", "op1");
                }
                if (op2 == double.NaN)
                {
                        Trace.TraceError("double.NaN passed to Subtract method.  Inputs
    should be validated.");
                        throw new ArgumentException("Both operands must be valid (and real)
    double values.", "op1");
                }
        return op1 - op2;
            }
        }
```

For the sake of simplicity, some details have been omitted. The hardcoded error strings should be replaced with strings from a resource file, and additional tests should be added to validate that the right exceptions are being thrown and that the right messages are being traced.

The final step to complete the task is to update the documentation for the new Subtract method, making sure that the new exceptions are documented:

```
        /// <summary>
        /// The subtract method returns the result of subtracting op2 from op1.
        /// </summary>
        /// <param name="op1">The first operand</param>
        /// <param name="op2">The second operand</param>
        /// <returns>The result of subtracting the second operand from the
    first.</returns>
        /// <exception cref="ArgumentException">op1 or op2 was equal to
    double.NaN.</exception>
        public double Subtract(double op1, double op2)
        {
    ...
```

Just to make sure that nothing was broken because of his changes, Bob runs a complete build and test cycle for the application, which shows everything building and passing okay. Bob then commits his code back to the test branch he created earlier. All of the files that he changed are now associated with a single change set in source control. The TortoiseSVN log window in Figure 13-3 shows the change set associated with Bob's comment that he finished task 5.

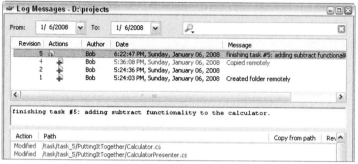

Figure 13-3

Anyone who comes along after Bob can easily see all of the changes he made to complete task 5.

All that remains to be done is to merge the changes made on the task branch back to the trunk so that they will be part of the next Continuous Integration build, and be visible to testers and other developers. Before committing the results of the merge, Bob makes sure that the latest build passed and that he has updated to the latest version, and then he runs a complete build and test again. Only if the build and test succeed will Bob commit his changes, so that the build will not break and everything will be left in a consistent state.

The merge step is specific to a particular source control system and so is omitted here. In this case, Bob only committed one change set to the task branch, but for a more complicated task, it might have taken multiple commits over several days. The task branch remains in source control as a record of each change set, so it is important that the comment associated with merging the task branch back to the trunk make some mention of which task branch it came from, in case that history needs to be understood later.

Bob can go on to his next task secure in the knowledge that he has done the right thing, and that his task will be consistent with the standards established by his team. His code will not cause problems for other developers or break the build, and it is ready to be passed off to testing.

Wrapping Up

Here's what Bob did:

❑   Bob completed his task according to his team's "done means done" criteria.

❑   He did his work on a separate task branch so that all of the changes associated with his task were recorded for later reference.

❑   He followed a Test-Driven Development process, writing his tests first to define the contract and then writing the code to make those tests pass.

❑   He checked the build server to make sure that he was starting with code that was functional and consistent.

- ❏ He wrote a mock view class to make sure that his presenter tests were only testing the presenter class.

- ❏ He followed the Model-View-Presenter pattern so that his application logic (such as it was) was testable independent of the user interface.

- ❏ He made sure that he had the appropriate error-handling and -tracing code in place to make his code easier to debug and support.

And here's what Bob didn't do:

- ❏ He didn't do any static analysis. This example was so simple that no such analysis was required. In the scope of a larger project, static analysis might be appropriate between iterations to keep track of changes in code complexity or dependencies.

- ❏ He didn't do any dependency injection. If the Calculator library were a part of a larger project, it might make sense to introduce dependency injection of some sort. It isn't necessary here.

- ❏ He didn't consider whether he should buy a calculator library instead of developing one himself. In reality a calculator is not something that you would write yourself. There are plenty of calculators on the market, so writing one doesn't provide an advantage.

If everyone on Bob's team follows the same policies, they will be turning out more code in less time at a higher level of quality. They will find it easier to work with their testers, and easier to work together. Best of all, Bob and his team will be learning to be better developers.

Index

C